BIZ TALK ·1
AMERICAN BUSINESS SLANG & JARGON

BIZ TALK ·1

*is now
available on cassette!*

See the coupon on the back page for details

BIZ TALK ·1
AMERICAN BUSINESS SLANG & JARGON

David Burke

Optima Books

Publisher: Optima Books
Editor: Robert Graul
Managing Editor: Debbie Wright
Editing, Design, and Production: Optima PrePress
Front Cover Illustration: Jim Graul
Inside Illustrations: Marc Chancer

ISBN 1-879440-17-2
Printed in the United States of America
93 10 9 8 7 6 5 4 3

This book is dedicated to Helen Kornblum... my "gura."

Preface

Visitors coming to America for the first time seem to have a common complaint:

"What are the natives saying?!
This isn't the English I learned in school!"

Anyone visiting or living in America is bound to encounter a confusing yet popular "inside" language used by the inhabitants; *slang and idioms.* This is an ever-changing, ever-evolving language which is like a code that tends to segregate non-native speakers. *Street Talk -1* and *Street Talk -2*, also by David Burke, are designed to open these seemingly closed doors quickly and help the non-native speaker integrate into American culture.

However, after learning everyday American slang and idioms, the business traveler is faced with an additional obstacle which *must* be conquered in order to transact business effectively in America.

BIZ TALK ·1 presents some of the most popular *business* slang terms and jargon which have infiltrated just about every profession and business situation. Without an understanding of this type of lingo, any non-native speaker conducting business in America is at a grave disadvantage, especially during important meetings and negotiations where it is common to hear expressions like:

- "to have the floor"
- "to stonewall"
- "to brainstorm"
- "to table a discussion" *etc.*

This is only the beginning! **BIZ TALK ·1** not only dedicates an entire chapter to slang and jargon used in meetings and negotiations, but also focuses on the lingo used in finance, marketing, advertising, computerese, business travel, sports terms used in business, offices in general, office parties, and more!

BIZ TALK ·1 takes a close look at the most popular terms and expressions used in American business as well as business terms adopted into everyday speech used by virtually everyone.

This easy-to-use textbook/workbook is divided into four parts:

- **DIALOGUE**

  Approximately twenty new business expressions and slang terms (indicated in boldface) are presented as they may be heard in an actual conversation. A translation of the dialogue in standard English is always given on the opposite page followed by an important phonetic version of the dialogue as it would actually be spoken by a native-born American. This page will prove vital to any non-native speaker since, as previously demonstrated, Americans tend to rely heavily on contractions, reductions, and shortcuts in pronunciation.

- **VOCABULARY**

  This section spotlights all of the slang words and expressions that were used in the dialogue and offers more examples of usage, synonyms, antonyms, and special notes.

- **PRACTICE THE VOCABULARY**

  These word games include all of the new terms and idioms previously learned and will help you to test yourself on your comprehension. (The pages providing the answers to all the drills are indicated at the beginning of this section.)

- **A CLOSER LOOK**

  This section offers the reader a further in depth look at common words used in slang expressions pertaining to the chapter's category.

If you've conquered the task of learning everyday American slang, you will undoubtedly be somewhat surprised to encounter a whole new world of colorful business phrases and terms usually reserved only for the native speaker...*until now!*

David Burke
Author

Acknowledgments

A special thanks goes to Janet Graul, Antonina Markoff and Bruce Fullerton for making the copyediting phase of this book so enjoyable. Their patience, expertise, and attitude were so appreciated.

I am very thankful to Jim Graul, our cover artist and Marc Chancer, our inside-illustrator. Their creativity, professionalism, and ability to produce exceptional images were astounding.

I owe an enormous amount of gratitude to Gordon McKee for his copyediting skills, his ability to turn a phrase, and assistance throughout the production of this book.

I am greatly appreciative of ESL teachers Joan Conway and June Quigley for their insight, support, and availability to my many questions.

I am particularly grateful for meeting Helen Kornblum of TESOL; to thank her for her patience and kindness just doesn't seem like enough.

Legend

expression

literal translation

an equivalent term or expression of the main entry in boldface

a term or expression opposite in meaning to the main entry in boldface

adjective

noun

useful information about the preceding entry

an entry preceded by a filled-in arrow refers to the main entry in boldface

an entry preceded by a hollow arrow refers to the preceding entry with a filled-in arrow

bracketed words in the main entry are optional

boldface words in parentheses are used before the main entry—they appear after the main entry for alphabetization purposes only: Example: *to call to order*

a common variation of the main entry in boldface

verb

work one's fingers to the bone (to) *exp.* to work very hard with one's hands.

bug *n.* ◆ (lit); an insect or pest • a flaw in a computer program.

◆ SYNONYM: **glitch** *n. I found a glitch in the program;* I found a flaw in the program.

◆ ANTONYM: **to debug a program** *v.* to remove the flaws in a computer program.

down (to be) *adj.* said of a computer which is inoperative.

circular *n.* a flyer or card advertising a product.

◆ NOTE: The term *"circular"* refers to the flyer or card (or other advertisement) which is being "circulated" to a number of people at the same time: not the shape of the advertisements.

◆ SYNONYM: **junk mail** *exp.* (a term known by those in and out of the advertising industry).

⇨ NOTE: Since consumers are constantly barraged with circulars in the mail, these advertisements tend to lose their effectiveness and are considered to be nothing more than junk by many people.

[way] off base (to be) *exp.* to be very wrong.

◆ ORIGIN: This expression is said of a baseball player who is not on a base and is therefore vulnerable to being tagged.

call to order (to) *exp.* to start a meeting • *The meeting was called to order at noon;* The meeting was started at noon.

◆ VARIATION: **to come to order** *exp.* • *This meeting will now come to order.*

boot (to) *v.* (said of computers) to start.

Contents

BIZ TALK ·1

AMERICAN BUSINESS SLANG & JARGON

General Office Slang

– "The Big Wigs" –

"Did you hear the **scuttlebutt** about Maggie getting **called on the carpet** by some of the **big wigs** today?"

Lesson One - GENERAL OFFICE SLANG

"The Big Wigs"

DIALOGUE

Anne and Sue are talking during lunch.

Anne: Did you hear the **scuttlebutt** about Maggie getting **called on the carpet** by some of the **big wigs** today? I wonder what happened!

Sue: Well, not only does Maggie **make it in** late every day, but she's **called in sick** all this week. Actually she's been spending her time at the beach! She's been asking everyone **to cover for** her **on phones**. That's why they called her in for a **pow-wow**, and you know what **slave drivers** they are. If she doesn't watch it, she's gonna find herself **pounding the pavement**, and it's not that easy **to make a buck** these days.

Anne: She should be thankful to have a **9 to 5**. It's terrible being **between jobs**! Well, if she doesn't **buckle down** and start **busting her buns** around here like the rest of us, she's sure to get **canned**.

Sue: You're right. If she can't **hold down this job**, she should just **hang it up** now. Maybe she'll find something she likes more. I mean, she does have a lot of **know-how**. She always mentioned that she wanted to be a **paper-pusher**. One of her best friends is a **head-hunter** who could probably find her a job in a day. Talk about good **contacts**!   *a brown noser.*

Anne: But her biggest problem is that she refuses **to kiss up** to the **execs** and sometimes you just have to. I certainly don't like having **to jump through hoops** and **kowtow** but sometimes you have no choice!

2

Lesson One - GENERAL OFFICE SLANG

Translation of dialogue in standard English

"The Big Wigs"

DIALOGUE

Anne and Sue are talking during lunch.

Anne: Did you hear the **rumors** about Maggie getting **reprimanded** by some of the **executives** today? I wonder what happened!

Sue: Well, not only does Maggie **arrive** late every day, but she's **called work to inform them she would be absent due to illness** all this week. Actually she's been spending her time at the beach! She's been asking everyone **to do her work for** her which is **answering telephones**. That's why they called her in for a **meeting**, and you know what **demanding administrators** they are. If she doesn't watch it, she's gonna find herself **looking for a new job**, and it's not that easy **to earn money** these days.

Anne: She should be thankful to have a **full-time job**. It's terrible being **jobless**! Well, if she doesn't **get organized** and start **working hard** around here like the rest of us, she's sure to get **discharged**.

Sue: You're right. If she can't **keep this job**, she should just **quit** now. Maybe she'll find something she likes more. I mean, she does have a lot of **ability**. She always mentioned that she wanted to be a **desk-worker**. One of her best friends is an **executive recruiter** who could probably find her a job in a day. Talk about good **influential friends**!

Anne: But her biggest problem is that she refuses **to accommodate** the **executives** and sometimes you just have to. I certainly don't like having **to go through a long burdensome process to achieve my goals** and **grovel** but sometimes you have no choice!

3

Lesson One - GENERAL OFFICE SLANG

Dialogue in slang as it would be heard

"The Big Wigs"

DIALOGUE

Anne and Sue are talking during lunch.

Anne: Didja hear the **scuddlebud** about Maggie gedding **called on the carpet** by some 'a the **big wigs** t'day? I wonder what happened!

Sue: Well, nod only does Maggie **make id in** lade ev'ry day, but she'z **called in sick** all this week. Acsh'ly she'z been spending 'er time at the beach! She'z been asking ev'ryone **ta cover for** her **on phones**. That's why they called 'er in fer a **pow-wow**, an' ya know what **slave drivers** they are. If she doesn' watch it, she'z gonna find 'erself **pounding the pavement**, an' it's not thad eazy **da make a buck** these days.

Anne: She should be thankful da have a **9 ta 5**. It's terr'ble being **b'tween jobs**! Well, if she doesn' **buckle down** 'n start **busting 'er buns** aroun' here like the rest of us, she'z sure da get **canned**.

Sue: Y'r right. If she can't **hold down this job**, she should just **hang id up** now. Maybe she'll find something she likes more. I mean, she does have a lodda **know-how**. She always mentioned that she wanted ta be a **paper-pusher**. One of 'er best friends is a **head hunter** who could prob'ly find 'er a job 'n a day. Talk about good **contacts**!

Anne: Bud 'er biggest problem is that she refuses **ta kiss up** ta thee **execs** 'n sometimes ya just haf to. I certainly don't like having **ta jump through hoops** 'n **kowtow** but sometimes ya have no choice!

4

Vocabulary

9-to-5 *n.* a regular job (which begins at 9:00 A.M. and ends at 5:00 P.M.) • *I'm so tired of working a 9-to-5. Maybe I should become an artist;* I'm so tired of working an ordinary job. Maybe I should become an artist.
 ♦ ALSO: **9-to-5er** *n.* one who works a 9-to-5 • *Look at him carrying that big gray lunch box. He's your typical 9-to-5er;* Look at him carrying that big gray lunch box. He's your typical person with an ordinary job.

between jobs (to be) *exp.* an optimistic description of someone who is unemployed • *I'm between jobs at the moment;* I'm unemployed at the moment.
 ♦ SYNONYM: **to be in transition** *exp.*

big-wig *exp.* executive • *Someday, I'm going to be a big-wig in a large company;* Someday, I'm going to be an executive in a large company.
 ♦ NOTE: This expression comes from the old court system in England where the attorneys, jurors, and judge all wore similar white wigs.

buckle down (to) *exp.* to make an extra effort to get work done • *I just found out that the project is due in a week! That means for the next few days, we're really going to have to buckle down;* I just found out that the project is due in a week! That means for the few days, we're really going to have to make an extra effort to get work done.

bust one's buns (to) *exp.* to work excessively hard • (lit); to break one's buttocks • *I'm tired of busting my buns for such a low salary!;* I'm tired of working excessively hard for such a low salary!
 ♦ NOTE: In this expression, any synonym for "buttocks" may be used in place of *"buns."*

call in sick (to) *exp.* to call one's place of work and inform the proper authorities of one's absence due to illness • *She called in sick eight times this month!;* She called work eight times this month and told them she would be absent due to illness!

called on the carpet (to be) *exp.* to be reprimanded by one's boss • *Tom got called on the carpet for being late to work again;* Tom got reprimanded by the boss for being late to work again.
⟐ VARIATION: **to be called on the mat** *exp.*

can someone (to) *v.* • to fire someone • *She canned her secretary for working too slowly;* She fired her secretary for working too slowly.
⟐ ALSO: **to get canned** *adj.* to get fired • *I got canned for no reason!;* I got fired for no reason!

cover for someone (to) *exp.* • **1.** to do someone else's job during his/her absence • *Would you mind covering for me while I'm on vacation?;* Would you mind doing my job for me while I'm on vacation? • **2.** to lie in order to protect someone from getting into a predicament • *You've got to stop taking two-hour lunches! The boss is asking too many questions and I'm tired of covering for you!;* You've got to stop taking two-hour lunches! The boss is asking too many questions and I'm tired of lying to protect you from getting into a predicament!

exec *n.* • a popular abbreviation of "executive" • *So, how does it feel to be a big exec now?;* So, how does it feel to be a big executive now?

good contacts (to have) *exp.* to know many influential people • *She shouldn't have any trouble finding a new job. She has a lot of good contacts in her field;* She shouldn't have any trouble finding a new job. She knows a lot of influential people in her field.

hang it up (to) *exp.* to quit a task; to give up • *You're never going to get the boss to give you a raise. Just hang it up!;* You're never going to get the boss to give you a raise. Just forget it!
⟐ SYNONYM (1): **to drop it** *exp.*
⟐ SYNONYM (2): **to give it up** *exp.*
⟐ ORIGIN: This expression conjures up an image of someone giving up a specific task and *"hanging it up"* where it will lay dormant.

head hunter *exp.* (very popular) employment agent, usually from an elite agency, hired by an employer to find qualified candidates; executive recruiter • (lit); a warrior who kills his victims and collects the heads as trophies • *A head hunter called me today to see if I was interested in a job supervising an entire department in a major company!;* An elite employment agent called me today to see if I was interested in a job supervising an entire department in a major company!

hold down a job (to) *exp.* to have a job • *It's difficult to hold down a job and raise two children at the same time;* It's difficult to have a job and raise two children at the same time.

  ♦ VARIATION: **to hold down a 9-to-5** *exp.* to have a job which begins at 9:00 A.M. and ends at 5:00 P.M.

jump through hoops (to) *exp.* to go through a long and burdensome process in order to achieve something • *The owner of the company made me jump through a lot of hoops to get my new position;* The owner of the company made me go through a long and burdensome process to get my new position.

  ♦ ORIGIN: This expression comes from animal trainers who teach animals various tricks such as jumping through hoops. It is applied to people who are forced to take a great deal of seemingly unnecessary and possibly humiliating steps in order to attain a goal.

kiss-up to someone (to) *exp.* to flatter someone in the hopes of being given preferential treatment • *Did you see that? The new guy just went and bought the boss lunch. I can't believe the way this guy is trying to kiss up to the boss!;* Did you see that? The new guy just went and bought the boss lunch. I can't believe the way this guy is trying to get preferential treatment from the boss!

know-how (to have) *exp.* to have expertise; to "know how" to do something • *Let him handle the account. He has a lot of know-how in this area;* Let him handle the account. He has a lot of expertise in this area.

kowtow (to) *v.* to bow and cater to someone's every desire • *If you want to advance in this company, you'll learn that you have to kowtow to the executives;* If you want to advance in this company, you'll learn that you have to cater to every desire of the executives.

  ♦ ORIGIN: This verb comes from Chinese literally meaning "to knock the head."

make a buck (to) *exp.* to make money • (lit); to make a dollar bill • *It's hard making a buck these days;* It's hard making money these days.

  ♦ VARIATION: **to make an honest buck** *exp.* to make money doing a reputable job • *No one wants to hire me! I just want to make an honest buck* *somewhere!;* No one wants to hire me! I just want to make money doing a reputable job somewhere!

▶ ORIGIN: The term *"buck,"* slang for "dollar," is a shortened version of "buckskin" which was used by American Indians for trade.

make it in (to) *exp.* to arrive at work • *I'm so exhausted after the party last night, I'm surprised I was able to make it in today;* I'm so exhausted after the party last night, I'm surprised I was able to arrive to work today.

paper-pusher *exp.* secretary; one who deals with a great deal of paper work • *I'm tired of being a paper-pusher in this company. I'm ready to do something more creative;* I'm tired of dealing with all this paper work. I'm ready to do something more creative.

▶ SYNONYM (1): **pencil-pusher** *exp.*

▶ SYNONYM (2): **pen-pusher** *exp.*

phones (to be on) *exp.* to be assigned to answer the telephones • *I hate being on phones!;* I hate being assigned to answer the telephones!

pound the pavement (to) *exp.* to look for employment • (lit); to walk from business to business seeking employment • *I've been pounding the pavement for three weeks and still can't find anything;* I've been looking for employment for three weeks and still can't find anything.

▶ SYNONYM: **to job search** *exp.*

pow-wow (to have a) *exp.* to hold a meeting • *We need to have a pow-wow in my office right away;* We need to have a meeting in my office right away.

▶ ORIGIN: This expression comes from American Indians who would regularly hold pow-wows (or meetings) with all the men in the tribe.

scuttlebutt *n.* the current scandalous rumor, gossip • *So, what's the scuttlebutt in the office?;* So, what's happening in the office?

▶ ORIGIN: It is said that most office rumors are started around the drinking fountain or water cooler since this is a convenient place for employees to gather. Unbeknownst to many native-born Americans, a *"scuttlebutt"* is a nautical term for a drinking fountain on a ship. The term worked its way on land and is used today to mean "gossip in general."

slave driver *n.* a supervisor who works his/her employees relentlessly as if they were slaves • *The boss insists we work the entire weekend! What a slave driver!*

PRACTICE THE VOCABULARY

(Answers to Lesson One, p. 219)

A. Underline the appropriate word that best completes the phrase.

1. Before you implement the change in policy, you'd better consult the
   big (**figs**, **wigs**, **rugs**).

2. I got called on the (**rug**, **linoleum**, **carpet**) for arriving late to work
   for the second time this week.

3. The supervisor just informed me that the president of the company
   will be here next week to review our progress! We're really going to
   have to buckle (**up**, **down**, **out**) for the next few days!

4. A (**buttocks**, **neck**, **head**) hunter just called me and offered me an
   executive position in a new company!

5. I didn't know you were holding (**up**, **down**, **out**) two jobs!

6. I have to go back for a fourth interview for this job! I swear, the
   executives are really making the applicants (**skip**, **hop**, **jump**)
   through hoops.

7. I don't think I'm going to be able to make it (**in**, **out**, **through**)
   today. I have a bad cold.

8. I've been (**hitting**, **pounding**, **slapping**) the pavement for two
   weeks now and I still can't find a job.

9. The boss expects us to work every weekend. What a slave (**driver**,
   diver, **dividend**)!

10. I'm tired of busting my (**rolls**, **loaves**, **buns**) at work while the boss
    is out playing golf!

B. Replace the word(s) in parentheses with the slang synonym(s) on the right.

1. He's a *(secretary who works with documents all day long)* __PAPER-PUSHER__ .

   A. **9-to-5**

2. Did you see the way she *(flattered)* __kissed-up to__ the boss yesterday?

   B. **hang it up**

3. My son just got his first *(job)* __9-to-5__ today!

   C. **called on the carpet**

4. I'll do anything to make *(money)* __a buck__ .

   D. **kissed-up to**

5. My boss expects everyone to *(bow and cater)* __kowtow__ to him.

   E. **a buck**

6. I'm *(unemployed)* __between jobs__ at the moment.

   F. **bust my buns**

7. The supervisor said the next person who arrives late to work is going to get *(reprimanded)* __called on the carpet__ .

   G. **between jobs**

8. The new employee has a great deal of *(expertise)* __know-how__ in her field.

   H. **know-how**

9. Just *(give up)* __hang it up__ ! The boss is never going to agree with you.

   I. **kowtow**

10. I *(work so hard)* __bust my buns__ — every day.

   J. **paper-pusher**

C. WORD SEARCH: Circle the words in the grid below that fit the following expressions. Words may be spelled up/down or diagonally. The first one has been done for you.

1. **to _____ for someone** *exp.* to do someone's job during his/her absense.

2. **to have good _____** *exp.* to know many influential people.

3. **to _____ up to someone** *exp.* to flatter someone in hopes of being given preferential treatment.

4. **to be called on the _____** *exp.* to be reprimanded by one's boss.

5. **to _____ someone** *v.* to fire someone.

6. **_____** *n.* the current scandalous rumor; gossip.

7. **to _____** *v.* to grovel and cater to someone's every desire.

8. **to _____ down** *exp.* to make an extra effort at getting work done.

9. **big _____** *n.* executive.

10. **paper _____** *exp.* one who deals with a great deal of paper work.

N	A	R	K	O	W	T	O	W	S	A	N	A	A
B	B	G	B	U	B	B	L	T	B	T	U	B	K
C	U	C	O	R	C	H	C	A	R	P	E	T	I
I	C	O	D	X	D	A	D	W	C	D	B	D	S
S	K	I	E	W	T	E	B	I	E	A	E	E	S
W	L	O	O	N	Y	F	L	G	B	F	N	F	F
H	E	G	O	G	G	L	F	G	C	G	K	U	P
E	L	C	O	V	E	R	H	B	H	K	E	E	L
F	P	I	S	C	U	T	T	L	E	B	U	T	T
E	R	P	J	P	U	S	H	E	R	J	L	P	J

A CLOSER LOOK (1):
Universal Business Slang, Idioms, & Jargon

Every group has it own unique slang (such as the jargon used among doctors, mechanics, lawyers, politicians, restaurateurs, etc.) which is incomprehensible to anyone on the outside. However, there is a universal business slang which transcends these barriers and is prevalent in just about every American company.

Anyone doing business in America should become familiar with the following terms as soon as possible since many of them will be encountered right away, starting with the receptionist!

"…and you are…?" *exp.* a common tactic used by receptionists whereby a pause is given in the hope that the other person will fill in the blank • *"… and you are…?" "… Ms. Graul."* • *"… and this is regarding…?" "… our contract with your firm."*

back on the front burner (to be) *exp.* said of an old news story that is noteworthy again • *Problems arising from severe rainstorms are back on the front burner again;* Problems arising from severe rainstorms are noteworthy again.
▶ ALSO: **to put something on the front burner** *exp.* to expedite something that has high priority • *The boss just told me that we have to finish the other project in two hours! We'd better put it on*
the front burner; The boss just told me that we have to finish the other project in two hours! We'd better expedite it since it has high priority.
▶ ANTONYM: **to be put on the back burner** *exp.* to take low priority • *Due to the emergency, everything else will have to be put on the back burner for a while;* Due to the emergency, everything else will have to take low priority for a while. • *I'm going to have to put fixing my car on the back burner for now. I have to leave town suddenly;* I'm going to have to postpone fixing my car for now. I have to leave town suddenly.
▶ NOTE: The term *"burner"* used in these expressions refers to the "burner of a stove." In the culinary world, elements such as gravies, sauces, etc. that are not

used at once are placed on the back burners of the stove where they are allowed to cook slowly or stay warm while the chef tends to the more immediate parts of the meal.

blow a deal (to) *exp.* to ruin a business arrangement with a potential client • *I can't believe you forgot to meet with the client! He got so mad that he decided to go with our competitor! How could you blow the deal like this?;* I can't believe you forgot to meet with the client! He got so mad that he decided to go with our competitor! How could you ruin the deal like this?

blue-collar worker *n.* one who does physical labor • *He may be a blue-collar worker now, but some day he'll be a manager;* He may do physical labor now, but some day he'll be a manager.
‣ ORIGIN: In America, a typical work shirt of a physical laborer used to consist of a sturdy blue long-sleeved shirt with a collar. Although originated due to a man's work shirt, this expression is also applied to women who are physical laborers.
‣ ALSO (1): **white-collar worker** *n.* one who is in a managerial position in a company • *I was the only white-collar worker at the office party!;* I was the only manager at the office party!

⇨ ORIGIN: It has always been common for men in management positions to wear formal clothing consisting of a suit, tie, and white shirt with a white collar. Although originating with men's formal clothing, this expression is also applied to women in management positions.
‣ ALSO (2): **pink-collar worker** *exp.* (outdated) a woman with a job typically filled only by other women such as a nurse, typist, secretary, etc. • *She's been a pink-collar worker ever since she got out of school;* She's worked a job typically filled only by other women ever since she got out of school.
⇨ ORIGIN: For years, Americans have considered "blue" a masculine color and "pink" a feminine color. Since just about any job is now filled by both sexes, the expression *"pink-collar worker"* is now outdated due to its sexist nature.

bottom line (to give someone the) *exp.* to proceed to the most relevant part of a story • *I don't need all that other information. Give me the bottom line! How are we doing financially?;* I don't need all that other information. Just give me the most important facts. How are we doing financially?
‣ NOTE: The *"bottom line"* refers to the actual bottom line of a financial report which indicates

either profit or loss, the most important indicator of a company's success.

breadwinner *n.* one who supports a family by earning money • *My wife is a surgeon. She's the real breadwinner of the family;* My wife is a surgeon. She's the one who really earns the money in the family.

bring someone up to speed (to) *exp.* to update someone • *A lot has happened while you were on vacation. Come into my office and I'll bring you up to speed;* A lot has happened while you were on vacation. Come into my office and I'll update you.

buck for a raise (to) *exp.* to fight for an increase in one's salary • *He's been bucking for a raise for two months but the boss still won't agree to it;* He's been fighting for a raise for two months but the boss still won't agree to it.
♦ ANTONYM: **to buck for a promotion** *exp.* to fight for an advancement in one's job position.

butt heads (to) *v.* to quarrel on a particular issue • *Gordon and David keep butting heads on the best way to run their department;* Gordon and David keep quarreling on the best way to run their department.
♦ ORIGIN: This verb comes from the act of two rams who literally butt heads as a way to claim territory.
♦ SYNONYM: **to lock horns** *exp.*

by the book (to do something) *exp.* to adhere fervently to the rules • *I was one minute late to work so the supervisor reported me to the president of the company! I swear, he does everything by the book;* I was one minute late to work so the supervisor reported me to the president of the company! I swear, he adheres fervently to the rules.

caps *n.pl.* abbreviation of *"capital letters."*
♦ NOTE: This abbreviation is only used when spoken (i.e. dictation). It is rarely used in written form: *Whenever you abbreviate Los Angeles, make sure that L.A. is in caps;* Whenever you abbreviate Los Angeles, make sure that L.A. is in capital letters.

card key *n.* a plastic card which is used like a key for access into a parking lot, building, room, etc. • *I forgot my card key, so I had to park in the street;* I forgot my plastic card which allows me into the parking lot, so I had to park in the street.

com *n.* abbreviation of *"comma."*
♦ NOTE: This abbreviation is only used when spoken (i.e. dictation). It is never used in written form: *Although your client fell in front*

of our building (com), we are not claiming responsibility.

come to a grinding halt (to) *exp.* said of a business or factory that shuts down abruptly • *The business came to a grinding halt when all the employees went on strike;* The business shut down abruptly when all the employees went on strike.

copy someone on something (to) *exp.* to send someone a copy of something • *Make sure to copy the boss on today's agenda;* Make sure to send the boss a copy of today's agenda.
♦ VARIATION: **to cc someone on something** *exp.* (cc is pronounced "C-C") • (lit); to send someone a carbon copy of something • *Don't forget to cc the executive board on this memo;* Don't forget to send a copy of this memo to the executive board.
♦ NOTE (1): Although carbon copies have been replaced by photocopies, the abbreviated verb *"to cc"* is still in common usage.
♦ NOTE (2): When sending copies of a correspondence to various people, it is common in business to list the recipients on the bottom of the last page next to the letters *"cc."* This way each recipient is aware of all those receiving the correspondence.
♦ NOTE (3): After the *"cc"* list, there may be an additional *"bcc"*

(blind carbon copy) list only on the file copy which does not circulate to the addressee(s). These are usually executives who also receive the correspondence yet prefer to remain anonymous.

crunch numbers (to) *exp.* to do mathematical calculations • *I was just offered two different jobs but I'm not sure which one will end up being the most profitable. I need to sit down tonight and crunch some numbers;* I was just offered two different jobs but I'm not sure which one will end up being the most profitable. I need to sit down tonight and do some mathematical calculations.

culture of the office (the) *exp.* the general atmosphere and feeling of the office • *"What's the culture of your new office?" "Very relaxed! I work with the nicest people!;"* "What's the mood of your new office?" "Very relaxed! I work with the nicest people!"
♦ VARIATION: **corporate culture** *exp.* the general atmosphere and feeling of an office or corporation • *The corporate culture at our office encourages greed;* The general atmosphere at our office encourages greed.

cush-job *exp.* an extremely easy and profitable job • *All day long he gives clients tours of the office. What a cush job!;* All day long he gives clients tours of the office. What an easy job!

cut a deal (to) *exp.* to make a business arrangement or contract • *After two days of negotiating, we're all finally ready to cut a deal;* After two days of negotiating, we're all finally ready to make a business arrangement.

deadline *n.* a point in time at which a specific project must be completed • *Tom has to work again this weekend because he has a Tuesday deadline;* Tom has to work again this weekend because his project must be completed by Tuesday.

desk jockey *n.* an employee who works behind a desk • *I prefer getting out and dealing with people. I guess I could never be a desk jockey;* I prefer getting out and dealing with people. I guess I could never be stuck working behind a desk.

double-time (to be on) *exp.* to be receiving twice one's regular wages for working beyond one's normal hours • *For the past three hours I've been on double-time. I'm really making a lot of money tonight!;* For the past three hours I've been receiving a compensation of twice my regular wages for working beyond my normal hours. I'm really making a lot of money

tonight!
♦ SEE: **time and a half (to be on)** *exp.*

draw up a contract (to) *exp.* to draft a contract • *Since we are all in agreement about our terms of working together, I think it's time to draw up a contract;* Since we are all in agreement about our terms of working together, I think it's time to draft a contract.

E-mail *exp.* electronic mail which is sent and retrieved through a computer screen • *I just received E-mail from the corporate office saying that the president of the company is going to be arriving in two hours!;* I just received electronic mail from the corporate office saying that the president of the company is going to be arriving in two hours! ♦ VARIATION: **to E-mail someone** *exp.* to send electronic mail to someone • *When I find out what time the meeting is, I'll E-mail you;* When I find out what time the meeting is, I'll send you electronic mail.

eat on the run (to) *exp.* to eat while rushing to an appointment • *I wish I could sit down and have lunch with you but I have to eat on the run again;* I wish I could sit down and have lunch with you but I have to eat while rushing to an appointment again.

embezzle (to) *v.* a common term meaning "to steal money from a company" • *He embezzled $1,000 each year from the company;* He stole $1,000 each year from the company.

‣ SYNONYM: **to misappropriate** *v.* (very popular) • *The new employee began misappropriating funds the day he began work!;* The new employee began stealing money the day he began work!

fall through (to) *exp.* to deteriorate (said of a business or a project) • *Just when we were about to sign contracts, the whole deal fell through;* Just when we were about to sign contracts, the whole deal deteriorated.

fax (to) *v.* to transmit a document from one location to another via a facsimile machine, also known as a fax machine • *Fax this letter to the corporate office right away!;* Transmit this letter to the corporate office right away!

FedEx *n.* a common abbreviation of "Federal Express," a well known express mail carrier which guarantees overnight deliveries • *Call FedEx right away! This package has to arrive in our satellite office tomorrow morning!;* Call Federal Express right away! This package has to arrive in our satellite office tomorrow morning!

‣ VARIATION: **to FedEx** *v.* to send something via Federal Express • *Could you please FedEx this package to France for me?;* Could you please send this package to France for me via Federal Express?

fill the bill (to) *exp.* to be appropriate for a job position • *I've finally found someone to fill the bill;* I've finally found someone appropriate for the job.

flunky *n.* one who does menial tasks • *My first job was as a flunky in a large office;* My first job was to do menial tasks in a large office.

fly (to) *v.* said of a business venture or idea that will succeed • *I don't think his idea to open a store in his little town will fly;* I don't think his idea to open a store in his little town will succeed.

‣ ANTONYM: **to go over like a lead balloon** *exp.* (humorous).

⇨ NOTE: This is a play-on-words on the expression *"to go over"* meaning "to be acceptable" • *When I demanded a raise, it didn't go over very well with the boss;* When I demanded a raise, it wasn't very acceptable with the boss. Therefore, something that *"goes over like a lead balloon"* is considered extremely unacceptable or unsuccessful • *My joke went over like a lead balloon at the meeting;* My joke was extremely unsuccessful at the meeting.

go over someone's head (to) *exp.* to go directly to someone's superior • *When Mr. Carlin wouldn't respond to my complaints, I decided to go over his head;* When Mr. Carlin wouldn't respond to my complaints, I decided to go directly to his supervisor.
◗ NOTE: The approach of *"going over someone's head"* is usually considered an insult to that person since you are implying that he/she is incompetent.

gopher *exp.* errand boy/girl • (lit); a rodent who lives underground • *She works as a gopher in a big movie studio;* She works doing errands in a big movie studio.
◗ ORIGIN: This term is actually a play-on-words describing someone whose job it is to *"go fer"* this and *"go fer"* that.
⇨ NOTE: The preposition "for" is commonly pronounced *"fer"* in colloquial American-English.

grapevine (to hear something through the) *exp.* to hear a rumor that has been passed along from one person to another • *Did you know she's been having an affair with the boss? I just heard it through the grapevine!;* Did you know she's been having an affair with the boss? I just heard it from several people!

graveyard shift (to work) *exp.* to work throughout the night (usually between 11:00 PM and 7:00 AM • *I work graveyard shift every other week;* I work throughout the night every other week.
◗ VARIATION (1): **to work the graveyard shift** *exp.*
◗ VARIATION (2): **to work graveyard** *exp.*

grind *n.* a difficult job (yet is commonly used in reference to a job in general • *That was a great lunch, but now it's back to the grind!;* That was a great lunch, but now it's back to work!
◗ VARIATION: **daily grind** *exp.* the repetitive drudgery of work • *My father is looking forward to retirement. He's so sick of the daily grind!;* My father is looking forward to retirement. He's so sick of the repetitive drudgery of work!

ground floor (to get in on the) *exp.* to invest in a company at its inception • *The company is just getting started and I've decided to invest now. I want to get in on the ground floor before everyone else discovers it's going to be extremely successful;* The company is just getting started and I've decided to invest now. I want to get involved at the company's inception before everyone else discovers it's going to be extremely successful.

hack it (to) *exp.* to cope successfully • *Jerry couldn't hack it as an accountant;* Jerry couldn't cope successfully as an accountant.

♦ SYNONYM: **to handle it** *exp.*

hang out one's shingle (to) *exp.* to open one's own business • *As soon as he got his medical degree, he hung out a shingle;* As soon as he got his medical degree, he opened his own practice.

♦ NOTE (1): The term *"practice"* is synonymous with "business" and is generally applied to professionals such as lawyers, doctors, accountants, etc.

♦ NOTE (2): Many years ago, merchants used to hang a rectangular piece of wood, or a *"shingle,"* in front of their shops indicating the name or type of the business.

hard-sell (to) *exp.* to attempt to sell something to someone by relentlessness, overstatement and pressure • *You don't need to hard-sell me. Just tell me about your product;* You don't need to try to get me to buy your product by overstating. Just tell me about your product.

♦ VARIATION: **hard-sell** *n.* an attempt to sell something to someone by relentlessness, overstatement and pressure • *I hate getting the hard-sell!;* I hate being sold something through relentlessness and overstatement!

hired hand *exp.* employee (especially on a ranch) • *Steve is our new hired hand;* Steve is our new employee.

"I'll scratch your back if you scratch mine" *exp.* "I'll do you a favor if you do me a favor" • *I'll be glad to loan you the money you need and in return, I'd like to get the names of some of your business contacts. I'll scratch your back if you scratch mine;* I'll be glad to loan you the money you need and in return, I'd like to get the names of some of your business contacts. I'll do you a favor if you do me a favor.

in full swing (to be) *exp.* • **1.** said of a company that is functioning at full capacity • *We've only been open three days and we're already in full swing;* We've only been open three days and we're already functioning at full capacity. • **2.** a function that has been going on for a while • *It looks like this meeting is in full swing;* It looks like this meeting has been going on for a while.

in/out of the loop (to be) *exp.* to be/not to be part of a job • *If there are problems with the job, don't call me. I'm out of the loop;* If there are problems with the job, don't call me. I'm not part of it.

job opening (a) *exp.* an available position in a company • *I hear there's a job opening at the computer store!;* I hear there's an available position in the computer store!

♦ VARIATION: • *Did you hear a job is opening at the computer store?;* Did you hear a job is opening at the computer store?

knock on doors (to) *exp.* to look for employment • *I've been knocking on doors all day and I still can't find a job!;* I've been looking for employment all day and I still can't find a job!

♦ SYNONYM: **to pound the pavement** *exp.*

knuckle down (to) *exp.* to become more strict • *The boss is knuckling down on employees who arrive late to work;* The boss is become more strict with employees who arrive late to work.

knuckle under (to) *exp.* to collapse (said of a person) • *She knuckled under because of all the pressure she had at work;* She collapsed because of all the pressure she had at work.

land an account (to) *exp.* to acquire an account • *We just landed a large account today;* We just acquired a large account today.

♦ NOTE: This is actually a play-on-words since the verb *"to land"* is typically used in the phrase *"to land a big fish"* meaning "to bring in a big fish."

lead time *n.* time available to prepare for an event or due date • *You want my report by next Tuesday? That doesn't give me much lead time!;* You want my report by next Tuesday? That doesn't give me much time to prepare!

let something slide (to) *exp.* to overlook something, to disregard something • *I was late but the boss said he would let it slide this time;* I was late but the boss said he would overlook it this time.

lunch (to do) *exp.* to have lunch with someone • *Let's do lunch tomorrow;* Let's have lunch together tomorrow.

♦ NOTE: This is a popular yet pretentious transformation of "to have lunch" and is stereotyped as being used primarily by pompous Hollywood agents.

make a killing (to) *exp.* to make a great deal of money in a business venture • *He opened his own business and made a killing!;* He opened his own business and made a great deal of money!

moonlight (to) *v.* to work an extra job at night • *I just found out the boss is moonlighting as a waiter! No wonder he's tired every day;* I just found out the boss is working as a waiter at night! No wonder he's tired every day.

Murphy's Law *exp.* an often quoted "law" (originated by developmental engineer Ed Murphy in the 1940s) which states: "Anything that can possibly go wrong, will go wrong" • *I can't believe I got a flat after just buying a whole new set of tires! It must be Murphy's law;* I can't believe I got a flat tire after just buying a whole new set of tires! Anything that can possibly go wrong, will go wrong.

office politics *exp.* competition among various management or executive levels within the office • *The new guy they hired as sales manager had better be careful or the office politics will cause him to be less effective than he thought he'd be;* The new guy they hired as sales manager had better be careful or the competition among various executives in the office will cause him to be less effective than he thought he'd be.

on board (to be) *exp.* to be employed • (lit); to be on a ship (whose decks are traditionally made of wooden boards) • *I've been on board with this company for three years;* I've been employed with this company for three years. • *Wait until the new vice president comes on board. Things will change!;* Wait until the new vice president starts working here. Things will change!

on lunch (to be) *exp.* to be on a lunch break • *Why don't you try back in an hour? Bob's on lunch until one o'clock;* Why don't you attempt to make contact again in an hour? Bob's at lunch until one o'clock.
‣ NOTE: The expression *"to try back"* is a common expression in business meaning "to attempt to make contact again."
‣ ALSO: **to be on break** *exp.* to be taking a pause from work.

on one's toes (to be) *exp.* to be alert and aware • *The president of the company will be here starting in the morning, so be on your toes!;* The president of the company will be here starting in the morning, so be alert and aware!

on the clock (to be) *exp.* to be accruing payable hours • *The boss said you have to stop chatting with the other employees while you're on the clock. He's right. You should be doing that on your own time;* The boss said you have to stop chatting with the other employees while you're accruing payable hours. He's right. You should be doing that when you're not getting paid.
‣ NOTE: This expression relates to a "time clock," utilized by many factories, which stamps (or *"punches"*) the employees' working hours on a card. It is

also common to hear the expression *"to punch in"* meaning "to begin work" and *"to punch out"* meaning "to end work."

on the job *exp.* in the course of one's job • *Did you know he drinks on the job?;* Did you know he drinks in the course of his job?

out of pocket (to be) *exp.* said of direct expenses that one incurs personally • *I hope I get reimbursed from the company soon. These expenses were all out of pocket!;* I hope I get reimbursed from the company soon. I paid for these expenses myself!

outsource (to) *v.* to use outside sources other then inhouse • *Due to time constraints, instead of printing our brochures here at our own company, I think we should outsource;* Due to time constraints, instead of printing our brochures here at our own company, I think we should use outside sources.

overnight something (to) *exp.* to send a document or package to a destination for delivery the next day • *We need to overnight these documents to our corporate office. They must arrive in time for an afternoon meeting tomorrow;* We need to send these documents so they arrive at our

corporate office the next day. They must arrive in time for an afternoon meeting tomorrow.

Pacific Standard Time *exp.* (seen as PST) The time zone for the United States west of the Rocky Mountains.
‣ ALSO (1): **Central Standard Time** *exp.* (seen as CST) The time zone in the central part of the United States which is two hours later than Pacific Standard Time.
‣ ALSO (2): **Eastern Standard Time** *exp.* (seen as EST) The time zone in the eastern part of the United States which is three hours later than Pacific Standard Time.

paren *n.* abbreviation of *"parenthesis."*
‣ NOTE: This abbreviation is only used when spoken (i.e. dictation). It is never used in written form: *Mr. Jones (open paren) (President of our company) (close paren) will be arriving at two o'clock in the afternoon.*

patch someone through (to) *exp.* to transfer someone to a designated telephone • *I'll patch you through to Mr. Smith;* I'll transfer you to Mr. Smith's telephone.
‣ NOTE: This expression originated several decades ago when operators would have to direct calls by plugging in (or *"patching in"*) the telephone

cable into the appropriate slot. Although this method is no longer used, the expression is still occasionally used.

pay cut (to take a) *exp.* to accept a decrease in one's salary • *The company is forcing everyone to take a pay cut since profits are so low;* The company is forcing everyone to accept a decrease in salary since profits are so low.
‣ VARIATION: **to take a cut in pay** *exp.*

plug away (to) *exp.* to work persistently • *He's been plugging away for the past three hours trying to get the problem solved;* He's been working persistently for the past three hours trying to get the problem solved.

politically correct (to be) *exp.* to use the most currently acceptable terminology when referring to certain groups • *In the '80s, it was politically correct to use the term "Black." However, in the '90s, the politically correct term is "African-American."*
‣ VARIATION: **to be P.C.** *adj.* an abbreviation for *"politically correct."*

put one's nose to the grindstone (to) *exp.* to work diligently • *I just got reprimanded by the boss for spending too much time talking on the job. She said I'd better put my nose to the grindstone or find another job!;* I

just got reprimanded by the boss for spending too much time talking on the job. She said I'd better start working more diligently or find another job!
‣ ORIGIN: Early grindstones, used to sharpen tools, required that the user get extremely close to the wheel during operation, giving an illusion of putting his/her nose on the grindstone itself.

put someone on hold (to) *exp.* to disconnect someone temporarily from the telephone line (where the caller will either hear silence or recorded music) • *When I called your office, some guy put me on hold while he went looking for you and never came back!;* When I called your office, some guy disconnected me temporarily while he went looking for you and never came back!
‣ ALSO: **to put something on hold** *exp.* to postpone a project • *Let's put this project on hold. We need to complete another assignment first;* Let's postpone this project. We need to complete another assignment first.
‣ SYNONYM: **to put someone on ignore** *exp.* (humorous) • *The operator put me on ignore for ten minutes!;* The operator left me in silence (or was possibly ignoring me) for ten minutes!

put someone through (to) *exp.* to transfer someone to someone else's telephone • *Mr. Jones just* *got off his phone. I'll put you through now;* Mr. Jones just got off his phone. I'll transfer you to him now.

♦ SYNONYM: **to ring someone through** *exp.*

put something on a rush (to) *exp.* to request that a service be done as fast as possible (which usually costs extra money) • *I need to get these negatives developed right away. Let's put it on a rush and I'll pay the extra costs;* I need to get these negatives developed right away. Let's request that the service be done as fast as possible and I'll pay the extra costs.

♦ VARIATION: **to put a rush on something** *exp.* • *Let's put a rush on these negatives;* Let's get these negatives made as soon as possible.

⇨ NOTE: This comes from the common practice of stamping the word *"RUSH"* on the outside of a package.

raise (to get a) *n.* to get an increase in one's salary • *I got a raise today!;* I got an increase in salary today!

♦ VARIATION: **to get raised** *exp.*

♦ ANTONYM: SEE - **pay cut (to take a)** *exp.*

rat race *exp.* the hectic day-to-day business life (where people seem to be running around like rats in a maze) • *I'm so tired of the rat race here in the city. Maybe I'll*

move to the country; I'm so tired of the hectic day-to-day business life here in the city. Maybe I'll move to the country.

red tape *exp.* excessive and seemingly unnecessary bureaucratic procedures • *I had to go through a lot of red tape to get a refund;* I had to go through a lot of excessive procedures to get a refund.

running late (to be) *exp.* to be late for an appointment • *If you don't want to get in trouble, you'd better call work and tell them you're running late;* If you don't want to get in trouble, you'd better call work and tell them you're late.

sales job on someone (to do a) *exp.* to try aggressively and somewhat over enthusiastically to sell a product or service to someone • *You don't have to do such a sales job on me! I'm already convinced I want to buy your product;* You don't have to try so hard to sell me your merchandise! I'm already convinced I want to buy your product.

♦ VARIATION: **to do a sell job on someone** *exp.*

♦ NOTE: sales pitch *exp.* an aggressive and somewhat overly enthusiastic speech used to attract a potential customer.

salt mines *n.pl.* work • *Lunch is over. Back to the salt mines!;* Lunch is over. Back to work!

‣ VARIATION: **mines** *n.pl.*

‣ ORIGIN: Since working in a salt mine is considered an extremely difficult, exhausting, and often painful task, the term *"salt mines"* or *"mines"* is commonly used in jest to refer to one's own job.

‣ SYNONYM (1): **coal mines** *n.pl.*

‣ SYNONYM (2): **gold mines** *n.pl.*

scab *n.* a derogatory term for a nonunion member who replaces a union worker while on strike • *When Steve heard that I was out on strike, he called my boss and told him he'd be glad to replace me. What a scab!*

‣ ALSO: **to scab** *v.*

secretarial pool *n.* a group of secretaries who wait to be called on assignment • *After being in the secretarial pool for almost a month, I finally got my first assignment in the company!;* After a month of being among the secretaries who aren't yet on assignment, I finally got my first assignment in the company!

sexual harassment *exp.* sexual advances or derogatory sexual remarks made by one's superior • *My boss said that if I didn't do exactly what he wanted sexually, he'd fire me! I've decided to bring him up on charges of sexual harassment;* My boss said

that if I didn't do exactly what he wanted sexually, he'd fire me! I've decided to bring him up on charges of making sexual advances toward me.

short-handed (to be) *exp.* to be low on personnel • *We weren't able to ship out all products to the customers because we were short-handed today;* We weren't able to ship out all products to the customers because we were low on personnel today.

‣ SYNONYM: **to be short-staffed** *exp.*

shred something (to) *exp.* to tear paper into little pieces (using a paper shredder) for security reasons • *Be sure to shred these extra copies of our budget before throwing them away;* Be sure to tear these extra copies of our budget into little pieces (using a paper shredder) before throwing them away.

‣ VARIATION: **to run/put it through the paper shredder** *exp.* • *Before you throw those papers away, make sure to run/put them through the shredder;* Before you throw those papers away, make sure to tear them into little pieces in the shredder.

slack off (to) *exp.* to shirk one's responsibilities • *He used to be such a good worker. Now he slacks off all the time;* He used to be such a good worker. Now he

shirks his responsibilities all the time.
♦ ALSO: **slacker** *n.* one who shirks his/her responsibilities.

"Speaking…" *n.* a very common term used to identify oneself as the person requested by the caller
• *"Is Mr. Burke in?"* *"Speaking;"* "Is Mr. Burke in?" "This is he."

step on someone's toes (to) *exp.* to infringe on someone's authority
• *If you make that decision without consulting Mr. Henderson, you'll be stepping on his toes;* If you make that decision without consulting Mr. Henderson, you'll be infringing on his authority.

step out (to) *v.* to leave temporarily
• *I'm afraid Mr. Chancer just stepped out. Would you like me to have him return your call?;* I'm afraid Mr. Chancer just left the office. Would you like me to have him return your call?

stet *n.* "ignore the change and keep the original."
♦ NOTE: When a copyeditor or proofreader makes a change in the text followed by the word *"stet,"* the original text should be kept and the change ignored.
♦ ORIGIN: This noun comes from the Latin verb *"stare"* meaning "to stand." Therefore, *"stet"* = **"let it stand."**

sweatshop *n.* factory (where the temperature is extremely warm and the work physically difficult)
• *My father worked in a sweatshop while he was going to school;* My father worked rigorously in a hot factory while he was going to school.
♦ ORIGIN: In the early 1900s, factories were typically located on the top floors or lofts of large manufacturing companies where temperatures were extremely high. These factories were referred to as *"sweatshops."*

take a big bite out of one's paycheck (to) *exp.* to be expensive • *What a beautiful new jacket! That must have taken a big bite out of your paycheck!;* What a beautiful new jacket! That must have been expensive!

take a break (to) *exp.* to take a short rest during the day • *If I don't take a break at some point during the day, I'm exhausted by the time I get home;* If I don't take a short rest at some point during the day, I'm exhausted by the time I get home.
♦ VARIATION: **to take a coffee break** *exp.*

take a letter (to) *exp.* to take dictation • *Ms. Johnson, would you please come into my office and take a letter?;* Ms. Johnson, would you please come into my office and take some dictation?

take a long weekend (to) *exp.* to take either Friday or Monday as a vacation day, creating a three-day weekend • *I'm taking a long weekend and renting a house at the beach;* I'm taking either Friday or Monday as a vacation day and renting a house at the beach.

take a mental health day (to) *exp.* to be absent from work in order to seek relaxation • *After these three weeks of stress, I'm taking a mental health day tomorrow!;* After these three weeks of stress, I'm going to be absent from work in order to relax tomorrow!

take a sick day (to) *exp.* to be absent from work and still receive pay.
♦ NOTE: For a certain number of days, large companies continue to pay their employees who are absent from work due to illness. If the employee has had no reason to use a *"sick day,"* he/she may opt to use one of these days as a vacation day: *I'm going to take a sick day on Friday and go skiing.*

take lunch (to) *exp.* to stop work in order to eat lunch • *I'm taking a late lunch today;* I'm eating lunch late today.

take on an employee (to) *exp.* **1.** to hire • *We took on three new employees today;* We hired three new employees today. • **2.** to

defy • *Why do you keep taking on the boss? Do you want to get yourself fired?;* Why do you keep defying the boss? Do you want to get yourself fired?

talk a good game (to) *exp.* to sound confident about one's own abilities or product while trying to make a sale • *That new employee talks a good game but I just don't believe he's really that experienced;* That new employee sounds confident about his abilities but I just don't believe he's really that experienced.
♦ SYNONYM: **to talk a good line** *exp.*

temp *n.* temporary employee • *Our receptionist called in sick this morning. We'd better get a temp to help out for the day;* Our receptionist called in sick this morning. We'd better get a temporary employee to help out for the day.
♦ ANTONYM: **perm** *adj.* a permanent employee • *I started out as a temp, now I'm perm;* I started out as a temporary employee, now I'm permanent.
♦ NOTE: Unlike *"temp,"* the term *"perm"* can only be used as an adjective when signifying "permanent employment." Therefore, it would be incorrect to say *"I'm a perm"* since the noun *"perm"* is used to mean a "hair permanent" which is a

process to make straight hair curly.

tied up (to be) *exp.* to be busy • *I'm afraid I'm going to be coming home late tonight. I'm tied up at work;* I'm afraid I'm going to be coming home late tonight. I'm going to be detained at work.

time and a half (to be on) *exp.* to be receiving one and a half times one's regular wages for working beyond one's normal hours • *Moving all these boxes is hard work but at least I'm on time and a half;* Moving all these boxes is hard work but at least I'm receiving one and one half times my regular wages for working beyond my normal hours.
 ‣ SEE: **double-time (to be on)** *exp.*

toe the line (to) *exp.* to follow the rules and policies established by a company • *At my father's company, if you don't toe the line, you'll be fired;* At my father's company, if you don't follow the company rules, you'll be fired.

toe-to-toe (to go) *exp.* to compete directly with a particular company (or other person) • *Although the Standard Trim Company has been in business for years, we should be big enough to go toe-to-toe with them in just a few months;* Although the Standard Trim

Company has been in business for years, we should be big enough to compete with them directly in just a few months.

troubleshoot (to) *v.* to identify and solve problems • *I need to hire someone who can troubleshoot the computer problems that occur so often;* I need to hire someone who can solve the computer problems that occur so often.
 ‣ ALSO: **troubleshooter** *n.* one who solves problems.

turn a profit (to) *exp.* to make a profit • *We turned a profit our first month in business!;* We made a profit our first month in business!

typo *n.* short for "typographical error" • *Look at all these typos he made! His work is really sloppy;* Look at all these typing errors he made! His work is really sloppy.

upper\lower *n.* a shortened version of "uppercase/lowercase."
 ‣ NOTE: Commonly seen written as u/l, this indicates to the typist that the first letter of each word should be capitalized.

V.P. *n.* a commonly used abbreviation of *vice president* • *I was just made V.P. of the company!;* I was just made vice president of the company!
 ‣ NOTE: Although it would be reasonable to assume that since

"V.P." is an abbreviation of "vice president," *"P."* would be an abbreviation of "president." This is *not* the case. The only abbreviation that can be applied to the noun "president" is *"pres."* whose usage is considered extremely casual.

voice-mail *exp.* a popular electronic telephone message-taking system • *I called her today but I got her voice mail;* I called her today but I got her electronic telephone message-taking system.
‣ SYNONYM: **phone-mail** *exp.*

walk (to) *v.* to strike • to abandon one's work and walk out the door • *If we don't get a raise, I think we should all walk!;* If we don't get a raise, I think we should all strike!
‣ NOTE: For years, a common synonym for "to strike" has been *"to walk out."* However, one of the biggest trends in slang and idiomatic speech of this decade is to drop the preposition after the verb. For example:
"to flip out" = *"to flip"* (to lose control of one's emotions)
"to be bummed out" = *"to be bummed"* (to be disappointed)
"to crank up" = *"to crank"* (to turn up the volume) etc.

watercooler gossip *exp.* rumors which are spread around the watercooler where employees can gather and look inconspicuous • *You actually believe all those rumors? That's nothing but watercooler gossip!;* You actually believe all those rumors? That's nothing but rumors spread by the employees who gossip around the watercooler!

wear several hats (to) *exp.* to have several responsibilities in a company • *I can't believe how busy I'm getting at work these days. I think I'm wearing too many hats!;* I can't believe how busy I'm getting at work these days. I think I have too many responsibilities!

well-connected (to be) *adj.* to have many important business relationships • *If you need any help finding a job, Kim can help you. She's very well-connected;* If you need any help finding a job, Kim can help you. She has many important business relationships.

white-out *n.* a white paint-like substance used to paint over an incorrectly typed letter (typed on white paper) so that it may be replaced by the correct letter • *I just can't type. I used an entire bottle of white-out trying to type one page!;* I just can't type. I used an entire bottle of correction fluid trying to type one page!
‣ NOTE: *"White-out"* is a brand name.

work one's fingers to the bone (to) *exp.* to work extremely hard with one's hands • *I worked my fingers to the bone yesterday preparing all that food!;* I worked extremely hard yesterday preparing all that food!

work overtime (to) *exp.* to work beyond one's normal hours • *I've had to work overtime every day this week!;* I've had to work beyond my normal hours every day this week!
♦ VARIATION: **to put in overtime** *exp.* • *Do you put in a lot of overtime at your job?;* Do you work beyond your normal hours often?

workaholic *n.* one who works constantly • *He works twelve hours a day and even on weekends. He's a real workaholic;* He works twelve hours a day and even on weekends. He works constantly.

workhorse (to be a) *exp.* to be an extremely hard and tireless worker • *Can you believe all the work he got done his first day on the job? He's a real workhorse!;* Can you believe all the work he got done his first day on the job? He's a real hard worker!
♦ NOTE: This term literally refers to a horse used for heavy work such a plowing, hauling, etc.

working stiff *n.* employee • *He's so professional I thought he* owned the company all these years. I found out he's really only a working stiff!; He's so professional I thought he owned the company all these years. I found out he's really only an employee!

Xerox (to) *v.* to photocopy • *Would you please Xerox this document for me?;* Would you please make a photocopy of this document for me?
♦ VARIATION: **to make a Xerox** *exp.* • *Would you please make five Xeroxes of this page for me?;* Would you please make five photocopies of this page for me?
♦ NOTE: *"Xerox"* is actually a company which makes photocopy machines. Their machines became so popular that the company's name itself has been adopted worldwide as a common synonym for the verb "to photocopy."

yes-man *n.* said of a man who avoids conflicts and is overly agreeable in order to stay in the good graces of his/her superiors • *He agrees with absolutely everything the boss says! I swear, he's such a yes-man!;* He agrees with absolutely everything the boss says! I swear, he's such a yes-man!
♦ NOTE: This term can only be used in the masculine form. Therefore, the term *"yes-woman"* does not exist.

Practice Using Universal Business Slang, Idioms, & Jargon

(Answers, p. 220)

A. Underline the correct word that best completes the phrase.

1. We have to put the current project on the (**back**, **side**, **lower**) burner and begin work right away on a new one.

2. I can't believe you forgot to meet the client for lunch today! Do you realize you (**blew**, **coughed**, **sneezed**) the deal?

3. I've been working in construction for several years. I really like being a (**red**, **white**, **blue**) collar worker.

4. My wife is a doctor. She's the real (**winner**, **prizewinner**, **breadwinner**) of the family.

5. Let me bring you up to (**seed**, **steed**, **speed**) on this project.

6. I arrive to work at noon and leave by four o'clock in the afternoon. This is such a (**cush**, **mush**, **tush**) job!

7. After negotiating for two days, we're finally ready to (**slice**, **dice**, **cut**) a deal.

8. If we're all in agreement on the terms we've discussed, I think we're ready to (**sketch**, **paint**, **draw**) up a contract.

9. Just when we were about to sign the contract, the whole deal fell (**through**, **up**, **in**).

10. You really shouldn't do personal work when you're still on the (**watch**, **clock**, **timer**).

11. The company is forcing everyone to take a pay (**cut**, **gash**, **slash**) since profits are so low.

12. I had to go through a lot of (**pink**, **red**, **purple**) tape in order to get a refund.

A CLOSER LOOK (2):
Office Party Jargon

It is common for many companies to throw office parties as a way to socialize with clients, heighten the morale of the employees, entertain potential business contacts, etc. Since these affairs are usually for both business and pleasure, two groups of slang are commonly present.

The following list should help to prepare you for just about any social function.

bash *n.* party • *The boss really threw a bash last night!;* The boss really threw a great party last night!
▶ NOTE: An extremely common expression meaning "to give a party" is *"to throw a party (bash, shindig, etc.)* • *I'm throwing a big bash for my parents;* I'm throwing a big party for my parents.
▶ SYNONYM: **shindig** *n.* This term originally referred to a raucous party in which men would begin fighting and kicking, digging each other in the shin with the toe of their boots. It is now used in jest to indicate a large, noisy, and fun party which may or may not have dancing • *Tonight, we're throwing a big shindig at my house;* Tonight, we're having a big party at my house.

fashionably late (to be) *exp.* to arrive purposely late after most of the other guests (in order to give others the impression you are important and have just arrived from yet another significant engagement) • *We must be sure to arrive fashionably late or everyone will know we have nothing else to do but come to this party!;* We must be sure to arrive purposely late (in order to give others the impression we are important and have just arrived from yet another significant engagement) or everyone will know we have nothing else to do but come to this party!

interface (to) *v.* to interact; to meet • *Let's make sure and interface tomorrow after the meeting;* Let's make sure and interact tomorrow after the meeting.

make an entrance (to) *exp.* to arrive just after the party has begun in order to attract everyone's attention upon entering (usually by dressing beautifully) • *You look beautiful! You sure did make an entrance!;*

You look beautiful! You sure did grab everyone's attention when you entered the room!

mingle (to) *v.* to socialize at a party by circulating throughout the room • *If you really want to meet someone here, you need to go mingle!;* If you really want to meet someone here, you need to go socialize by circulating throughout the room!

network (to) *exp.* to meet people who are influential in the business world (for one's personal gain) • *The reason you're not getting anywhere in your field is because you don't network enough!;* The reason you're not getting anywhere in your field is because you don't meet enough influential people in the business world!

pick someone up (to) *exp.* to look for someone for romantic encounters • (lit); to lift someone (and carry him/her away) • *The new client keeps trying to pick me up!;* The new client keeps trying to approach me on a romantic level!
 ♦ VARIATION: **to pick up on someone** *exp.* • *Is he still trying to pick up on you?;* Is he still trying to approach you on a romantic level?

put in an appearance (to) *exp.* to go to a party just long enough for the host (and other guests) to know you were there • *I'll be home from the party early. I'm just going to put in an appearance;* I'll be home from the party early. I'm just going long enough for the host (and other guests) to know I was there.

rub elbows with someone (to) *exp.* to socialize with influential people • *It's important for me to go to the party tonight and rub elbows;* It's important for me to go to the party tonight and socialize with influential people.

seen (to be) *exp.* said of one who goes to important functions (usually dressed lavishly to attract attention) in order *"to be seen"* by influential people • *The only reason she goes to so many parties is to be seen!;* The only reason she goes to so many parties is to be seen by influential people.

shmooze (to) *v.* to take advantage of a party by socializing with the influential people in attendance to further one's career • *There's my boss. I'm gonna go shmooze;* There's my boss. I'm going to go socialize with him (in the hopes of furthering my career).

small talk (to make) *exp.* to make superficial conversation • *I'm so tired of going to parties! I can't stand having to make small talk!;* I'm so tired of going to parties! I can't stand having to make superficial conversation!

suck-up party *exp.* (crude yet popular) a party where people seek out influential people with whom to socialize in order to further their careers • *The boss is having a party at his house tonight. It's going to be nothing but a suck-up party!;* The boss is having a party at his house tonight. There will only be people trying to socialize with him in order to further their careers!

work a party (to) *exp.* to take advantage of a party by going around meeting virtually everyone (usually hoping to make new business contacts) • *She really knows how to work a party!;* She really knows how to take advantage of a party!
  ‣ SYNONYM: **to work a room** *exp.*

Practice Using Office Party Jargon

(Answers, p. 220)

B. Replace the italicized word(s) using the list below.

bash	to be fashionably late	mingle
make an entrance	put in an appearance	shmooze
	small talk	

1. I'm so tired of going to parties because I'm not good at making *superficial conversation* _____ .

2. If you really want to make new friends here, you need to go *socialize by circulating throughout the room* _____ .

3. The party started an hour ago and Judy still isn't here. I guess she's trying *to arrive purposely late* _____ .

4. This is really a great *party* _____ !

5. You look beautiful! You sure did *grab everyone's attention when you entered* _____ .

6. There's my boss. I'm going to go *take advantage of this party by socializing with him in order to further my career* _____ .

7. I'll be home from the party early. I'm just going *long enough for the everyone to know I was there* _____ .

A CLOSER LOOK (3):
Common Slang Synonyms for Business-Related Terms

Needless to say, if you are a business traveler from another country, it is extremely important to be familiar with the everyday slang used in the business world or you face being at a serious disadvantage.

However, even after you've learned a popular slang equivalent of any given term, you still face the many other slang synonyms which are also commonly used for that term. Knowing several slang synonyms for a particular item (such as the examples in the following list) shows you to be impressively fluent in the language as well as a true aficionado of slang.

"Business"

bag *n.* (outdated) that in which one is greatly involved, either a hobby or business • *So, what's your bag?;* So, what business are you in?
♦ NOTE: Although this term is outdated, it is occasionally still used by the older generation, in old movies, or in jest.

biz *n.* 1. an abbreviation for "business" • *I'm getting out of the business;* I'm leaving this business. • **2.** an abbreviation for "show business" (also known as the entertainment industry) or more commonly *"showbiz"* • *How long have you been in the biz?;* How long have you been in show business?

♦ NOTE: The difference in connotation between definitions **1.** and **2.** depends on the context.

fly-by-night operation *exp.* said of a business which is not well established, transitory, and only interested in making fast money • *The new computer I just bought broke after one day. When I tried to return it, the store was closed! What a fly-by-night operation!;* The new computer I just bought broke after one day. When I tried to return it, the store was closed! What a cheating business!

game *n.* used commonly in the following expression: *David Burke's the name, writing's my game;* My name is David Burke and I'm a writer.

♦ NOTE: This term, although outdated, is still occasionally heard in old movies and in jest.

gold mine *n.* an extremely successful business • (lit); a quarry or tunnel where gold is extracted • *Can you believe all the money our business made in one day! We have a gold mine!;* Can you believe all the money our business made in one day! We have an extremely successful business!

line *n.* one's profession (used primarily in the expression "line of work") • *What line of work are you in?;* What profession are you in?

♦ NOTE: This term used to be heard commonly by itself: *What's your line?;* meaning "What profession are you in?" This usage is now considered somewhat outdated.

Ma and Pa shop *exp.* a small family-owned business • *I always find you get extra good service whenever you go to a Ma and Pa shop. Since they own the business, they really care about your satisfaction;* I always find you get extra good service whenever you go to a family-owned shop. Since they own the business, they really care about your satisfaction.

♦ VARIATION: **Mom and Pop shop** *exp.*

megacorp *n.* a very large corporation often composed of many smaller corporations • *When the company first opened, it had trouble due to lack of finances. Now, it's a megacorp!;* When the company first opened, it had trouble due to lack of finances. Now, it's a large corporation!

multinational *adj.* having operations in several countries • *The opening of our new Tokyo office has turned us into a multinational corporation;* The opening of our new Tokyo office has turned us into an international company.

operation *n.* • (lit); that which operates or functions • *What kind of operation does she have?;* What kind of business does she have?

racket *n.* **1.** business; one's occupation (gangster talk, now used in jest) • *What's your racket?;* What profession are you in? • **2.** scam, a business which cheats people • *He gets people to invest in his invention, and then steals their money! What a racket!;* He gets people to invest in his invention, and then steals their money! What a cheating business!

rat race *exp.* daily hectic life of business • *I'm tired of the rat race in the city. Someday I want to go live in the country;* I'm tired of the hectic life of business in the city. Someday I want to go live in the country.

set up shop (to) *exp.* to open a new business • *A new ice cream parlor just set up shop across the street!;* A new ice cream parlor just opened across the street!

shoestring (to be on a) *exp.* said of a person or business with little money • *They have a shoestring operation;* They have a business which operates on little money. / *I'm on a shoestring budget;* I'm on a very small budget.

small time (to be) *exp.* **1.** said of a modest business • *His business is small time but at least he doesn't have many worries;* He has a modest business but at least he doesn't have many worries. • **2.** said of a person of little importance • *He can't hurt your business. He's small time;* He can't hurt your business. He's of little importance.

what one is into *exp.* **1.** one's profession or current hobby • *You always seem so busy. What are you into?;* You always seem so busy. What profession are you in? (or: What hobby are you doing?) • **2.** what one enjoys sexually • *Before we spend the night together, tell me what you're into;* Before we spend the night together, tell me what you enjoy sexually. • **3.** what drugs one is taking • *I think he's into cocaine;* I think he's using cocaine. • **4.** what mischief one is doing • *You look guilty. What are you into?* You look guilty. What mischief are you doing? • **5.** to enjoy greatly • *He's really into sports;* He really enjoys sports.

white elephant *n.* a venture which turns out to be an obvious failure • *Our new product turned out to be a real white elephant;* Our new product turned out to be an enormous failure.

Executive

[big] boss lady *exp.* female employer or supervisor • *I can't believe she's the [big] boss lady here. She's so young!;* I can't believe she's the supervisor here. She's so young!
‣ ANTONYM: **[big] boss man** *exp.*

big cheese *n.* the head of a company; the boss • *There's Mr.*

Malin. He's the new big cheese at this company; There's Mr. Malin. He's the new boss at this company
‣ SYNONYM: **head honcho** *n.*

[big] mucky-muck *n.* an executive
• *She's a [big] mucky-muck in the largest movie studio in the United States;* She's a [big] executive in the largest movie studio in the United States.

big shot *exp.* **1.** executive of a company • *Mr. Olson is one of the big shots here;* Mr. Olson is one of the executives here. • **2.** important person • *Look at how he's dressed. He thinks he such a big shot!;* Look at how he's dressed. He thinks he such an important person.

big wheel *exp.* • *One of the big wheels wants to see you right away!;* One of the executives wants to see you right away!
‣ NOTE: This expressions refers to the largest wheels in the company "machine" which make it successful.

biggies *n.pl.* • *She's one of the biggies in the company;* She's one of the executives in the company.

brains *n.pl.* (humorous) • *Don't ask me what to do next! I'm the brawn, you're the brains!;* Don't ask me what to do next! I do the

physical work, you do the thinking!
‣ NOTE: This term comes from old gangster movies which refer to the head member of a particular mob as the *"brains"* since he's the one who conceives of all the illegal schemes.

brass (the) *n.* (humorous) • *He's the brass around here;* He's the boss around here.
‣ NOTE: This term comes from military slang referring to a high-ranking officer who wears many brass medals, buttons, etc.
‣ VARIATION: **the top brass** *exp.*

C.E.O. *n.* abbreviation for Chief Executive Officer • *My father is the C.E.O. of a large corporation;* My father is the Chief Executive Officer of a large corporation.

C.F.O. *n.* abbreviation for "Chief Financial Officer" • *I just got a job as C.F.O. at one of the largest companies in the city!;* I just got a job as Chief Financial Officer at one of the largest companies in the city!

C.O.O. *n.* abbreviation for "Chief Operating Officer" • *How did he ever get to be C.O.O. of the company? He's so disorganized!;* How did he ever get to be Chief Operating Officer of the company? He's so disorganized!

chief *n.* • *She's the chief of the firm;* She's the director of the firm.
♦ NOTE: When used as an address, *"chief"* (whose original meaning is the "head of an indian tribe") takes on a humorous tone: *Whatever you say, Chief!;* I'll do whatever you say, Boss!

head *n.* • *She's the head of the company;* She's the executive of the company.
♦ VARIATION: **head man/woman** *exp.*

head honcho *exp.* • *My mother is the head honcho of a major corporation;* My mother is the head honcho of a major corporation.

higher ups *n.pl.* • *If you want to see a change made in the company, go talk to one of the higher ups;* If you want to see a change made in the company, go talk to one of the executives.
♦ NOTE: Oddly enough, it would be extremely rare, and somewhat jarring, to hear this term used in the singular form: *He's a higher up.* The correct usage would be: *He's one of the higher ups.*

king of the hill *exp.* (humorous) • *May I help you? I'm king of the hill around here;* May I help you? I'm the boss around here.

kingfish *n.* (humorous) • *If you have a complaint, you may want*
to speak with the kingfish himself; If you have a complaint, you may want to speak with the boss himself.

kingpin *n.* the most important person or central figure in a company • (lit); the head pin in a group of bowling pins • *He can't quit! He's the kingpin of the company!;* He can't quit! He's the most important person in the company!

man (the) *n.* • *Now's your chance to ask for a raise. There's the man!;* Now's your chance to ask for a raise. There's the boss!
♦ NOTE: Although women have moved up the ranks in business over the years, this term is rarely used in the feminine form: *"the woman/lady."*
♦ VARIATION: **the main man** *exp.*

man upstairs (the) *exp.* • *The man upstairs wants to see you;* The boss wants to see you.
♦ NOTE: This expression refers to: **1.** a male executive whose office is located on a floor above the employees • **2.** God (since he sits "upstairs").

mastermind *n.* one who conceives masterful plans to make his/her company successful • *So, you're the mastermind behind this corporation;* So, you're the one who makes this corporation successful.

Mr. Big *exp.* (humorous) • *If you want to take a vacation next week, you'd better ask Mr. Big;* If you want to take a vacation next week, you'd better ask the boss.

♦ NOTE: This expression comes from old gangster movies which often presented mob members with nicknames fitting their personalities such as Baby Face, Fingers (the safecracker), Scar Face, Itchy Finger (the gunman), etc.

queen bee *exp.* (humorous) female boss • *Don't get her mad. She's the queen bee around here;* Don't get her mad. She's the boss here.

♦ NOTE: In nature, the queen bee is known for being the largest and most sought after in the bee kingdom.

run the show (to) *exp.* said of one who is in charge • *Why are you taking orders from him? I'm running the show!;* Why are you taking orders from him? I'm the

one in charge!

♦ NOTE: This expression comes from theatre and is used to refer to the stage manager who is in charge of *running the show.*

slave driver *exp.* a very demanding boss who works his/her employees like slaves • *He wants us to work twelve hours a day! What a slave driver!;* He wants us to work twelve hours a day! What a demanding boss!

super *n.* abbreviation for "supervisor" • *The super isn't coming in today. I guess we can all take long lunches!;* The supervisor isn't coming in today. I guess we can all take long lunches!

top dog *exp.* • *You'd better ask his permission if you want to leave work early today. After all, he's top dog;* You'd better ask his permission if you want to leave work early today. After all, he's the boss.

♦ VARIATION: **top banana** *exp.*

To Fire (someone)

axe someone (to) *v.* • (lit); to kill someone with an axe • *I heard the boss is planning to axe three people from the department;* I heard the boss is planning on firing three people from the

department.

♦ VARIATION: **to give someone the axe** *exp.* • *I gave Cathy the axe for stealing from the company;* I fired Cathy for stealing from the company.

▶ ALSO: **to get the axe** *exp.* to get fired • *After working for the company nearly nine years, Steve just got the axe;* After working for the company nearly nine years, Steve just got fired.

boot someone (to) *exp.* • (lit); to remove someone from a location by means of kicking him/her with a boot • **1.** to fire someone • *I don't believe this! The boss said I lied about my qualifications so he booted me!;* I don't believe this! The boss said I lied about my qualifications so he fired me! • **2.** to force someone to leave • *She booted me from her office;* She forced me to leave her office.
▶ VARIATION: **to give someone the boot** *exp.* • *The boss is going to give you the boot if you come to work late again;* The boss is going to fire you if you come to work late again.
▶ ALSO: **to get the boot** *exp.* to get fired • *My father got the boot after being with the company for thirty years!;* My father got fired after being with the company for thirty years!

cut back (to) *exp.* to reduce one's operating costs • *Since our profits are down, we're going to have to cut back this year;* Since our profits are down, we're going to have to reduce our operating costs this year.
▶ ALSO: **to make cutbacks** *exp.* •

I just heard the company is going to make cutbacks soon. I hope that doesn't mean I'm going to lose my job!; I just heard the company is going to reduce operating costs soon. I hope that doesn't mean I'm going to lose my job!

downsize (to) *v.* to reduce a company's operating costs in order to be competitive with other similar companies • *Southern Shoe Leather is going to have to downsize in order to survive;* Southern Shoe Leather is going to have to reduce operating costs by firing workers in order to survive.
▶ NOTE: The verb *"to downsize"* is commonly used as a euphemism for "taking drastic measures such as firing employees or lowering salaries."

dump someone (to) *v.* • (lit); to dispose of someone • *I've had it with her attitude! I'm dumping her!;* I've had it with her attitude! I'm firing her!
▶ ALSO: **to get dumped** *adj.* • **1.** to get fired, dismissed • *The company is cutting back so I was one of the first to get dumped;* The company is cutting back so I was one of the first to get dismissed. • **2.** to get abandoned in a relationship • *I just heard Susan got dumped by her*

boyfriend; I just heard Susan got abandoned by her boyfriend.

give someone the gate (to) *exp.* • *He kept arriving to work late so his boss gave him the gate;* He kept arriving to work late so his boss fired him.
‣ NOTE: This expression is outdated and heard only in old movies or in jest.

give someone the ol' heave-ho (to) *exp.* • *You're not going to believe this. The boss just gave me the ol' heave-ho!;* You're not going to believe this. The boss just fired me!
‣ NOTE (1): The interjection *"Heave ho!"* was originally a nautical command given to sailors to pull hard on a rope or line.
‣ NOTE (2): The adjective "old" is commonly reduced to *"ol'"* and used to mean "familiar:" *There's my old boyfriend! I'm getting that ol' feeling again;* There's my old boyfriend! I'm getting that familiar feeling again.

kick someone out (to) *v.* • (lit); to remove someone from a location by delivering a kick • **1.** to fire someone • *Mark was rude to a customer, so the boss kicked him out!;* Mark was rude to a customer, so the boss fired him. • **2.** to eject someone • *He stayed at my house for over a week. I finally kicked him out!;* He

stayed at my house for over a week. I finally ejected him!
‣ ALSO: **to get kicked out** *exp.* • **1.** to get fired • **2.** to get ejected from a location.

lay off (to) *exp.* • **1.** to dismiss someone from a job (supposedly temporarily) due to lack of finances • *I just heard that eight people are going to be laid off because the company didn't make high enough profits this year;* I just heard that eight people are going to be dismissed from their jobs because the company didn't make high enough profits this year. • **2.** to leave someone alone • *Why do you always have to harass him? Can't you just lay off [him]?;* Why do you always have to harass him? Can't you just leave him alone?
‣ ALSO: **lay-off** *n.* • *Is the company planning to make lay-offs soon?;* Is the company planning to make dismissals of personnel soon?
‣ SEE (1): **cut back (to)** *exp.*
‣ SEE (2): **downsize (to)** *v.*

let someone go (to) *exp.* • *I'm afraid we're going to have to let you go;* I'm afraid we're going to have to dismiss you.
‣ ALSO: **to get let go** *exp.* to be fired, dismissed • *I just got let go!;* I just got fired!

oust someone (to) *v.* • (lit); to remove someone from a location • *The boss ousted the new employee the moment he was caught stealing!;* The boss fired the new employee the moment he was caught stealing! • *She ousted him from her office;* She ejected him from her office.
‣ ALSO: **to get ousted** *adj.* to get fired, ejected.

ride someone out of town on a rail (to) *exp.* to be removed unceremoniously from a company • *When Mark hit the customer, the boss rode him out of town on a rail!;* When Mark hit the customer, the boss fired him!
‣ ORIGIN: Years ago when rail travel was the predominant form of transportation in small towns, an undesirable person would be put physically onto a train (or railway) and "ridden" out of town.

sacked (to get) *v.* to get fired • *He got sacked because he kept making mistakes;* He got fired because he kept making mistakes.

send someone packing (to) *exp.* to fire, eject someone • (lit); to make someone pack up his/her belongings and leave • *The moment the boss caught her breaking into his office, he sent her packing;* The moment boss caught her breaking into his office, he fired her.

show someone the door (to) *exp.* • *If you yell at the boss, don't be surprised if he responds by showing you the door;* If you yell at the boss, don't be surprised if he responds by firing you.

throw someone out on one's ear (to) *exp.* to eject someone angrily or forcibly • *The boss was so angry with the new employee that he threw him out on his ear the first day!;* The boss was so angry with the new employee that he fired him the first day!

trim the fat (to) *exp.* to discharge the employees who are not productive • (lit); to cut the fat off an otherwise desirable piece of meat • *I'm tired of working with so many people in the company who aren't productive. I think it's time to trim the fat;* I'm tired of working with so many people in the company who aren't productive. I think it's time to get rid of the less useful people.

walking papers (to be handed one's) *exp.* to be fired • *As soon as I arrived at work, I was handed my walking papers!;* As soon as I arrived at work, I was fired!
‣ SYNONYM: **to get one's pink slip** *exp.*

♦ NOTE: A "pink slip" refers to one's notice of termination as well as to the ownership

certificate to one's car. The difference in connotation depends on the context.

To Quit
(permanently or just for the day)

bail (to) *v.* an abbreviated form of *"to bail out"* • (lit); to empty water from a boat by pouring water over the side • *I can't stand this job! I'm bailing!;* I hate this job! I'm quitting!

call it a day (to) *exp.* to quit for the day • *I've worked ten hours straight. I'm calling it a day;* I've worked ten hours straight. I'm quitting for the day.

call it quits (to) *exp.* • **1.** to abandon a thing • *We've been trying to figure out the answer to this problem for over a week! I think we should call it quits;* We've been trying to figure out the answer to this problem for over a week! I think we should abandon it. • **2.** to abandon a person • *You have to admit we just don't get along anymore. I think we should call it quits;* You have to admit we just don't get along anymore. I think we should abandon this relationship.

knock off (to) *exp.* to quit work • *What time are you knocking off*

today?; What time are you quitting today?

hang it up (to) *exp.* • *I'm hanging it up early today;* I'm quitting early today.

out of here (to be) *exp.* (pronounced: *outta here*) • *I'm outta here! See you tomorrow;* I'm leaving! See you tomorrow.

pack it up (to) *exp.* to leave either permanently or for the day • (lit); to pack up one's belongings • *I just can't bear working here anymore. I'm packing it up;* I just can't bear working here anymore. I'm quitting.

run out on a job (to) *exp.* to quit a job abruptly • *She got a better offer and just ran out on the job!;* She got a better offer and just suddenly quit her job!

sew it up (to) *exp.* to finalize something • *We sewed up the deal in about fifteen minutes;* We finalized the deal in about fifteen minutes.

throw in the towel (to) *exp.* to give up completely • *This job is just too hard. I'm throwing in the towel!;* This job is just too hard. I give up!
♦ ORIGIN: This expression comes from boxing where the manager of the losing fighter would throw a towel into the ring, indicating defeat.

wind it up (to) *exp.* to finish a task
• *Your father said he'll be winding it up at work in about an hour;* Your father said he'll be finishing work in about an hour.

wrap it up (to) *exp.* to finish a task
• *I think we've all worked hard enough for one day. Let's wrap it up;* I think we've all worked hard enough for one day. Let's quit.
♦ NOTE: A variation of this expression is extremely popular in the film industry: *"That's a wrap!"* meaning "We're finished!"

Practice Using Common Slang Synonyms for Business-Related Terms

(Answers, p. 220)

C. Circle the synonym(s) which do not belong to the group.

1. **business**:
   a. biz
   b. gold mine
   c. big wheel
   d. line
   e. Ma and Pa Shop
   f. big shot

2. **executive**:
   a. big cheese
   b. line
   c. big wheel
   d. big shot
   e. slave driver
   f. the brass

3. **to fire (someone)**:
   a. to call it quits
   b. to axe someone
   c. to cut back
   d. to downsize
   e. to boot someone
   f. to bail

4. **to quit**:
   a. to lay off
   b. to downsize
   c. to bail
   d. to knock off
   e. to pack it up
   f. to wind it up

Computer Slang

– *"The New PC Clone"* –

*"I just bought a **PC clone** with all sorts of **bells and whistles**!"*

Lesson Two - COMPUTER SLANG

"The New PC Clone"

DIALOGUE

David is at Gordon's house admiring his new personal computer.

David: Is that the new computer you're using for **desktop publishing**?

Gordon: Yeah! It's a **clone** with all sorts of **bells and whistles**, even a **joystick**. In fact, my **PC** has a **monitor** which shows everything in **WYSIWYG** and it **calls up docs** much faster than my **laptop**!

David: As long as it's **user-friendly**! Just be careful. Sometimes you can get a **glitch** in your **software** which will make your computer **crash** and **zap** all your data. That happened to me once as soon as I **booted** the computer. My **system** was **down** for a week! Luckily I had a **backup** of most of the **files**. It was probably caused by a **virus** that I **downloaded** from a **BBS**. So it doesn't happen to you, I'll **modem** you an **antidote**. Just make sure to keep it on **floppy** in case you need it again.

Lesson Two - COMPUTER SLANG

Translation of dialogue in standard English

"The New PC Clone"

DIALOGUE

David is at Gordon's house admiring his new personal computer.

David: Is that the new computer you're using for **in-house typesetting**?

Gordon: Yes! It's a **copy of a more expensive brand** with all sorts of **useless yet enticing features**, even a **computer control shaped like a stick**. In fact, my **personal computer** has a **screen** which shows everything **exactly how it will appear when printed** and it **retrieves computer documents** much faster than my **small portable computer**!

David: As long as it's **easy to use**! Just be careful. Sometimes you can get a **minor malfunction** in your **computer program** which will make your computer **fail** and **delete** all your data. That happened to me once as soon as I **started** the computer. My **computer** was **inoperative** for a week! Luckily I had a **diskette copy** of most of the **computer documents**. It was probably caused by a **hidden instruction in the computer program meant to destroy data** that I **received from another computer** through a **Bulletin Board System**. So it doesn't happen to you, I'll **electronically transmit** you a **remedy**. Just make sure to keep it on **removable disk** in case you need it again.

Lesson Two - COMPUTER SLANG

Dialogue in slang as it would be heard

"The New PC Clone"

DIALOGUE

David's at Gordon's house admiring 'is new personal compuder.

David: Izat the new compuder yer using fer **desktop publishing**?

Gordon: Yeah! It's a **clone** with all sorts 'a **bells 'n whistles**, even a **joystick**. In fact, my **PC** has a **monider** which shows ev'rything 'n **wizee-wig** 'n it **calls up docs** much faster than my **laptop**!

David: As long as it's **uzer-friendly**! Jus' be careful. Sometimes ya c'n ged a **glitch** 'n yer **software** which'll make yer compuder **crash** 'n **zap** all yer dadah. That happen' ta me once as soon as I **booded** the compuder. My **system** was **down** fer a week! Luckily I had a **backup** of most 'a the **files**. It was prob'ly caused by a **virus** thad I **downloaded** from a **BBS**. So it doesn' happen ta you, I'll **modem** you 'n **antidote**. Jus' make sher da keep id on **floppy** 'n case ya need id again.

Vocabulary

antidote *n.* a program used to "cure" a computer of a "virus" • *I think the computer has a virus which is why it's having trouble saving each document. Hopefully, this new program is the antidote;* I think the computer has a virus which is why it's having trouble saving each document. Hopefully, this new program is the cure.
▶ SEE: **virus** *n.*

backup *n.* a copy of one's computer work on diskette or tape • *Be sure to make a backup of your work before leaving today;* Be sure to make a diskette (or tape) copy of your work before leaving today.
▶ VARIATION: **to backup** *v.* • *Don't forget to backup your work every day;* Don't forget to make a copy of your work on diskette (or tape) every day.

BBS *n.* an acronym for "Bulletin Board System" which is an electronic bulletin board system accessed through a modem-equipped computer where users may leave messages for each other or converse using the keyboard • *I wanted to find out where to buy a good printer so I left a message with one of the BBSs. Someone left me a reply that day;* I wanted to find out where to buy a good printer so I left a message with one of the electronic bulletin board systems. Someone left me a reply that day.
▶ SEE: **modem (to)** *v.*

bells and whistles *exp.* unnecessary yet enticing features • *This computer is so expensive because it comes with a special tape backup system, scanner, and modem. I just don't want to pay for all those bells and whistles!;* This computer is so expensive because it comes with a special tape backup system, scanner, and modem. I just don't want to pay for extra features I don't need!

boot (to) *v.* to start • *For some reason, the computer is having problems booting;* For some reason, the computer is having problems starting.
▶ SYNONYM: **to boot up** *v.* • *Your computer seems to take a long time booting up!;* Your computer seems to take a long time starting!

call up a document (to) *exp.* to retrieve a computer document on the screen • *Would you please call up the document we worked on yesterday? We need to make some changes;* Would you please retrieve the document we worked on yesterday? We need to make some changes.

clone *n.* a personal computer that has similar functions to a name brand such as the IBM Personal Computer • *I never thought I could afford a personal* *computer, so I bought a clone;* I never thought I could afford a personal computer, so I bought a reproduction which is really the same thing only cheaper.

crash (to) *v.* • **1.** said of a computer which stops working unexpectedly due to a slight malfunction • *I was in the middle of working on my document and suddenly my computer crashed!;* I was in the middle of working on my document and suddenly my computer stopped functioning! • **2.** said of a computer which stops working unexpectedly due to a serious malfunction causing lose of valuable data • *All the operators were working on their terminals when suddenly the entire mainframe crashed! Everyone's files were instantly destroyed!;* All the operators were working on their terminals when suddenly the entire mainframe lost data! Everyone's files were instantly destroyed!
♦ SEE: **mainframe** *n.* (p. 66).
♦ ALSO: **system crash** *n.* a serious computer failure (resulting in loss of data) • *At two o'clock in the afternoon, we had a system crash which destroyed all the files we had been working on for the past three weeks!;* At two o'clock in the afternoon, we had a serious computer failure which destroyed all the files we had been working on for the past three weeks!

desktop publishing *n.* (also called "DTP") a name given to the growing field of computer users who typeset in-house publications on a small scale using a personal computer • *We've just begun to do desktop publishing for all our newsletters;* We've just begun to do in-house typesetting for all our newsletters.
♦ ALSO: **to desktop publish** *v.* • *Did you desktop publish this brochure?;* Did you typeset this brochure in-house?

down (to be) *adj.* said of a computer which is inoperative • *This computer is down right now. Why don't you try the one in my office?;* This computer is not working right now. Why don't you try the one in my office?
♦ ANTONYM: **to be up** *adj.* to be functioning • *The computer will be down for a while. We hope to have it up around noon;* The computer will be down for a while. We hope to have it functioning around noon.

download (to) *v.* to receive a file from another computer via a modem • *Before I download your file, how large is it? I want to be sure I have enough room on my hard disk;* Before I receive your file, how large is it? I want to be sure I have enough room on my hard disk.
♦ SEE: "A CLOSER LOOK" section: **hard disk** *n.* (p. 65).
♦ ANTONYM: **upload (to)** *v.* to transfer a file from one computer to another via a modem • *I'm going to upload the file to you. As soon as you get it,*

print it out and give it to the president of our company; I'm going to transfer the file to you. As soon as you get it, print it out and give it to the president of our company.

file *n.* a computer-generated document • *Don't forget the name of the file you created or you'll have trouble retrieving it!;* Don't forget the name of the document you created on the computer or you'll have trouble retrieving it!

floppy *n.* a shortened version of *"floppy disk"* which is a removable disk (typically measuring either 31/2" or 51/4" in diameter) where data is stored • *Make sure not to expose your floppy disk to extreme heat or it could destroy the data;* Make sure not to expose your removable disk to extreme heat or it could destroy the data.

‣ NOTE: The flexible or *"floppy"* disks are housed in a square plastic envelope.

‣ SYNONYM: **diskette** *n.*

glitch *n.* a minor computer malfunction • *This computer doesn't seem to be working very well. It must have a glitch;* This computer doesn't seem to be working very well. It must have a malfunction.

joystick *exp.* a cursor devise resembling the control stick of an aircraft used for positioning the cursor on the computer screen • *Now that I have a joystick, I can play all sorts of computer games;* Now that I have a stick control, I can play all sorts of computer games.

‣ SEE: **mouse** *n.* (p. 66).

laptop *n.* a small portable computer which fits on the operator's lap • *Whenever I go on business trips, I bring my laptop with me;* Whenever I go on business trips, I bring my small portable computer with me.

modem (to) *v.* to transmit a document electronically from one computer to another by way of a modem (a "computer-to-telephone" interface enabling one computer to communicate with another through the telephone lines) • *I'll modem the document to you tonight;* I'll transmit the document to you through the modem tonight.

‣ NOTE: The term *"modem"* is short for "**mo**dulator/**dem**odulator."

monitor *n.* a computer screen resembling a television screen • *I just bought a monochrome monitor because the color ones are just too expensive;* I just bought a computer screen which displays in a single color because the color ones are just too expensive.

PC *n.* an abbreviation for the IBM "Personal Computer" but is commonly used to describe any desktop computer • *I finally threw away my old typewriter and bought a PC;* I finally threw away my old typewriter and bought a personal computer.

▸NOTE: In computer advertisements, *"PC"* is rarely seen with periods: *P.C.*

software *n.* refers to computer programs in general • *What kind of software are you using in your computer?;* What kind of computer programs are you using in your computer?

system *n.* short for "computer system" • *Our expensive system isn't working correctly;* Our expensive computer system isn't working correctly.

user-friendly (to be) *adj.* easy to use • *This typesetting program is very user-friendly. It tells you what to do every step of the way;* This typesetting program is very easy to use. It tells you what to do every step of the way.

virus *n.* a hidden instruction in a computer program intended to cause the computer to malfunction (causing possible loss of data) • *It's a good idea to backup the computer data every day in case it turns out to have a virus;* It's a good idea to backup the computer data every day in case it turns out to have a hidden instruction somewhere which may destroy the data.

WYSIWYG *n.* (pronounced "wisee-wig" or "wizee-wig") an acronym for *"What you see is what you get"* meaning "What you see on the computer screen is exactly what you'll see when the page is printed" • *The display you see on the screen is WYSIWYG. So if it doesn't look right on the screen, it won't look any better when it's printed!;* The display you see on the screen matches what the printed page will look like. So if it doesn't look right on the screen, it won't look any better when it's printed!

zap (to) *v.* to erase • *I don't need that computer file anymore. Go ahead and zap it;* I don't need that computer file anymore. Go ahead and erase it.

PRACTICE THE VOCABULARY

(Answers to Lesson Two, p. 221)

A. Underline the appropriate definition.

1. **bells and whistles:**
   a. an old and noisy computer
   b. unnecessary yet enticing features on a computer

2. **antidote:**
   a. a program used to get rid of a computer "virus"
   b. a special program to help the computer process data faster

3. **file:**
   a. a computer screen
   b. a computer-generated document

4. **to be down:**
   a. said of a computer which processes slowly
   b. said of a computer which is inoperative

5. **monitor:**
   a. a computer screen
   b. a computer instructor

6. **desktop publishing:**
   a. a name given to the growing field of computer artists
   b. a name given to the growing field of computer users who typeset in-house publications on a small scale using a home computer

7. **laptop:**
   a. a large heavy computer which sits on a surface above one's lap
   b. a small portable computer which fits on the operator's lap

8. **glitch:**
   a. a minor computer malfunction
   b. a major computer malfunction

9. **WYSIWYG:**
   a. an acronym for *"What you spend is what you get"* meaning "You need to spend a little more money in order to get a good computer"
   b. an acronym for *"What you see is what you get"* meaning "What you see on the computer screen is exactly what you'll see when the page is printed"

10. **to zap:**
    a. to erase (a computer file)
    b. to type quickly

11. **to be user-friendly:**
    a. said of a happy computer operator
    b. said of a computer or program which is easy to use

12. **PC:**
    a. a popular abbreviation for "personal computer"
    b. a popular abbreviation for "precise calculating"

B. FIND-THE-WORD-SCREEN

Step 1: Fill in the blanks with the most appropriate word using the list below.

Step 2: Find and circle the word in the grid on the opposite page. The first one has been done for you.

backup	**BBS**	**boot**
clone	**crashed**	**down**
glitch	**joystick**	**modem**
PC	**friendly**	**WYSIWYG**

1. While I was working on my computer, it suddenly _____ for no apparent reason!

2. My computer seems to be taking a long time to _____ .

3. I posted a message on the _____ that I'm looking for a used computer.

4. Now that I bought a _____ , I can't imagine ever using a typewriter again.

5. This computer's so easy to use! It's really user-_____ .

6. This program isn't working right. It must have a _____ somewhere.

7. The computer in the office is going to be _____ for a few days while it's being repaired.

8. I need to work with your document on my computer. Instead of mailing it to me, why don't you just _____ it?

9. I just bought a _____ for my computer so my little brother can play games on it.

10. My computer screen shows everything I type in _____ .
    That way I know exactly how it's going to look when it's printed.

11. I think my computer document got destroyed. Luckily, I made a
    _____ of everything yesterday.

12. My new computer is a _____ which is identical to one
    of those more expensive brands.

C. Replace the italicized word(s) with the appropriate slang synonym(s) from the right column.

1. That computer sure has a lot of *unnecessary yet enticing features* _____!

   A. **down**

2. I tried to *retrieve* _____ my computer file but I can't find it.

   B. **system**

3. Every time I *start* _____ my computer, it takes about five minutes.

   C. **downloading**

4. My computer is going to be *inoperative* _____ for a day.

   D. **software**

5. I can't find my file in the computer. I must have put it on a *diskette* _____ .

   E. **user-friendly**

6. What kind of *computer programs* _____ are you using to do your artwork?

   F. **call up**

7. Before I begin *receiving your file from your computer via a modem* _____ , how large is your file? I want to be sure I have enough room on my hard disk.

   G. **boot**

8. This computer program is so *easy to use* _____ !

   H. **floppy**

9. I'm running out of room in my computer. I guess I'd better *erase* _____ some files to make room for more.

   I. **zap**

10. How's your new *computer* _____ ?

    J. **bells and whistles**

A CLOSER LOOK:
Advanced Computer Slang & Jargon

Anyone who has ever decided to buy a personal computer has undoubtedly been assaulted by advertisements, computer enthusiasts, salespeople, etc. all reeling off unintelligible technical jargon which seems like another language. In fact, much of this lingo (commonly called *"computerese"*) is actually created by computer manufacturers who hope the more complex the computer terminology, the more desirable the product will seem in the eyes of the consumer.

The following list contains some of the most popular terms and expressions used in the computer world as well as in advertisements nationwide. Whether you work in an office with computers or are planning on buying your own *"PC,"* this list will prove to be invaluable!

486-50 *n.* a computer system based on the Intel 486 processor (the "brain" of the computer) operating at a 50-megahertz clock speed (generally, the higher the clock speed the faster the computer).
 ‣ SEE: **Intel 486 chip** *n.*

abort (to) *v.* to terminate a program • *I had the document on the computer screen but suddenly the program started malfunctioning, so I aborted;* I had the document on the computer screen but suddenly the program started malfunctioning, so I terminated it.

artificial intelligence *n.* (often referred to as *"AI"*) a concept in which the computer, with the appropriate program, can be made to imitate the capabilities of human reasoning • *Our medical computer is equipped with an artificial intelligence system to aid in diagnosis;* Our medical computer is equipped with human reasoning capabilities to aid in diagnosis.

batch file *n.* a group or "batch" of computer commands which runs by activating a single command • *I just created a batch file which automatically brings today's calendar on the screen when I turn on the computer;* I just created a group of computer commands which automatically brings today's calendar on the screen when I turn on the computer;

♦ NOTE: This is also referred to as a *"bat file"* since this type of file is named using a three-character extension: *"bat."*

baud rate *n.* the speed at which data is transmitted from one computer to another via a modem • *Most modems transmit files at a baud rate of 1200, 2400, or 9600;* Most modems transmit files at a speed of 1200, 2400, or 9600.

bit *n.* the smallest unit of information that a computer works with.

♦ ALSO (1): **byte** *n.* a group of eights bits which is the amount a computer needs in order to store a character.

♦ ALSO (2): **kilobyte** *n.* (also referred to as a *"K-byte"* or simply *"K"*) Computer data is always measured in kilobytes which equals 1024 bytes. For example, this actual page which was created using a computer, takes up three kilobytes of computer memory.

♦ ALSO (3): **megabyte** *n.* (also referred to as a *"M-byte"* or *"meg"*) A megabyte is 1,048,576 bytes. Computer hard drives commonly can store hundreds of megabytes of information. It is common to see advertisements for computers where the size of the hard drive is highlighted in megabytes.

breadboard (to) *n.* to build an experimental electronic circuit for purposes of testing before doing an expensive final design.

bug *n.* • (lit); an insect or pest • **1.** a flaw in a computer program • *The computer program doesn't seem to be operating correctly. It must have a bug;* The computer program doesn't seem to be operating correctly. It must have a flaw. • **2.** a flaw in a strategy • *I think your strategy has a bug in it somewhere;* I think your strategy has a flaw in it somewhere **3.** a cold or virus • *I think I caught a bug from my niece;* I think I caught a cold from my niece.

♦ ANTONYM: **to debug a program** *v.* to remove the flaws in a computer program.

bulletproof (to be) *adj.* said of a computer program which is very well designed and resistant to failure • *Don't worry about having your little brother use your computer. All the programs are bulletproof;* Don't worry about having your little brother use your computer. All of the programs are very resistant to failure.

burn in (to) *v.* to run a computer for a period of time, typically 48 hours, before selling it (ideally, defective components will fail during *"burn in"* at which time repairs can be made before the customer takes delivery) • *My new computer quit the first day I bought it. I wonder if the manufacturer burned it in;* My new computer quit the first day I bought it. I wonder if the manufacturer ran it for a period of time before selling to me.

cache *n.* a high speed storage area in the computer where data can be quickly retrieved • *Since I have to use both programs, I have them both in cache so that I can access each one quickly;* Since I have to use both programs, I have them both in a high speed storage area in the computer so that I can access each one quickly.

CD Rom *n.* short for *"Compact Disc read only memory"* removable storage device that holds approximately 650 megabytes of computer information.

CGA *n.* an abbreviation of *"Color Graphics Adaptor."*
▸ NOTE: This refers to the first color monitor produced for the IBM Personal Computer.

chip *n.* a small silicon wafer that can be used to process and store computer data.

chiphead *n.* a computer enthusiast • *All she ever talks about is her new computer. She's a real*

chiphead!; All she ever talks about is her new computer. She's a real computer enthusiast!
▸ SEE: **chip** *n.*

click on something (to) *v.* to use a "mouse" to move the cursor to the appropriate position on the screen by pressing the mouse button (which makes a clicking sound) to begin the command • *If you click on that word, the computer will give you a list of synonyms;* If you put the cursor on that word and press the mouse button, the cursor will give you a list of synonyms.
▸ SEE: **mouse** *n.*

compatible *n.* any computer system capable of running programs written for the IBM Personal Computer • *This program is IBM compatible;* This program will operate on IBM computers.

computer hacker *n.* one who is proficient at using a computer • *I didn't know you were a computer hacker;* I didn't know you were proficient at using computers.
▸ SYNONYM: **computer buff** *n.*

computer nerd *exp.* a stereotypical computer fanatic who dresses poorly, speaks in an annoying voice (usually high-pitched and nasal), wears glasses, and keeps a plastic pocket protector full of pens in his shirt pocket • *My sister is dating the biggest* *computer nerd!;* My sister is dating a computer fanatic who fits the stereotype!

♦ NOTE: This expression is also used in jest: *So, I hear you're a computer nerd!;* So, I hear you love computers!

computerese *n.* slang and jargon associated with computers • *I can't understand all the computerese used by computer sales people;* I can't understand all the slang and jargon used by computer sales people.

corrupted (to be) *adj.* said of a computer file whose data has become defective • (lit); to be dishonest and unscrupulous • *For some reason, the program I've been using for months is suddenly no longer working. I guess it got corrupted!;* For some reason, the program I've been using for months is suddenly no longer working. I guess it became defective!

CPU *n.* an abbreviation for "central processing unit" which is the primary chip in a computer system (although referred to by many users as the main chassis of a computer system) • *I always keep the CPU on the table with the monitor sitting on top;* I always keep the computer's central processing unit on the table with the monitor sitting on top.

crunch (to) *v.* • **1.** to perform a mathematical function, to calculate • *I just entered all of our expenditures for the year. The computer is now crunching all the numbers to give us a total of the money we've spent since the company first opened;* I just entered all of our expenditures for the year. The computer is now calculating all the numbers to give us a total of the money we've spent since the company first opened. • **2.** said of an accountant • *I don't know how he can spend every day crunching numbers!;* I don't know how he can spend every day doing accounting!

cyberpunk *n.* an enthusiast of high technology • *You should see Gordon's house. Every appliance looks like something from the future. I never knew he was such a cyberpunk!;* You should see Gordon's house. Every appliance looks like something from the future. I never knew he was such a high-technology enthusiast!

daisy wheel *n.* a wheel, resembling a daily, which is used in impact printers (as opposed to laser printers) and holds a character at the end of each "pedal" striking the ink ribbon to imprint the page • *I need to buy a laser printer. My daisy wheel printer takes too long to print each page!;* I need to buy a laser printer. My character-by-character printer takes too long to print each page!

dedicated (to be) *adj.* said of a computer which has only one purpose • *I don't know why she bought a dedicated word processor when a personal computer can do so many different tasks including word processing!;* I don't know why she bought a computer which only can do word processing when a personal computer can do so many different tasks including word processing!

default *n.* a preset condition of a computer program that will hold unless changed by the operator • *My word processing program automatically double-spaces my documents. I'm going to change the default to single-space;* My word processing program automatically double-spaces my documents. I'm going to change the preset condition to single-space.

display *n.* that which is being "displayed" on the computer screen; • *The display just went blank;* The computer screen just went blank.

do a directory (to) *exp.* to examine the contents of "directory" of the computer • *Do a directory of your C-drive. I think the file you're looking for is there;*

Examine the directory of your C-drive. I think the file you're looking for is there.

docs *n.pl.* abbreviation for "documents" or "documentation" • *Did the manufacturer send us some docs on this program?;* Did the manufacturer send us some documentation on this program?

DOS *n.* an abbreviation for "Disk Operating System" which is the most common program used on the IBM PC and compatibles.

DPI *n.* an abbreviation for "dots per inch" which refers to the resolution of a laser printer • *Most laser printers print 300 DPI;* Most laser printers print 300 dots per inch.
  ♦ NOTE: Each character printed by a laser printer is made of little dots. The more dots which make up a character, the higher the resolution.

drive *n.* a generic term for *"floppy," "CD Rom,"* or *"hard disk"* storage • *Put the diskette in the "A" drive.*
  ♦ NOTE: Drives are usually designated in alphabetical order starting with "A." "C" is typically the first hard drive.
  ♦ SEE (1): **CD Rom** *n.*
  ♦ SEE (2): **floppy** *n.*
  ♦ SEE (3): **hard disk** *n.*

end user *n.* a consumer of software or computer equipment • *The* *manufacturer sells directly to the end user as opposed to selling to a store first;* The manufacturer sells directly to the computer customer as opposed to selling to a store first.

"EXE" file *n.* (pronounced "x-ee file") a special type of computer program which executes when its name is typed — for example: *to run the PRINT.EXE program, type "PRINT" and press the ENTER key.*

execute (to) *v.* to run a computer program • *It takes about ten minutes to execute the program;* It takes about ten minutes to run the program.

font *n.* typeface • *Which font do you want to use for this document?;* Which typeface do you want to use for this document?

footer *n.* that which appears automatically on the bottom portion (or "foot") of each page such as a page number • *Instead of typing the page number at the bottom of each page, just create a footer;* Instead of typing the page number at the bottom of each page, just have the computer print it automatically on every page.
  ◊ ANTONYM: **header** *n.* that which appears automatically on the top portion (or "head") of each page such as the name of

the document or book title • *Instead of typing the name of the book at the top of each page, just create a header;* Instead of typing the name of the book at the top of each page, just have the computer print it automatically on every page.

garbage (to spit out) *exp.* said of a computer which outputs nonsense or incorrect characters on the screen or printer • *The computer's spitting out all sorts of garbage on the screen. The program must be corrupted;* The computer's spitting out all sorts of random characters on the screen. The program must be corrupted.

global search *n.* (often referred to as a *"global"*) a function of the computer where a search can be made through a large amount of information for a particular file, word, character, etc. • *I didn't know where the other computer operator stored the file, so I did a global and found it right away;* I didn't know where the other computer operator stored the file, so I did an automatic search through the entire computer and found it right away.

handshake (to) *v.* said of two machines which connect electronically such as a computer and printer • *For some reason, the printer isn't receiving the* *signal from the computer. I guess they didn't handshake when I started them;* For some reason, the printer isn't receiving the signal from the computer. I guess they didn't receive each other's signals when I started them.

hard copy *n.* an actual printed copy of a document generated on a computer • *As a safety precaution, make sure to print out a hard copy of the document as soon as you're done;* As a safety precaution, make sure to print out an actual copy of the document as soon as you're done.

hard disk *n.* a nonremovable magnetic disk within the computer where data is stored • *My hard disk is just about full. I'd better transfer some of my files onto a floppy disk;* My computer's permanent disk is just about full. I'd better transfer some of my files onto a removable diskette.
  ‣ SYNONYM: **hard drive** *n.*
  ‣ SEE - "VOCABULARY" Section: floppy disk *n.* (p. 53)

hardware *n.* refers to the computer equipment • *How did you afford all your new computer hardware?;* How did you afford all your new computer equipment?

housekeeping *n.* refers to organizing the computers' hard disk which includes getting rid of old files, making backups, etc. • *My computer has so many files in it I never use. I think it's time to do some housekeeping;* My computer has so many files in it I never use. I think it's time to get rid of my old files.
  ‣ SYNONYM: **housecleaning** *n.*

icon *n.* a computer command represented on the screen by a picture or pictogram • *To enter the word processing program, choose the icon of the computer and press the enter key;* To enter the word processing program, choose the picture of the computer and press the enter key.

IDE Hard Drive *n.* an abbreviation for "Integrated Drive Electronics," a common type of hard drive (nonremovable storage as opposed to a "floppy disk.").
  ‣ SEE - "VOCABULARY" Section: **floppy disk** *n.* (p. 53)

Mac *n.* a popular abbreviation for a "Macintosh" brand computer • *I work off a Mac;* I use a Macintosh computer.

Mac head *n.* one who uses nothing but Macintosh computers • *He's a real Mac head. He'll never use a personal computer;* He's a real enthusiast of Macintosh. He'll never use a personal computer.

macro *n.* a single instruction which executes a series of instructions by pressing only one key • *You'll need to go into the document and boldface each technical term. Instead of doing each one with a series of keystrokes, just set up a macro so you can do it quickly;* You'll need to go into the document and boldface each technical term. Instead of doing each one with a series of keystrokes, just record your keystrokes as one instruction so you can do it quickly.

mainframe *n.* a large computer system to which many computer terminals are connected enabling multiple operators to retrieve files from a common source • *All the computers in our office are connected to a mainframe. That way when one operator is finished working on a file, a different operator can continue working on the same file from another terminal;* All the computers in our office are connected to a large primary computer which stores all the files. That way when one operator is finished working on a file, a different operator can continue working on the same file from another terminal.
‣ SYNONYM (1): **host** *n.*
‣ SYNONYM (2): **server** *n.*

menu *n.* a list of options available to the computer operator • *Choose the program you want from this menu;* Choose the program you want from this list.
‣ ALSO (1): **pop-up menu** *n.* a menu which suddenly appears on the screen by pressing a particular keystroke sequence or by moving the mouse cursor to a particular location and pressing the mouse button.
‣ ALSO: **pull-down menu** *n.* a menu which appears on the screen by pressing the mouse button, dragging the mouse cursor to a particular location, and releasing the mouse button.

micro *n.* short for "microcomputer" which refers to any small computer including portable systems • *Micro computers have really come down in price this year!;* Small portable computers have really come down in price this year!

mouse *n.* a small hand-controlled pointing device that, when rolled across a surface, makes the cursor move accordingly on the computer screen • *You really need a mouse to be able to work with this program. Otherwise, you'll have to use the keyboard which moves the cursor slowly, step by step;* You really need a device that moves the cursor quickly to be able to work with this program. Otherwise, you'll have to use the keyboard which moves the cursor slowly, step by step.

nerd pack *n.* a plastic pocket protector which holds pens and is stereotypically used by computer fanatics • *I think a guy who wears a nerd pack is so unsexy!;* I think a guy who wears a plastic pocket protector is so unsexy!

off-the-shelf (to be) *n.* said of a computer which is ready to be used without any modification • *When you buy your computer, try and find one that is off-the-shelf. A customized system will be much too expensive;* When you buy your computer, try and find one that ready to use without any modification. A customized system will be much too expensive.

peripherals *n.pl.* external attachments to a computer such as the printer, scanner, mouse, etc. • *Look at all the new peripherals I got to go along with my computer!;* Look at all the supplementary equipment I got to go along with my computer!

plain vanilla (to be) *adj.* to be ordinary; said of a computer with no special features • *Your computer wasn't very expensive because it's plain vanilla;* Your computer wasn't very expensive

because it doesn't have any special features.

prompt *n.* a symbol or instruction on the computer screen indicating that the computer is now ready to receive a command from the operator • *The prompt on the bottom of your screen says to choose selection A or B;* The instruction on the bottom of your screen says to choose selection A or B.
⯈ NOTE: After a personal computer (or PC) is turned on, the symbols "C:\" will usually appear on the screen, indicating that the computer is ready to receive its first command. This is referred to as the *"C prompt."*

QWERTY *n.* (pronounced "querty") refers to a keyboard whose second row of keys reads, from left to right, QWERTY as opposed to foreign keyboards whose keys are in a different orientation • *When I lived in France, I sat down at my friend's computer but couldn't type because they don't use the QWERTY keyboard;* When I lived in France, I sat down at my friend's computer but couldn't type because they don't use the same keyboard as we do in America.

run a program (to) *exp.* to execute a computer program • *Which word processing program are* *you running on your computer?;* Which word processing program are you operating on your computer?

scroll (to) *v.* to move up or down through the text on the screen • *Scroll down through the text and try to find where you began typing in boldface;* Move down through the text and try to find where you began typing in boldface.

spell check (to do a) *exp.* to verify the spelling of a document automatically • *Before you print the document, make sure to do a spell check;* Before you print the document, make sure to verify the spelling automatically.

techie *n.* technician • *Bob is a computer techie;* Bob is a computer technician.

time bomb *n.* a hidden instruction in a computer program which is triggered by the computer's internal clock (the effect may range from annoying to very destructive) • *My brother was working on his computer when all of a sudden his entire*

manuscript was deleted. Maybe someone planted a time bomb in the program he was using!; My brother was working on his computer when all of a sudden his entire manuscript was deleted. Maybe someone, without warning, planted an instruction to delete his data in the program he was using.
◗ SYNONYM: **Trojan horse** *n.*

trashed (to get) *v.* said of a computer document that gets erased • *When I tried to find the document in the computer, it wasn't there! Somehow it got trashed!;* When I tried to find the document in the computer, it wasn't there! Somehow it got erased!

write-protected (to be) *exp.* said of a program or diskette that cannot be altered by the computer operator • *I want to be able to customize this program but I can't because it's write-protected;* I want to be able to customize this program but I can't because it's been "locked" by the programmer.

Practice Using Advanced Computer Slang & Jargon

(Answers, p. 222)

A. Circle the word that best completes the phrase.

1. I had the document on the computer screen but suddenly the program started malfunctioning, so I decided to (**transport, deport, abort**).

2. The computer program doesn't seem to be operating correctly. It must have a (**bug, pest, flu**).

3. Since I have to use both programs, I have them both in (**cachet, cache, coach**) so that I can access each one quickly.

4. If you (**click, lick, flick**) on that word, the computer will give you a list of synonyms.

5. I just entered all of our expenditures for the year. The computer is now (**munching, punching, crunching**) all the numbers to give us a total of the money we've spent since the company first opened.

6. My word processing program automatically double-spaces my documents. I'm going to change the (**default, defrost, defeat**) to single-space.

7. Put the diskette in the "A" (**dive, pilot, drive**).

8. The manufacturer sells directly to the (**front, end, last**) user as opposed to selling to a store first.

9. All the computers in our office are connected to a (**mainframe, refrain, strain**). That way when one operator is finished working on a file, a different operator can continue working on the same file from another terminal.

10. I want to be able to customize this program but I can't because it's (**read, write, draw**)-protected.

Meeting/Negotiation Jargon

"A Brainstorming Session!"

*The staff is **brainstorming** about some problems that need to be **laid on the table** right away.*

Dialogue In Slang

"A Brainstorming Session!"

DIALOGUE

The **Chairman**, Mr. Holm, has already **called the meeting to order**. The **minutes** have just been read.

Mr. Holm: As we mentioned in our last meeting, it's essential that we **brainstorm** about some problems that need to be **laid on the table** right away.

Mr. Jones: Mr. Chairman!

Mr. Holm: **The chair recognizes** Mr. Jones.

Mr. Jones: Several of our **officers** are out of town today and we don't have a **quorum**-

Ms. Benstein: Mr. Chairman, I think that...

Mr. Holm: I'm sorry Ms. Benstein. You're **out of order**. Mr. Jones **has the floor**.

Mr. Jones: As I was about to say, I **move** that we **table the discussion** until our next meeting when everyone is present.

Ms. Brown: I **second** the motion.

Mr. Holm: The motion has been **moved and seconded**. All those in favor, say **"aye."** All those opposed, say **"nay."** The "ayes" have it. **The motion carries**. We'll **hold** our next meeting a week from Monday at the new **facility**. This meeting **stands adjourned**.

Lesson Three - MEETING/NEGOTIATION JARGON

Translation of dialogue in standard English

"A Brainstorming Session!"

DIALOGUE

The **moderator**, Mr. Holm, has already **started the meeting**. The **record of events of the previous meeting** have just been read.

Mr. Holm:	As we mentioned in our last meeting, it's essential that we **try together to arrive at some solutions** to some problems that need to be **discussed** right away.
Mr. Jones:	Mr. Chairman!
Mr. Holm:	**As the moderator, I give you permission to speak**, Mr. Jones.
Mr. Jones:	Several of our **executives who hold positions of authority in our organization** are out of town today and we don't have a **minimum number of persons present needed to transact business**.
Ms. Benstein:	Mr. Chairman, I think that...
Mr. Holm:	I'm sorry Ms. Benstein. You're **not adhering to the rules of this meeting by speaking out of turn**. Mr. Jones **presently has permission to speak**.
Mr. Jones:	As I was about to say, I **propose** that we **postpone our discussion** until our next meeting when everyone is present.
Ms. Brown:	I **agree with the proposal**.
Mr. Holm:	The motion has been **proposed and agreed upon**. All those in favor, say **"I am in favor."** All those opposed, say **"I am not in favor."** The "ayes" have it. **The proposal will be acted upon**. We'll **conduct** our next meeting a week from Monday at the new **location**. This meeting **is dismissed**.

Lesson Three - MEETING/NEGOTIATION JARGON

Dialogue in slang as it would be heard

"A Brainstorming Session!"

DIALOGUE

The **Chairm'n**, Mr. Holm, has already **called the meeding ta order**. The **minutes**'ve jus' been read.

Mr. Holm: As we mentioned in "R" our last meeding, it's essential that we **brainstorm** about s'm problems that need ta be **laid on the table** ride away.

Mr. Jones: Mr. Chairman!

Mr. Holm: **The chair recognizes** Mr. Jones.

Mr. Jones: Several of "R" **officers** 'r oud of town t'day 'n we don't have a **quorum**-

Ms. Benstein: Mr. Chairman, I think that...

Mr. Holm: I'm sorry Ms. Benstein. Yer **oud of order**. Mr. Jones **has the floor**.

Mr. Jones: As I w'z about ta say, I **move** that we **table the discussion** 'til "R" next meeding when ev'ryone's present.

Ms. Brown: I **secon'** the motion.

Mr. Holm: The motion has been **moved 'n seconded**. All those 'n favor, say **"aye."** All those opposed, say **"nay."** The "ayes" have it. **The motion carries**. We'll **hold** "R" next meeding a week fr'm Monday at the new **facilidy**. This meeding **stands adjourned**.

Vocabulary

aye *n.* used to indicate a positive vote or "I am in favor" • *How many people are in favor of opening a new office downtown? Signify by saying "aye."* *The "ayes" have it;* How many people are in favor of opening a new office downtown? Signify by saying "yes." The "yes" votes prevail.

▸ SYNONYM: **yea / yah** *n.*

▸ ANTONYM: **nay** *n.* used to indicate a negative vote or "I am not in favor" • *The nays have it;* The majority of the members in this meeting are not in favor.

brainstorm (to) *v.* to gather in a group and spontaneously contribute ideas for solving problems • *We need to find a solution to this problem right away. I think we should have a meeting tomorrow with all the executives and brainstorm for a while;* We need to find a solution to this problem right away. I think we should have a meeting tomorrow with all the executives and study this for a while.

▸ ALSO (1): **brainstorming session** *exp.* a meeting where people gather and collectively arrive at decisions or solutions to a problem • *We're having a brainstorming session tomorrow to see how we can go about finding new clients;* We're having a decision-making meeting tomorrow to see how we can go about finding new clients.

▸ ALSO (2): **to have a brainstorm** *n.* to have a sudden clever idea • *I just had a brainstorm!;* I just had a great idea!

▸ SYNONYM (1): **to have a meeting of the minds** *exp.* • *We need to have a meeting of the minds in order to find a proper solution;* We need to have a meeting where we all try and arrive at a solution together.

▸ SYNONYM (2): **to put heads together** *exp.* • *I'm sure that if we put our heads together, we'll be able to come up with a great new product!;* I'm sure that if we think about this together, we'll be able to come up with a great new product!

call to order (to) *exp.* to start a meeting • *The meeting was called to order at nine o'clock in the morning;* The meeting was started at nine o'clock in the morning.

▸ VARIATION: **to come to order** *exp.* • *This meeting will now come to order.*

chairperson *n.* moderator • *She's going to be the chairperson for the conference;* She's going to be the moderator for the conference.

▸ NOTE: The term *"chairperson"* is a transformation of the noun "chairman."

Since a chairman can be either a man or a woman, the term was deemed sexist by feminist groups and was transformed into a nongender-specific noun.

facility *n.* the location where a meeting will be held • *We're going to hold the meeting at a new facility in Chicago;* We're going to hold the meeting at a new location in Chicago.
‣ SYNONYM: **site** *n.*

have the floor (to) *exp.* to have permission to speak • *It's not your turn to speak. Mr. Smith has the floor;* It's not your turn to speak. Mr. Smith has permission to speak.
‣ VARIATION (1): **to obtain the floor** *exp.* to get permission to speak.
‣ VARIATION (2): **to yield the floor** *exp.* to relinquish one's right to speak in order that another topic be discussed.

hold a meeting (to) *exp.* to conduct a meeting • *The meeting will be held tomorrow at noon;* The meeting will be conducted tomorrow at noon.

lay something on the table (to) *exp.* to present a matter for discussion • *I think we need to lay this matter on the table before we proceed;* I think we need to discuss this matter before we proceed.

minutes *n.pl.* a record of events of a previous meeting by times • *Please read the minutes from yesterday's meeting;* Please read the record of events from yesterday's meeting.

move (to) *v.* to propose • *I move that we adjourn the meeting;* I propose that we adjourn the meeting.

officer *n.* an executive who holds a position of authority or trust in an organization • *Ms. Rich has just been appointed as one of the new officers in our corporation;* Ms. Rich has just been appointed as one of the new executives in our corporation.

out of order (to be) *exp.* said of one who is not adhering to the rules of a meeting such as speaking out of turn, yelling, etc. • *Mr. Chancer, you're out of order! I'll have to ask you to either take your seat or be excused from this meeting;* Mr. Chancer, you're not adhering to the rules of this meeting! I'll have to ask you to either take your seat or be excused from this meeting.

quorum *n.* (Latin) minimum number of persons present at the meeting of a committee or organization, usually a majority, needed to transact business • *The vote couldn't be taken because we didn't have a quorum;* The vote couldn't be taken because we didn't have the minimum number of persons needed to transact business present.

second a motion (to) *exp.* to agree with a proposal • *"I second the motion." "The motion has been seconded;"* "I agree with the proposal." "The motion has been agreed upon by one of our members."

◗ NOTE: After a motion is made, it requires that one of the members in the meeting agree with its terms by saying *"I second the motion."* At that time, a general vote may be taken.

◗ ALSO: **to make a motion** *exp.* to make a proposal • *I make a motion to give all the employees a raise;* I make a proposal to give all the employees a raise.

stand adjourned (to) *v.* to be dismissed (said of a meeting) • *This meeting stands adjourned;* This meeting is dismissed.

table a discussion (to) *exp.* to postpone a discussion for a later time • *Let's table the discussion for now because we have something more important to address;* Let's postpone the discussion for now because we have something more important to address.

"The chair recognizes [name]" *exp.* "As the chairperson, I give permission for [name] to speak."

◗ NOTE: This is a common expression used by the leader of a meeting who permits others to speak one at a time. In this expression, the *"chair"* refers to the "chairperson."

"The motion carries" *exp.* "The proposal will be acted upon."

◗ NOTE: This is a common expression used by the leader of a meeting to indicate that a vote for a particular proposal has been accepted.

PRACTICE THE VOCABULARY

[Answers to Lesson Three, p. 222]

A. Underline the word that best completes each phrase.

1. All those in favor, signify by saying "(**aye, you, them**)."

2. This meeting is now called to (**command, rule, order**).

3. Why don't we meet tomorrow and (**thunderstorm, rainstorm, brainstorm**) about some solutions.

4. Ms. Pearlman, you have the (**floor, ceiling, door**).

5. The vote couldn't be taken because we didn't have a (**forum, decorum, quorum**).

6. I (**push, budge, move**) that we adjourn the meeting.

7. Janet Graul was just elected as our new chair (**human being, person, individual**).

8. Why don't we (**table, davenport, chair**) this discussion for later.

9. We're now going to hear the (**hours, minutes, seconds**) from our last meeting.

10. Mr. Clement, you're out of (**mortar, order, reorder**)!

B. Complete the phrases by choosing the appropriate words from the list below.

floor	**minutes**	**quorum**
adjourned	**recognizes**	**carries**
hold	**brainstorm**	**aye**

1. We all need to meet tomorrow and _____ about how we can increase our sales.

2. The chair _____ Mr. Smith. Please speak loudly.

3. The meeting stands _____ . Have a good weekend.

4. Since we have a _____ at our meeting, we can take a vote on this important issue.

5. All those in favor of starting our meetings an hour earlier, signify by saying " _____ ."

6. Ms. Chambers, you have the _____ . What is your opinion about this matter?

7. Will the secretary please read the _____ from our last meeting?

8. It may be a good idea to _____ our meetings in the morning before work.

9. The motion _____ . From now on, our meetings will start at eight o'clock in the morning.

C. Match the columns.

☐ 1. Let's postpone this discussion until our next meeting.

☐ 2. The meeting was started at noon.

☐ 3. The meeting took place at our new location.

☐ 4. We need to gather and contribute some ideas about this problem.

☐ 5. You have permission to speak.

☐ 6. The proposal will be acted upon.

☐ 7. We just elected new people to hold positions of authority in our organization.

☐ 8. Where should we conduct tomorrow's meeting?

☐ 9. I think we need to discuss this matter before we proceed.

☐ 10. I agree with the proposal.

☐ 11. As the chairperson, I give you permission to speak, Ms. Hirsch.

☐ 12. This meeting is dismissed.

A. **This meeting stands adjourned.**

B. **The motion carries.**

C. **I think we need to lay this matter on the table before we proceed.**

D. **We need to brainstorm about this problem.**

E. **We just elected new officers.**

F. **The chair recognizes Ms. Hirsch.**

G. **You have the floor.**

H. **The meeting was called to order at noon.**

I. **I second the motion.**

J. **The meeting took place at our new facility.**

K. **Where should we hold tomorrow's meeting?**

L. **Let's table this discussion until our next meeting.**

A CLOSER LOOK (1):
More Jargon Relating to Meetings

As seen in the opening dialogue of this lesson, there are several terms and idioms which are used primarily in a meeting situation.

Below are some additional words and expressions to add to an already full list.

bitch session *n.* a meeting where people get together and do nothing but complain (in a nonconstructive manner) • *I was hoping to find some solutions to the problems the employees are having with management, but the meeting just turned into one giant bitch session!;* I was hoping to find some solutions to the problems the employees aren having with management, but the meeting just turned into one giant gathering where people did nothing but complain without discussin any solutions!
▸ NOTE (1): The verb *"to bitch"* is a popular, yet somewhat coarse, slang term meaning "to complain."
▸ NOTE (2): A *"bitch,"* literally a "female dog," is a somewhat coarse term used to describe a shrewish, unpleasant woman. Furthermore, a *"son of a bitch"* refers to a despicable man *or* woman and is, oddly enough, stronger than *"bitch."*

conference call *exp.* a telephone meeting between people in different locations • *We're going to have a meeting tomorrow with all of our representatives from around the world. The conference call will begin at noon our time;* We're going to have a meeting tomorrow with all of our representatives from around the world. The telephone meeting will begin at noon our time.

open a meeting (to) *exp.* to begin a meeting • *I'd like to open the meeting by welcoming our new employees;* I'd like to begin the meeting by welcoming our new employees.
▸ ANTONYM: **to close a meeting** *exp.*

"Point of order!" *exp.* "I question whether or not the present proceedings are allowed or "in order" with the rules of parliamentary procedure!"

proxy vote *n.* a vote made by someone appointed to act as one's representative • *The board member voted as proxy in favor of the proposal to paint the office building;* The board member's representative voted in favor of the proposal to paint the office building.

▸ ALSO: **to vote by proxy** *exp.* to vote through one's representative • *She wasn't able to attend the meeting, so she voted by proxy;* She wasn't able to attend the meeting, so she voted through her representative.

stonewall (to) *v.* to inhibit a process, i.e. negotiations, plans, etc. • *Why are you stonewalling our decision?;* Why are you standing in the way of our decision?

take a meeting (to) *exp.* a common transformation of "to have a meeting" • *I think we'd better take a meeting and discuss this situation;* I think we'd better have a meeting and discuss this situation.

A CLOSER LOOK (2):
More Jargon Relating to Negotiations

It cannot be stressed enough that any non-native speaker without a considerable knowledge of the slang and jargon typically used during negotiations, is at an enormous and grave disadvantage. Without an understanding of this type of lingo, important discussions and agreements are bound to be misinterpreted.

The following list is destined to clear up any potential confusion.

arbitrator *n.* one who settles disputes between two or more people involved in a legal proceeding • *Since we can't seem to agree on this issue, maybe we should get an arbitrator;* Since we can't seem to agree on this issue, maybe we should get someone who can settle our dispute.

▸ SYNONYM: **mediator** *n.*

at a standstill (to be) *exp.* said of two negotiating parties who refuse to yield further • *Since I'm not accepting the terms you've* *offered me, and you've refused to revise them, it looks like we're at a standstill;* Since I'm not accepting the terms you've offered me, and you've refused to revise them, it looks like these negotiations can't proceed further.

▸ SYNONYM (1): **to be at an impasse** *n.*

▸ SYNONYM (2): **to be at a standoff** *n.*

▸ SYNONYM (3): **to be deadlocked** *adj.*

▸ SEE: **parties** *n.pl.*

back down (to) *exp.* to yield in one's position during a negotiation • *I know he's going to try and make you lower your price but just don't back down!;* I know he going to try and make you lower your price but just don't yield!

barter (to) *v.* to negotiate • *Since we're both interested in each other's services, maybe we can barter something that's mutually beneficial;* Since we're both interested in each other's services, maybe we can negotiate something that's mutually beneficial.

come back with something (to) *exp.* to return to the potential client with a revised offer • *I told him that I wasn't interested in having him do distribution for my product under the terms he proposed. Well, you won't*

believe what he came back with!; I told him that I wasn't interested in having him do distribution for my product under the terms he proposed. Well, you won't believe what his revised offer was!

come down (to) *exp.* to lower the price of one's product • *We simply can't afford to pay that much money for your product. Can you come down a little?;* We simply can't afford to pay that much money for your product. Can you lower the price a little?

come in low (to) *exp.* to offer a potential customer a substandard sum of money for a product or service • *I told both buyers that I would hire whomever gave me the best deal. I decided to go with the second company because the first company came in low;* I told both buyers that I would hire whomever gave me the best deal. I decided to go with the second company because the first company offered me a low price.

cut someone a deal (to) *exp.* to make a financial arrangement with someone • *After speaking with the president of our company, I'm ready to cut you a deal;* After speaking with the president of our company, I'm ready to make you a financial offer.

▸ SYNONYM: **to work out a deal** *exp.*

dicker (to) *v.* to negotiate over the price of something • *We spent an hour dickering over the price he wanted to charge us;* We spent an hour negotiating over the price he wanted to charge us.
‣ SYNONYM: **to haggle** *v.*

get something at a steal (to) *exp.* to sell someone something at an incredibly low price • *I got the car at a steal!;* I bought the car at an incredibly low price!

give a little (to) *exp.* to compromise • *When you negotiate, you have to learn to give a little;* When you negotiate, you have to learn to compromise.

give and take *exp.* compromising • *Negotiating always requires a certain amount of give and take;* Negotiating always requires a certain amount of compromising.

hammer out a deal (to) *exp.* to take a long time to negotiate a deal • *After several days of negotiating, we finally hammered out a good deal for both parties;* After several days of negotiating, we finally negotiated a good deal for both parties.
‣ SEE: **parties** *n.pl.*

knock down the price (to) *exp.* to bring one's price down • *If you're willing to knock down your price by 15%, you've got a sale!;* If you're willing to bring your price down by 15%, you've got a sale!;

‣ SYNONYM: **to drop the price** *exp.*

let someone walk away with something for [price] (to) *exp.* to bring one's price down to [price] • *After negotiating for almost an hour, the salesperson let me walk away with my new boat for half the price!;* After negotiating for almost an hour, the salesperson brought the price of my new boat down by half!
‣ VARIATION: **to let someone walk out the door with something for [price]** *exp.*

make an offer (to) *exp.* to make a financial proposal for one's product or service • *After giving the matter a great deal of thought, I'm ready to make you an offer for your product;* After giving the matter a great deal of thought, I'm ready to make you a financial proposal to obtain your product.
‣ ALSO: **to make a counter-offer** *exp.* to make a revised version of one's original financial proposal • *After the client rejected our original offer, we made a counter-offer that the client finally accepted;* After the client rejected our original offer, we made a revised version of our original proposal that the client finally accepted.

parties *n.pl.* two or more people involved in a legal proceeding • *All of the parties involved are* *from the United States;* All of the people involved in this legal proceeding are from the United States.

rock-bottom offer *exp.* the lowest price that one can offer to sell something • *Here is my rock-bottom offer. I'll sell you the car for $9,000;* Here is my lowest price. I'll sell you the car for $9,000.

sickout *n.* a protest conducted by angry employees (hoping to get their requests met) where each worker informs the company of his/her absence under the pretense of sickness • *If we don't give the employees an increase in salary, there's going to be a sickout starting tomorrow!;* If we don't give the employees an increase in salary, they're all going to call in sick starting tomorrow!
  ♦ ALSO: **blue flu** *exp.* a protest conducted by angry police officers (hoping to get their requests met) where each officer informs the company of his/her absence under the pretense of sickness. This expression originated due to the blue color of the typical uniform of the police officer.

strike (to) *v.* said of employees who cease work and demonstrate until their requests (usually for higher wages or improved conditions) are met • *If the boss doesn't give*
us what we want, we're going to strike; If the boss doesn't give us what we want, we're going to stop working.
  ♦ VARIATION (1): **to be on strike** *exp.*
  ♦ VARIATION (2): **sit-down strike** *n.* a peaceful yet disruptive demonstration where employees stop work and sit down in public as a way of protesting.
    ⇨ SYNONYM: **sit-in** *n.*
  ♦ ALSO (1): **strike** *n.* a cessation of work by employees until their requests are met • *The employees are planning a strike;* The employees are planning to stop work until their requests are met.
    ⇨ SYNONYM: **walk-out** *n.* • *We're planning a walk-out tomorrow morning;* We're planning to stop work tomorrow until our requests are met. (See: **sickout**).

"Take it or leave it" *exp.* a common expression used in negotiations meaning "Either accept my terms or let's abandon further negotiations" • *I just gave you my final offer. Take it or leave it;* I just gave you my final offer. Either accept my terms or let's abandon further negotiations.

undercut someone (to) *exp.* to bring one's price down more than one's competitor in order to attract an undecided client • *I'm willing to undercut my competitor if you'll make the* *deal with me;* I'm willing to bring my price down lower than my competitor if you'll make the deal with me.

wheel and deal (to) *exp.* to negotiate • *Whenever you buy a car, never pay the asking price. You have to wheel and deal with the salesperson;* Whenever you buy a car, never pay the asking price. You have to negotiate with the salesperson.

▸ ALSO: **wheeler-dealer** *n.* one who enjoys negotiating.

win-win situation *exp.* said of a condition where two individuals (or groups) benefit from the same situation • *Let's have the meeting at the client's office. That way the client won't have to drive in traffic for an hour to get here and we'll get to meet some of his wealthy investors! That's the perfect win-win situation!;* Let's have the meeting at the client's office. That way the client won't have to drive in traffic for an hour to get here and we'll get to meet some of his wealthy investors! That's the perfect way for everyone to benefit from the same situation!

▸ ANTONYM: **no-win situation** *exp.* said of a condition where no one wins • *If I don't invite my boss to the party, he'll be angry and hurt. If I do invite him, the rest of the guests will be mad at me because no one likes him! I'm in a real no-win situation;* If I don't invite my boss to the party, he'll be angry and hurt. If I do invite him, the rest of the guests will be mad at me because no one likes him! I'm in a situation where I just can't win.

work someone down (to) *exp.* to convince someone to bring down the price of one's product • *His price is way too high. Can't you work him down a little?;* His price is way too high. Can't you convince him to lower it a little?

Practice Jargon
Used in Meetings & Negotiations

(Answers p. 223)

A. Choose the word(s) that go(es) with the appropriate definition.

back down	**come down**	**cut**
standstill	**proxy**	**stonewall**
barter	**give and take**	**win-win**
	rock-bottom	

1. _____ **(to)** *v.* to inhibit a process, i.e. negotiations, plans, etc.

2. _____ **vote** *n.* a vote made by someone appointed to act as one's representative.

3. **at a** _____ **(to be)** *exp.* said of two negotiating parties who refuse to yield further.

4. _____ **(to)** *exp.* to yield in one's position during a negotiation.

5. _____ **(to)** *v.* to negotiate

6. _____ **(to)** *exp.* to lower the price of one's product.

7. _____ **someone a deal (to)** *exp.* to make a financial arrangement with someone.

8. _____ *exp.* compromising.

9. _____ **offer** *exp.* the lowest price that one can offer to sell something.

10. _____ **situation** *exp.* said of a condition where two individuals (or groups) benefit from the same situation.

A CLOSER LOOK (3):
*How to Ruin a Deal Unintentionally!**

Learning American gestures is a *necessity* for anyone doing business in America! In fact, since meetings and negotiations are often attended by people from several different countries, gestures in general need to be understood.

Many non-native speakers interpret our gestures (which in America are considered humorous, light, and simply second nature) as being offensive, malicious, and even combative.

In meetings and negotiations in particular, these types of misinterpretations can be very critical and even irreconcilable. For example, in America one might wish you luck in landing a contract by crossing his/her fingers whereas this gesture has the very different meaning of "vagina" in countries such as Vietnam and parts of China. Even something as typical and certainly unoffensive as crossing one's legs (inadvertently showing the bottom of one's shoe) is considered the height of disrespect to someone from Japan and can adversely affect a negotiation.

The following examples should help prevent any likely misunderstanding when meeting, negotiating with, or simply encountering any native born American (or international business person).

– The "OKAY" Gesture –

An extremely offensive gesture in countries such as Brazil and Greece.

U.S.A.

CANADA

BRAZIL   GREECE

---

* *Parts of this section are taken from **BLEEP!** -* **A Guide to Popular American Obscenities**, *Chap. 8, starting on page 153 (also by David Burke).*

– *Indicating "Two"* –

Even before we learn the alphabet, we are taught how to count using our fingers. Holding up fingers to indicate numbers one through five seems to be almost second nature to anyone born in America. However, if you do this same seemingly innocent gesture to someone from England, instead of receiving two of something, you may receive two black eyes!

In England, to hold up two fingers with the back of the hand facing the other person represents two phallic symbols.

An extremely offensive gesture in England.

In England (and other parts of Europe), the correct way to gesture "two" is to hold up your thumb and index finger. Unlike Americans who start counting with the index finger, Europeans begin with the thumb.

ENGLAND

– *The Beckoning Gesture* –

When gesturing for someone to approach you, it is common in America to use the index finger. However, it would certainly not be advisable to use this gesture when inviting a Yugoslavian or Malaysian to join you since this gesture is only used with animals and would cause great offense.

Most importantly, if you were to use this gesture with a woman in Indonesia or Australia, you would either be slapped or find yourself with a companion for the evening as this is the gesture for summoning prostitutes.

U.S.A.

CANADA

AUSTRALIA

INDONESIA

"Come here."   **"I'd like to buy your services for the evening."**

In many European and Latin American countries the correct way to beckon someone is to turn the hand upside-down with the palm facing the ground. The thumb is held still while the other four fingers extend straight then curl several times.

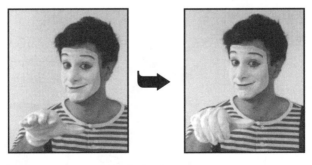

"Come here."

– *The "Stop" or "Wait" Gesture* –

The "stop" or "wait" gesture is commonly used all over America. It is simply meant to add emphasis whether in anger or nonchalantly. However, this gesture is commonly misinterpreted by Greeks, since for them, this sign has a very different and crude meaning.

An extremely offensive gesture in Greece.

– *The "Thumbs Up" Gesture* –

To convey agreement or satisfaction, it is common practice to give a *"thumbs up"* sign by making a fist and extending the thumb straight up. This gesture is also commonly followed by a slight upward jerk of the entire fist.

Any American who has used this gesture in front of an Australia has learned quickly that its meaning is extremely offensive and may bring potentially disastrous results to a negotiation.

An extremely offensive gesture in Australia.

– A Gesture of Greeting –

Many natives of Tibet must surely feel that Americans are extremely unfriendly upon first meeting. After all, when greeted by a Tibetan, many Americans seem aloof, annoyed, even disgusted. There is a simple reason for this. The Tibetan is unaware that the traditional greeting of sticking out the tongue as a gesture of friendship is interpreted by Americans as being rude and insolent.

TIBET   U.S.A.   CANADA

– The American "Hand-In-The-Lap" Gesture –

In American families, we are told to keep our elbows off the table since it is considered bad manners. It is therefore quite common to eat or simply sit with one hand resting in one's lap.

If an American does this in the presence of a European (especially someone from France), this could be misinterpreted as being rather obscene since you may be suspected of either playing sexually with yourself or your neighbor!

U.S.A.   FRANCE

CANADA

– *Gesturing Yes and No* –

This can lead to great confusion and misunderstanding between Americans and Bulgarians. In America, we nod our heads up and down to signify "yes" and back and forth to signify "no." However, in Bulgaria it's just the opposite!:

U.S.A.   **"Yes"**   **"No"**

BULGAR   **"No"**   **"Yes"**

Business Travel Jargon

– *"The Red-Eye"* –

Dialogue In Slang

"The Red-Eye"

DIALOGUE

Joe boards the plane with just moments to spare.

Bob: What happened? I thought you were going to miss the flight!

Joe: As soon as I got to the airport, the **skycap** helped me **check my luggage** which suddenly sprang open and dumped all over the place! I guess that's what I get for not **traveling light**. Then, it turned out that the office **booked me** on the wrong flight, so I had **to go standby** on this one!

Bob: At least they **bumped you up** to **business class** so we could sit together. Now you won't have to eat the **plastic food** they serve you in **coach**.

Joe: I think I'm just tired of taking these **red-eyes**.

Bob: At least it's nice **to get away**. Sure, I'd prefer to be able **to check into** a nice **B&B** somewhere and not have to worry about meetings, but at least we're away from the office!

Joe: I guess so. By the way, I heard we may be **laid over** in Chicago for a while because the other airport is **fogged in**.

Bob: Before you got **on board**, they announced from the **cockpit** that we'll be experiencing **head winds** so we're already going to be an hour late **getting in**, too. At least they said it should be **smooth sailing** most of the way.

Joe: I swear, when you travel, you either need to worry about delays or **jet lag**. Take your pick.

Lesson Four - BUSINESS TRAVEL JARGON

Translation of dialogue in standard English

"The Red-Eye"

DIALOGUE

Joe boards the plane with just moments to spare.

Bob: What happened? I thought you were going to miss the flight!

Joe: As soon as I got to the airport, the **airport attendant** helped me **register my luggage** which suddenly sprang open and dumped all over the place! I guess that's what I get for not **traveling with less baggage**. Then, it turned out that the office **arranged to put me** on the wrong flight, so I had to **wait for an available seat** on this one!

Bob: At least they **upgraded you** to **the more expensive class** so we could sit together. Now you won't have to eat the **institutional food** they serve you in **standard class**.

Joe: I think I'm just tired of taking these **all-night flights**.

Bob: At least it's nice **to leave town**. Sure, I'd prefer to be able **to register myself into** a nice **inn that offers sleeping accommodations as well as breakfast** somewhere and not have to worry about meetings, but at least we're away from the office!

Joe: I guess so. By the way, I heard we may be **delayed** in Chicago for a while because the other airport is **thick with fog**.

Bob: Before you got **on the airplane**, they announced from the **pilot's compartment** that we'll be experiencing **winds blowing against us** so we're already going to be an hour late **arriving**, too. At least they said it should be **a smooth flight** most of the way.

Joe: I swear, when you travel, you either need to worry about delays or **being tired due to the time change**. Take your pick.

Lesson Four - BUSINESS TRAVEL JARGON

Dialogue in slang as it would be heard

"The Red-Eye"

DIALOGUE

Joe boards the plane with just moments ta spare.

Bob: What happened? I thought you were gonna miss the flight!

Joe: As soon as I got ta thee airport, the **skycap** help't me **check my luggage** which suddenly sprang open 'n dumpt all over the place! I guess that's whad I get fer not **trav'ling light**. Then, it turned out that thee office **book't me** on the wrong flight, so I had **ta go stan'by** on this one!

Bob: At least they **bump't you up** ta **business class** so we could sit t'gether. Now ya won' haf ta eat the **plastic food** they serve you 'n **coach**.

Joe: I think I'm jus' tired of taking these **red-eyes**.

Bob: At least it's nice **ta ged away**. Sher, I'd prefer da be able **ta check into** a nice **B&B** somewhere 'n not haf ta worry about meetings, bud at least we're away from thee office!

Joe: I guess so. By the way, I heard we may be **laid over** in Chicago fer a while b'cause thee other airpord is **fogged in**.

Bob: B'fore ya god **on board**, they announc't fr'm the **cockpit** that we'll be experiencing **head winds** so we're already gonna be 'n hour late **gedding in**, too. At leas' they said it should be **smooth sailing** most 'a the way.

Joe: I swear, when ya travel, ya either need ta worry about delays or **jet lag**. Take yer pick.

Vocabulary

B&B *n.* This is a common abbreviation for a *"Bed and Breakfast"* which is an inn that offers sleeping accommodations as well as breakfast • *While we were on vacation, we found a great inexpensive B&B;* While we were on vacation, we found a great inexpensive inn which serves breakfast.

book a hotel, flight, room, etc. (to) *exp.* to reserve a hotel, flight, room, etc. in advance • *I had a lot of trouble booking my flight to Paris because all the planes were full! Luckily, there was a cancelation at the last minute;* I had a lot of trouble arranging my flight to Paris because all the planes were full! Luckily, there was a cancelation at the last minute.

bump someone up (to) *exp.* to upgrade someone's accommodations • (lit); to force someone to move by pushing him/her with a sudden jolt • *When the hotel manager found out my mother was a big executive, she was bumped up to the luxury suite!;* When the hotel manager found out my mother was a big executive, she was upgraded to the luxury suite!
▸ ALSO: **to bump someone** *exp.* to replace someone in a particular situation (such as a flight, a project, etc.) • *I got bumped from the flight for being a minute late!;* I got replaced on the flight for being a minute late!

business class *exp.* the class between first class and coach • *I couldn't afford to travel first class so I settled for business class;* I couldn't afford to travel first class so I settled for the class between first class and coach.
▸ NOTE: *"Business Class"* is also commonly referred to as *"Executive Class."*

check into a hotel (to) *exp.* to register oneself into a hotel • *I believe Mr. Hammond just checked in;* I believe Mr. Hammond just registered himself (into the hotel).
▸ ANTONYM: **to check out of a hotel** *exp.*

check one's luggage (to) *exp.* to relinquish one's luggage to a special airline agent in exchange for a claim ticket • *We'd better arrive at the airport a little early so you can check your luggage;* We'd better arrive at the airport a little early so you can relinquish your luggage to the airline agent in exchange for a claim ticket.
▸ NOTE: A passenger usually checks his/her luggage at the *"Baggage*

Check-In" desk. Although the term "luggage" is a common synonym for "baggage," it would be very rare to see a sign for "Luggage" Check-In.

coach *n.* an economical class of accommodations in an airplane or train • *I always travel coach so I can spend my money on the good restaurants!;* I always travel economically so I can spend my money on the good restaurants!

cockpit *n.* the front of the plane where the pilot controls the airplane • *My father is a pilot and always lets me sit with him in the cockpit;* My father is a pilot and always lets me sit with him in the front of the airplane.

fogged in (to be) *exp.* said of an area which is so thick with fog as to impede all traffic • *The flight is delayed because the airport is fogged in;* The flight is delayed because the airport is thick with fog.
 ‣ SYNONYM: **to be socked in** *exp.*

get away (to) *exp.* to leave one's problems by taking a vacation • (lit); to extricate oneself from a situation • *After working on this project for sixty hours a week, it'll be nice to get away tomorrow!;* After working on this project for sixty hours a week, it'll be nice to take a vacation away from work!
 ‣ ALSO: **getaway** *n.* said of a vacation place far away from everyday pressures • *Our new cabin is the perfect mountain getaway;* Our new cabin is the perfect place in the mountains to escape from everyday pressures.

get in (to) *exp.* to arrive • *Can you believe this new employee? She got in at noon today! When the boss finds out, she could lose her job;* Can you believe this new employee? She arrived at noon today! When the boss finds out, she could lose her job.

head winds *exp.* winds which blow toward the aircraft, slowing it down • *We're going to be about ten minutes late arriving in Los Angeles due to head winds;* We're going to be about ten minutes late arriving in Los Angeles due to winds blowing toward the aircraft.
 ‣ ANTONYM: **tail winds** *exp.* winds which blow in the same direction as the aircraft helping to increase its speed.

jet lag (to have) *exp.* said of one who has traveled to a location in a different time zone and whose body has not yet adapted to the time change • *I know it's midnight but I'm wide awake. It must be jet lag from my trip;* I know it's midnight but I'm wide awake. It must be that my body hasn't adapted to the time change yet.

laid over (to be) *exp.* said of a flight which makes a stop (of undetermined length) before continuing to its final destination • *It looks like we're going to be laid over here for a few hours due to fog;* It looks like we're going to be stopped here for a few hours due to fog.
> ♦ ALSO: **lay-over** *n.* a stop made by an aircraft before continuing to its final destination • *We're going to have an hour lay-over in San Francisco;* We're going to have an hour stop in San Francisco.

on board (to be) *exp.* to be in a ship, aircraft, car, etc. • *We can't leave until the vice president is on board!* We can't leave until the vice president is in the aircraft!
> ♦ ORIGIN: The expression *"to be on board"* originally applied to being on a ship since the old vessels were all made of wood. The expression is still used today but refers to any means of transportation.

"plastic food" *exp.* humorous name given to the institutional food served in economy class on typical airlines (which often comes wrapped in plastic).

red-eye *n.* an airplane flight which travels during the night (causing the passenger to loose a night's sleep and arrive at the destination with *"red eyes"*) • *I'm catching a red-eye to New York tonight;* I'm catching a night-plane to New York tonight.

skycap *n.* employee of an airline in charge of assisting passengers with checking in their luggage • *I think we'd better ask a skycap to assist us with our luggage.*

smooth sailing (to be) *exp.* said of a situation or journey which is calm and steady • *Once we finish with the difficult drawings on this portion of the building, the rest will be smooth sailing;* Once we finish with the difficult drawings on this portion of the building, the rest will be calm and steady (like a sailboat traveling on a tranquil sea).

stand-by (to be on) *exp.* said of a person who does not have a reserved seat on an airplane and must therefore wait at the airport for a cancelation • *I've been on stand-by for three hours!;* I've been waiting for a cancelation for three hours!

travel light (to) *exp.* to commute with very little luggage • *Whenever I go out of town on business, I try to travel light;* Whenever I go out of town on business, I try to take very little luggage with me.

PRACTICE THE VOCABULARY

(Answers to Lesson Four, p. 223)

A. Underline the definition of the expression in boldface.

1. **to bump someone up:**
   a. to push someone over
   b. to lift someone up
   c. to upgrade someone's accommodations

2. **to book something:**
   a. to reserve something in advance
   b. to leave in a hurry
   c. to cancel an arrangement

3. **B&B:**
   a. an inn which offers "Bed & Bathroom"
   b. an inn which offers "Bed & Brunch"
   c. an inn which offers "Bed & Breakfast"

4. **to travel coach:**
   a. to travel standard class
   b. to travel by foot
   c. to travel by air

5. **to get away:**
   a. to arrive at one's destination
   b. to leave one's problems by taking a vacation
   c. to arrive at work after a long vacation

6. **to be laid over:**
   a. to be extremely sick
   b. to be on time
   c. said of a flight which makes a stop before continuing to its final
      destination

7. **to get in:**
   a. to arrive
   b. to leave
   c. to remain in one place

8. **to travel light:**
   a. to travel in cool clothing
   b. to wear pastel colors when traveling
   c. to travel with very little luggage

9. **red-eye:**
   a. an all-night flight
   b. a turbulent flight
   c. a flight where liquor is served

10. **to be smooth sailing:**
    a. said of a situation or journey which is clam and steady
    b. said of someone who sleeps soundly while traveling
    c. said of an aircraft which lands smoothly

B. Fill in the blank with the corresponding letter of the word that best completes the phrase.

1. I hope I get on this flight. I've been on stand- _____ for an hour!
   a. **off**   b. **by**   c. **up**

2. I need to _____ my flight now if I want to get a good price.
   a. **magazine**   b. **newspaper**   c. **book**

3. We'd better arrive at the airport a little early so we have time to _____ our luggage.
   a. **check**   b. **verify**   c. **examine**

4. The airline _____ me up to first class for free!
   a. **lumped**   b. **dumped**   c. **bumped**

5. Everytime I travel abroad, I'm usually exhausted for several days because of the jet _____ .
   a. **lag**   b. **bag**   c. **hag**

6. We may be late landing at the airport because of all the _____ winds we're experiencing.
   a. **neck**   b. **foot**   c. **head**

7. It looks like the plane will have to be rerouted to another city since the airport in San Francisco is fogged _____ .
   a. **in**   b. **up**   c. **out**

8. She actually likes the _____ food they serve you on these flights!
   a. **plastic**   b. **cement**   c. **glass**

9. I hate carrying all this luggage with me. Next trip, I'm definitely going to travel _____ .
   a. **white**   b. **bright**   c. **light**

10. We'd better ask one of the _____ to help us with all this luggage.
    a. **kneecaps**   b. **skycaps**   c. **hubcaps**

C. Complete the boxes by choosing the appropriate words from the list below.

WORD LIST		
book	bump	business
check	coach	cockpit
fogged	head	lag
laid	board	light

1. to be in a ship, aircraft, car, etc.

T	O		B	E		O	N	

2. to commute with very little luggage.

T	O		T	R	A	V	E	L	

3. to reserve something (such as a hotel, flight, room, etc.)

T	O	■	■				
S	O	M	E	T	H	I	N	G

4. said of an area which is so thick with fog as to impede all traffic.

T	O	■	B	E	■					
I	N									

5. to upgrade someone's accommodations.

T	O	■				
S	O	M	E	O	N	E	■	U	P

6. the front of the plane where the pilot controls the airplane.

7. winds which blow toward the aircraft.

				■	W	I	N	D	S

8. the class between first class and coach, also called Executive Class."

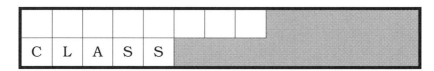

C	L	A	S	S		

9. said of a flight which makes a stop before continuing to its final destination.

T	O	█	B	E	█				
O	V	E	R						

10. an economical class of accommodations in an airplane or train.

11. said of one who has traveled to a location in a different time zone and whose body has not yet adapted to the time change.

T	O	█	H	A	V	E	█	J	E	T	

12. to register oneself into a hotel.

T	O	█					█	I	N	T	O
A	█	H	O	T	E	L					

A CLOSER LOOK (1):
Business Travel Slang & Jargon

As seen in Lesson One, general business slang and jargon are quite extensive and certainly important to understand due to their enormous popularity. However, once these universal terms and expressions have been learned, there is yet another category that must be mastered by anyone who does extensive business traveling.

The following terms are not only common to any American business traveler, but to *anyone* who is vacationing, planning a trip, or simply dropping someone off at the airport.

aisle seat *n.* a seat next to the aisle (in an aircraft, theatre, etc.) • *I prefer an aisle seat to a window seat so I don't have to climb over people when I want to use the lavatory;* I prefer a seat next to the aisle to a seat next to the window so I don't have to climb over people when I want to use the restroom.
♦ NOTE: In airplanes, the restroom is commonly referred to as the *"lavatory."*

baggage carousel *n.* a large revolving belt where all the luggage from a particular flight is sent to be retrieved by the passengers • *Look at all the suitcases on the baggage carousel! How am I ever going to be able to find mine?* Look at all the suitcases on the revolving belt! How am I ever going to be able to find mine?

baggage claim *n.* an area of the airport terminal where passengers retrieve their luggage • *Baggage Claim is downstairs;* The area where passengers retrieve their luggage is downstairs.
♦ NOTE: Although the term "luggage" is a common synonym for "baggage," it would be very rare to see a sign for "Luggage" Claim.

barf bag *n.* humorous term given to the traditional air sickness bag found in each seat pocket of a passenger aircraft • *The flight was so rough I thought I was gonna need to use the barf bag;* The flight was so rough I though

I was going to need to use the air sickness bag.

board a plane (to) *v.* to enter a plane • *We have to board the plane in one hour;* We have to enter the plane in one hour.
‣ ANTONYM: **to deplane** *v.* • *Be careful deplaning. The stairs are slippery from the rain;* Be careful exiting the plane. The stairs are slippery from the rain.

boarding pass *n.* an authorization card given to each passenger allowing access onto the aircraft • *After you purchase your ticket, you'll have to pick up a boarding pass at the gate;* After you purchase your ticket, you'll have to pick up an authorization card at the gate which will allow you access onto the aircraft.

cabin *n.* the inside of an aircraft • *Feel free to move about in the cabin;* Feel free to move about inside the aircraft.

carryon *n.* a briefcase, bag, small suitcase, etc. which can be carried onto the aircraft and easily stored • *Most airlines permit passengers to board an aircraft with a maximum of two carryons;* Most airlines permit passengers to board an aircraft with a maximum of two small bags or suitcases which can be

easily stored.
‣ VARIATION: **carryon luggage** *adj.* small luggage which may be easily carried onto an aircraft and easily stored.

commuter *n.* an aircraft which travels regularly between two destinations • *I'm going to take a commuter to Los Angeles for a meeting this afternoon.*

Concorde *n.* a supersonic passenger jet used exclusively for transatlantic flights • *The Concorde actually travels the speed of sound and at twice the altitude of conventional aircrafts.*
‣ NOTE: The Concorde is also called the *"S.S.T."* meaning "Supersonic Transport."

customs *n.* an area where passengers traveling abroad are required to report for clearance before entering the country of destination • (lit); the convention or practices of a people • *It may take us a long time to get home because we have to pass through Customs first;* It may take us a long time to get home because we have to pass through the clearance area first.

duty free shop *exp.* a shop found at any port of entry where an import tax is not charged to the customer • *I always save money by* *purchasing my cameras at the duty free shop;* I always save money by purchasing my cameras at the shop where I don't have to pay an import tax.

first class *exp.* the best and most expensive class of travel (originally started with ocean liners) • *I don't know how Alicia can afford to travel first class everywhere!;* I don't know how Alicia can afford to travel the best and most expensive class!

flight attendant *n.* one who works in a commercial aircraft tending to the needs of the passengers • *He just got a job as a flight attendant;* He just got a job working in a commercial aircraft tending to the needs of the passengers.

⬧ NOTE: In America, there is a large movement to get rid of gender-specific terms such as waitress, actress, businessman, etc. These have been changed to "waiter," "actor," and "business person," which may be applied to either sex. Those who work in the capacity of serving airline passengers used to be separated into two gender-specific groups: *"stewardesses"* and *"stewards."* Both have been changed to the nongender-specific term: *"flight attendant."*

floatation *n.* the act of resting on the surface of the water.

⬧ NOTE: This term is included here since anyone traveling in the U.S. is likely to hear one of the flight crew announce, *"Your seat cushion may be used for floatation,"* which means "Your seat cushion may be used as a life preserver if we are forced to land on the water."

⬧ VARIATION: **flotation** *n.*

Frequent Flyer Plan *exp.* This is a common plan whereby the air traveler receives special points for each mile traveled. These points are then redeemed in the way of discounts when purchasing future tickets.

⬧ SYNONYM: **Mileage Plus Plan** *exp.*

galley *n.* the kitchen of an aircraft (or ship) • *Let me see what kind of drinks we have left in the galley;* Let me see what kind of drinks we have left in the kitchen.

gate *n.* the terminal door from which passengers enter and exit the plane • *Flight 349 is now leaving from Gate 2;* Flight 349 is now leaving from Door 2.

L-1011 • 747 • DC-10 *n.* these are the most common "wide bodied" or "jumbo" jets used for commercial transportation —

other popular smaller jets are the **727** and **737**.

♦ NOTE: These large aircraft are commonly referred to as *"wide bodies:" I took a wide body to Paris… it's the only way to fly!;* I took a jumbo jet to Paris… it's the only way to fly!

moving sidewalk *n.* a long moving ramp where a person can simply stand and be carried forward to avoid having to walk through the typically long airport corridors.

overhead compartment *n.* an area located above the passenger seats used for storage of small items such as bags, briefcases, small pieces of luggage, etc.

♦ SYNONYM: **overhead bin** *n.*

"Please bring your seat backs and tray tables to their full and upright position" *exp.* This announcement is included here due to its frequent use by aircraft personnel. For safety reasons, flight regulations state that during take off and landing it is prohibited to have the seat in a reclining position or the tray tables down.

porter *n.* employee of a hotel in charge of carrying guests' luggage to their rooms • *Would you please call a porter to take my luggage to my room?*

run a movie (to) *exp.* to show a movie • *During today's flight, we'll be running a two-hour comedy;* During today's flight, we'll be showing a two-hour comedy.

sit in an exit row (to) *exp.* to sit in a row (of an airplane) which is next to an emergency exit • *If you are sitting in an exit row and don't feel you are capable of opening the emergency door, please notify your flight attendant so that we may change your seat assignment;* If you are sitting in a row next to an emergency exit and don't feel you are capable of opening the emergency door, please notify your flight attendant so that we may change your seat assignment.

♦ NOTE: This expression has been included here since anyone traveling in the U.S. is likely to hear it announced by the flight crew.

take off (to) *v.* (said of an airplane) to lift off the ground via propulsion • *We should be taking off soon;* We should be lifting off the ground soon.

♦ NOTE: This verb is also commonly used in general to mean "to leave."

♦ ANTONYM: **to land** *v.*

♦ ALSO (1): **takeoff** *n.* During takeoff, your ears may pop;

While the aircraft rises in flight, your ears may pop.

▶ ALSO (2): **to set sail** *exp.* (said of a ship or boat) to embark.

▶ ALSO (3): **to blast off** *exp.* (said of a rocket ship) to embark.

taxi (to) *v.* (said of an airplane) to move on the ground • *Please remain seated until we're at the gate. We will be taxiing for another couple of minutes;* Please remain seated until we're at the gate. We will be moving on the ground for another couple of minutes.

"The white zone is for immediate loading and unloading of passengers only" *exp.* This announcement is included here due to its repeated use by airport personnel. Each airline typically has an area directly in front of the terminal entrance designated for the sole purpose of dropping off passengers. Since this is also an ideal place to park one's car being so close to the entrance, this announcement is repeated on a regular basis and will surely be heard within a few moments of entering the terminal.

wake-up call *exp.* a telephone call (made by the hotel) whose only purpose is to serve as an alarm clock for a particular guest • *Front desk? I'd like a wake-up call for six o'clock in the morning please;* Front desk? I'd like you to ring my telephone at six o'clock in the morning please.

white courtesy telephone (the) *exp.* an in-house telephone located in an airport terminal where passengers may get messages • *Irene Rich, please pick up a white courtesy telephone;* Irene Rich, please pick up an in-house telephone to retrieve a message.

wind shear *exp.* a sudden and dangerous change in wind direction from horizontal to vertical, forcing the aircraft to lose altitude suddenly • *Due to wind shear, the plane was rerouted to another airport;* Due to the vertical direction of the wind, the plane was rerouted to another airport.

window seat *n.* a seat next to a window of a vehicle or aircraft • *I want to have a window seat so I can look at the view;* I want to have a seat next to the window so I can look at the view.

Practice Using
Business Travel Slang & Jargon

(Answers, p. 226)

A. Fill in the crossword puzzle on the opposite page by choosing the correct word from the list below.

lag	check	barf
flotation	stand	shear
attendant	customs	plus
	wake	

Across

1. **jet _____ (to have)** *exp.* said of one who has traveled to a location in a different time zone and whose body has not yet adapted to the change.

4. **_____ one's luggage (to)** *exp.* to relinquish one's luggage to a special airline agent in exchange for a claim ticket.

6. **_____ bag** *n.* humorous term given to the traditional air sickness bag found in each seat pocket of an airplane.

8. **_____** *n.* the act of resting on the surface of the water.

9. **_____-by (to be on)** *exp.* said of a person who does not have a reserved seat on an airplane and must therefore wait at the airport for a cancellation.

10. **wind _____** *exp.* a sudden and dangerous change in wind direction from horizontal to vertical, forcing the aircraft to loose altitude suddenly.

Down

2. **flight _____** *n.* one who works in a commercial aircraft tending to the needs of the passengers.

3. **_____-up call** *exp.* a telephone call (made by the hotel) whose only purpose is to serve as an alarm clock for a particular guest.

5. **_____** *n.* an area where passengers traveling abroad are required to report for clearance before entering the country of destination.

7. **mileage _____** *exp.* a program offered by many airlines where a certain number of miles traveled may be redeemed for a free flight.

A CLOSER LOOK (2):
Slang Names for Popular Cities

Most non-native speakers who have studied English for years are thoroughly confused when they hear native-born American converse. And why not? There is a slang synonym for just about everything; verbs, adjectives, people, animals, food, clothing, modes of transportation, even cities! After all, we often give nicknames to old friends, and to many business travelers who return to the same city time and time again, these cities are like familiar faces and are given affectionate names.

The following list will let you in on the *"inside"* nicknames of popular cities usually known only by native speakers.

CITY	(STATE)	SLANG NICKNAME
Atlanta	(Georgia)	**Hot Lanta** *(Due to its hot summer weather)*
Boston	(Massachusetts)	**Bean Town** *(Due to the large Irish popular and their famous bean dishes such as Boston baked beans)*
Chicago	(Illinois)	**Chi Town** *(Chi from "Chi" in "Chicago")* **The Windy City** *(Due to the frequent high winds)* **Shakeytown**
Dallas	(Texas)	**Big D** *(Since Texas is the largest state in the U.S., everything in the state is considered to be big. In fact, many of the tourist souvenirs are actually oversized such as giant fly swatters for the giant flies, etc.)*
Denver	(Colorado)	**The Mile High City** *(The city is approximately one mile in elevation)*

CITY	(STATE)	SLANG NICKNAME
Detroit	(Michigan)	**Motown** **The Motor City** *(This is where the first cars were made and is still the home of the majority of car manufacturers)*
Hollywood	(California)	**Hollyweird** *(Hollywood has always encouraged open expression making it common to see "weird" characters with the strangest clothing and hairdos of different colors)* **Tinsel Town** *(Hollywood is known for being very glitzy and bright because of all the movie premieres and lights. All of this sparkle gave Hollywood the nickname "Tinsel Town.")*
Indianapolis	(Minnesota)	**Indy** *(An affectionate shortened version of "Indianapolis")*
Las Vegas	(Nevada)	**Lost Wages** *(A humorous play-on-words implying that, due to all the gambling, it is a place where many people have "lost their wages")* **Luck Town** *(Many people have come to Las Vegas and have had great "luck" at winning enormous amounts of money by gambling)* **Vegas** *(An affectionate shortened version)*
Los Angeles	(California)	**LA** *(Pronounced L-A; an extremely common abbreviation used by the inhabitants)* **La-La Land** *(from LA)*

CITY	(STATE)	SLANG NICKNAME
Louisville	(Kentucky)	**Derbyville** *(This is where the Kentucky Derby horse race takes place every year)*
Milwaukee	(Wisconsin)	**Beer Town** *(Home of many large breweries)*
Minneapolis/ St. Paul	(Minnesota)	**The Twin Cities** *(These two cities are directly across the river from each other)*
New York City	(New York)	**The Big Apple** *(This comes from the story of Adam & Eve, suggesting that New York City has many temptations)* **The Concrete Jungle** *(Due to its compact size)*
Oakland	(California)	**Oaktown** *(Due to the numerous oak trees that used to fill the city)*
Philadelphia	(Pennsylvania)	**Philly** *(An affectionate shortened version of "Philadelphia")* **The Big Pretzel** **The City of Brotherly Love**
San Francisco	(California)	**Bagdad By The Bay** **Frisco** *(Considered disrespectful terms invented by gangsters who used to live in San Francisco - the use of these nicknames is actually offensive to many of its inhabitants due to the gangster reference)*
Seattle	(Washington)	**Sea Town** *(Due to the many sea ports)*
St. Louis	(Missouri)	**St. Louie** *(An affectionate shortened version of the name "Louis")*

A CLOSER LOOK (3):
State Mottos

As just seen, many popular cities have nicknames which represent their uniqueness or the specialty within their particular state. However, each of the fifty United States has its own distinct motto or characteristic worn with pride. Any business traveler is destined to encounter those creeds since they are commonly displayed at airports, many ports of entry into the U.S., on banners, license plates, and more.

It should be noted that the *only* two states which share a common motto are Florida and South Dakota which are both known as *"The Sunshine State."*

STATE (and State Flag)	CREED
Alabama	*Heart of Dixie*
Alaska	*Great Land*
Arizona	*Grand Canyon State*
Arkansas	*Land of Opportunity*
California	*Golden State*
Colorado	*Centennial State*
Connecticut	*Constitution State*
Delaware	*First State*

STATE (and State Flag)	CREED
Florida	*Sunshine State*
Georgia	*Empire State of the South*
Hawaii	*Aloha State*
Idaho	*Gem State*
Illinois	*Land of Lincoln*
Indiana	*Hoosier State*
Iowa	*Hawkeye State*
Kansas	*Sunflower State*
Kentucky	*Bluegrass State*
Louisiana	*Pelican State*
Maine	*Pine Tree State*
Maryland	*Old Line State*
Massachusetts	*Bay State*

STATE (and State Flag)		CREED
Michigan		Great Lakes State
Minnesota		Gopher State
Mississippi		Magnolia State
Missouri		Show Me State
Montana		Treasure State
Nebraska		Cornhusker State
Nevada		Silver State
New Hampshire		Granite State
New Jersey		Garden State
New Mexico		Land of Enchantment
New York		Empire State
North Carolina		Tar Heel State
North Dakota		Flickertail State

STATE (and State Flag)	CREED
Ohio	*Buckeye State*
Oklahoma	*Sooner State*
Oregon	*Beaver State*
Pennsylvania	*Keystone State*
Rhode Island	*Ocean State*
South Carolina	*Palmetto State*
South Dakota	*Sunshine State*
Tennessee	*Volunteer State*
Texas	*Lone Star State*
Utah	*Beehive State*
Vermont	*Green Mountain State*
Virginia	*Old Dominion*
Washington	*Evergreen State*

STATE (and State Flag)		CREED
West Virginia		*Mountain State*
Wisconsin		*Badger State*
Wyoming		*Equality State*

Marketing Jargon

– *"A Cash Cow"* –

Lesson Five - MARKETING JARGON

"A Cash Cow"

DIALOGUE

Emily, president of Powell Marketing Group, is discussing a new product with her staff.

Emily: We need **to position** the new **line** of Biff's Hair Care for Men very carefully because it could turn out to be a real **cash cow**, even though the product is somewhat **gender-biased**. Since the **demographics** of this product are primarily **yuppies**, we need to come up with ideas for a new **corporate image** as well as effective ways **to target** this **market**.

Roger: What if we start by **counter-marketing** other products like it? After all, it's supposedly the best **on the market** and it's **on the cutting edge** of hair care technology. In fact, we **test-marketed** the products and everyone in the **focus group** loved them!

Irene: Once we get a good **hook**, we should begin a **marketing blitz** to really **move the product**. I think we should start by contacting a **list broker** and get names of men who subscribe to fashion magazines and then do **cold calls**. We could even tell them we'll offer a **rebate** if they order now.

Jack: It may also be a good idea to plan a **rollout** during the holiday season. That way we can do a **tie-in** with some other popular products we're planning to **launch** in December.

Lesson Five - MARKETING JARGON

Translation of dialogue in standard English

"A Cash Cow"

DIALOGUE

Emily, president of Powell Marketing Group, is discussing a new product with her staff.

Emily: We need **to devise a careful marketing strategy** for the new **product** under Biff's Hair Care for Men because it could turn out to be a real **money-maker**, even though the product is somewhat **geared toward one sex over the other**. Since the **aim** of this product is primarily toward **young urban professionals**, we need to come up with ideas for a new **attractive "personality" for the company** as well as effective ways **to focus** on this **specific section of the general public**.

Roger: What if we start by **convincing the public not to buy** other products like it? After all, it's supposedly the best **available** and it's **in the forefront** of hair care technology. In fact, we **pretested the effectiveness** of the product and everyone in this **carefully selected group** loved it!

Irene: Once we create an **enticing advertisement**, we should begin an **extremely aggressive marketing campaign** to really **sell the product**. I think we should start by contacting **someone who can sell us a list of potential customers** and get names of men who subscribe to fashion magazines and then make **unsolicited telephone calls to obtain sales**. We could even tell them we'll offer a **partial refund** if they order now.

Jack: It may also be a good idea to plan **national distribution of the product** during the holiday season. That way we can **share advertising costs** with some other popular products we're planning on **introducing to the public** in December.

Lesson Five - MARKETING JARGON

Dialogue in slang as it would be heard

"A Cash Cow"

DIALOGUE

Emily, president of Powell Markeding Group, is discussing a new product with 'er staff.

Emily: We need **ta position** the new **line**'v Biff's Hair Care fer Men very carefully b'cuz it could turn out ta be a real **cash cow**, even though the product is somewhat **gender-biased**. Since the **demagraphics** of this product 'r primarily **yuppies**, we need ta come up with ideas fer a new **corp'rate image** as well as effective ways **ta target** this **market**.

Roger: Whadef we start by **counter-marketing** other products like it? After all, it's supposedly the best **on the market** an' it's **on the cutting edge** of hair care technology. In fact, we **test-markeded** the products 'n ev'ryone 'n the **focus group** loved it!

Irene: Once we ged a good **hook**, we should b'gin a **markeding blitz** ta really **move the product**. I think we should start by contacting a **list broker** 'n get names of men who subscribe ta fashion magazines 'n then do **cold calls**. We could even tell 'em we'll offer a **rebate** if they order now.

Jack: It may also be a good idea ta plan a **rollout** during the holiday season. That way we c'n do a **tie-in** with s'm other popular products we're planning to **launch** 'n December.

Vocabulary

cash cow *n.* a product which makes money simply by being on the market without expensive advertising • *This new food processor is a real cash cow! We haven't done any advertising at all and it just keeps selling!;* This new food processor attracts customers just by being on the market! We haven't done any advertising at all and it just keeps selling!

cold call *n.* a marketing strategy where an unsolicited telephone call (or personal visit) is made to a potential customers in the hope of making a sale • *I hate making cold calls because many of the people who answer the phone resent that I'm bothering them at home;* I hate making unsolicited telephone calls to potential customers because many of the people who answer the phone resent that I'm bothering them at home.

corporate image *n.* the general impression the public has about a company's "personality" (i.e. friendly, helpful, service-oriented, etc.) • *We need to change your corporate image in order to attract more customers. Right now when people think of your company, they think of a company that is indifferent to their needs;* We need to change the general impression the public has about your corporation in order to attract more customers. Right now when people think of your company, they think of a company that is indifferent to their needs.

countermarketing *n.* the act of a company convincing people *not* to buy the product of another company • *Did you hear about the countermarketing our competitor is doing? I just heard a radio commercial that said "Our new laundry soap is much more effective than SPIFF Soap which doesn't rinse out all the way!";* Did you hear how our competitor is trying to convince people not to buy our product? I just heard a radio commercial that said "Our new laundry soap is much more effective than SPIFF Soap which doesn't rinse out all the way!"

cutting edge (to be on the) *exp.* to be the leader in setting trends, to be in the forefront • *Paris is on the cutting edge of fashion;* Paris is the leader in setting trends in fashion. • *MBI is on the cutting edge of computer technology;* MBI is the leader in computer technology.

demographics *n.* a popular marketing term which refers to the characteristics of the population by specific groups such as age, race, religion, sex, income, etc. • *The demographics of Los Angeles shows a* *growing number of women. Therefore, our marketing efforts for women's perfume should be concentrated in that city;* An increasing group in Los Angeles is made up of women. Therefore, our marketing efforts for women's perfume should be concentrated in that city.

focus group *n.* a carefully selected cross section of consumers hired by a manufacturer to give their reaction to a particular product • *Let's bring in a focus group to test our new soft drinks. The drink that gets the best overall reaction is the one we'll release to the market;* Let's bring in a cross section of consumers to test our new soft drinks. The drink that gets the best overall reaction is the one we'll release to the market.

gender-biased (to be) *adj.* to be aimed more to one sex over the other • *It would be easier to market those tennis shoes if they weren't gender-biased. They need to look less masculine and more neutral;* It would be easier to market those tennis shows if they weren't aimed toward one sex over the other. They need to look less masculine and more neutral.

hook *n.* **1.** a marketing idea that attracts or *"hooks"* the customer or media • *The toy company recently came up with a good hook for their slogan: "Our toys are safe. If you care about your child's safety, you'll look at ours first."* The toy company recently came up with a good marketing slogan: "Our toys are safe. If you care about your child's safety, you'll look at ours first;" • **2. the part of a commercial which the customer remembers** • *The part of the commercial where the children sing the product name in harmony is a great hook;* The part of the commercial where the children sing the product name in harmony is extremely memorable.
    ‣ ALSO: **to hook a client** *exp.* • *Our new slogan should really hook clients;* Our new slogan should really attract clients.

launch a product (to) *exp.* to introduce a product to the public with an aggressive advertising campaign • *In just two weeks, we're going to launch our new shampoo product;* In just two weeks, we're going to introduce our new shampoo product to the public.

line *n.* (term also known by those outside marketing) a group of products carrying the same name within a specific category such as health products, bathroom products, etc. • *Let me show you our new line of evening wear;* Let me show you our new collection of evening wear.

list broker *n.* one who supplies (and sells) lists of potential clients to companies about to embark on a direct mail campaign • *Let's find a list broker who can give us the names and addresses of people who have a degree in linguistics;* Let's find a specialist who can give us the names and addresses of people who have degrees in linguistics.

market • **1.** *v.* to promote, distribute, and sell a product • *This new laundry soap will be easy to market. It's the only one like it!;* This new laundry soap will be easy to promote, distribute, and sell. It's the only one like it! • **2.** *n.* a specific section of the general public made up of consumers • *There is a large market for skin care products;* There is a large section of the general public who will buy skin care products.

marketing blitz *n.* an extremely aggressive marketing campaign • *If this marketing blitz doesn't sell this product, nothing will!;* If this aggressive marketing campaign doesn't sell this product, nothing will!

move a product (to) *exp.* to sell a product • *Your product is certainly in demand. I don't think we'll have any problem moving it;* Your product is certainly in demand. I don't think we'll have any problem selling it.

on the market (to be) *exp.* said of a product which is available in stores • *This is the best soap I've ever used. It's new on the market;* This is the best soap I've ever used. It's new in the stores.

position a product (to) *exp.* to generate product sales among a certain group of the population by means of a well-conceived strategy • *The best way to position this book in a busy city like Los Angeles is to call it "The Ultimate Survival Guide for Every Driver;"* The best way to generate sales of this book in a busy city like Los Angeles is to call it "The Ultimate Survival Guide for Every Driver."

rebate *n.* a partial refund offered a consumer as an enticement to buy a product • *The dealer is offering a $150 rebate with the purchase of their computer;* The dealer is offering a partial refund of $150 with the purchase of their computer.

rollout *n.* the national distribution of a product • *When do you think the best time would be to do a rollout;* When do you think the best time would be to begin national distribution of the product?

target (to) *v.* to focus on a particular group of consumers • *We need to target our expensive perfumes toward the wealthy group of consumers and our swim wear toward students;* We need to focus our expensive perfumes toward the wealthy group of consumers and our swim wear toward students.

test-market a product (to) *v.* to test the effectiveness of a particular product before it is widely distributed by getting comments from people who have been chosen to use the product for a specified amount of time • *It's a good thing we test-marketed our new soft drink. We would have never known that only a few people like the taste!;* It's a good thing we tested the effectiveness on our new soft drink. We would have never known that only a few people like the taste!

tie-in *n.* a campaign where two companies share advertising costs by combining or *"tying in"* each other's products • *World Amusement Park is interested in doing a tie-in with us where the consumer will receive a discount to the park for buying our product;* World Amusement Park is interested in combining advertising costs with us where the consumer will receive a discount to the park for buying our product.

yuppie *n.* an abbreviation for *"young urban professional,"* a young, well-paid, pretentious, executive who tends to buy products of a trendy nature • *We need to target our new fashionable shoes to the yuppie;* We need to target our new fashionable shoes to the young, well-paid executive who would be attracted to anything fashionable.
‣ NOTE: In the gay world, the term has been modified to *"guppi"* meaning "gay urban professional."
‣ ALSO: **to be yuppified** *exp.* to acquire the traits of a yuppie • *He became so yuppified ever since he got his new job;* He acquired all the traits of a yuppie ever since he got his new job.

PRACTICE THE VOCABULARY

[Answers to Lesson Five, p. 227]

A. Circle the letter corresponding to the correct synonym of the word(s) in boldface.

1. **to launch a product**:
   a. to send a product into orbit
   b. to introduce a product to the public
   c. to eat something for lunch

2. **hook**:
   a. a marketing idea that attracts the customer
   b. a group of products carrying the same name within a specific category
   c. a partial refund offered a consumer as an enticement to buy a product

3. **to target**:
   a. to sell a product
   b. to introduce a product to the public
   c. to focus on a particular group of consumers

4. **rebate**:
   a. a partial refund offered a consumer as an enticement to buy a product
   b. the national distribution of a product
   c. a carefully selected cross section of consumers hired by a manufacturer to give their reaction to a particular product

5. **to position a product**:
   a. to focus on a particular group of consumers
   b. to generate product sales among a certain group of the population by means of a well-conceived strategy
   c. to move a product over in order to make room for another product

6. **cash cow**:
   a. a product which makes money simply by being on the market without expensive advertising
   b. a marketing strategy where an unsolicited telephone call or personal visit is made to a potential customer in the hope of making sale
   c. a group of products carrying the same name within a specific category

7. **cold call**:
   a. a product which makes money simply by being on the market without expensive advertising
   b. a marketing strategy where an unsolicited telephone call or visit is made to a potential customer in the hope of making a sale
   c. a group of products carrying the same name within a specific category

8. **countermarketing**:
   a. the national distribution of a product
   b. the act of a company convincing people not to buy the product of another company
   c. an extremely aggressive marketing campaign

B. FIND-THE-WORD CUBE

Step 1:   Fill in the blanks with the correct word using the list below.

Step 2:   Find and circle the word in the grid on the opposite page. The first one has been done for you.

cutting	blitz	tie
target	cold	yuppies
line	launch	focus
list	hook	rebate

1. We're planning a huge marketing _____ starting next week to try and sell the product.

2. The city of Paris is on the _____ edge of fashion.

3. The manufacturer is offering a $5 _____ .

4. We need to come up with a good _____ in our marketing campaign to really attract the potential customer.

5. Let's do a _____ -in with Galaxy Studios where if customers buy our product, they'll get a discount to the studio tour!

6. I think we should contact a _____ broker to get names and adresses of women who have bought similar products to ours.

7. The best time to make _____ calls is either at night or on the weekends when potential customers are home.

8. _____ are known for buying trendy products.

9. We need to _____ the suntan lotion toward people who love going to the beach.

10. Just before the end of summer, we're going to _____ a new car that's affordable to teenagers.

11. It may be a good idea to bring in a _____ group to test the new softdrink before we begin our marketing campaign.

12. Have you tried our new _____ of men's skin care products?

FIND-THE-WORD CUBE

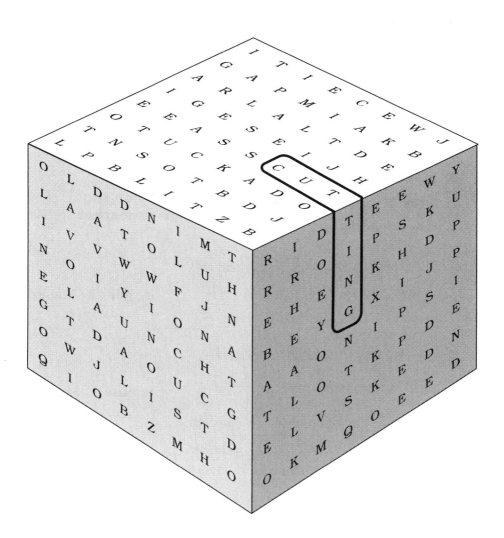

C. Replace the italicized word(s) with the appropriate slang synonym(s) from the right column.

1. Let me show you our new

   group _____ of dresses.

   A. **marketing blitz**

2. If this *aggressive marketing campaign*

   _____ doesn't sell

   this product, nothing will!

   B. **cold calls**

3. The manufacturer is offering a *partial*

   refund _____ if you buy

   their new product.

   C. **on the market**

4. These products are being bought primarily

   by *young urban professionals*

   _____ .

   D. **gender-biased**

5. Our company is *the leader in setting*

   trends _____ .

   E. **line**

6. Every time I make *unsolicited phone calls*

   to sell products _____ , people

   get angry that I'm bothering them at home.

   F. **on the cutting edge**

7. The product has been *available to the*

   public _____ for a long time.

8. It would be a lot easier to market

   those tennis shoes if they weren't

   aimed toward one sex over the

   other _____ .

   G. **yuppies**

   H. **rebate**

A CLOSER LOOK:
Advanced Marketing Jargon

Everywhere we go, we are surrounded by various forms of marketing, from flyers to billboards, testimonials to jingles, word-of-mouth to skywriting, and much more. Just about every marketing technique has its own jargon which, to the outsider, must seem entirely nonsensical and confusing. Many of the terms conjure up some pretty bizarre images. What could a marketer possibly mean by a *"bell cow,"* a *"bangtail,"* or a *"flanker?"*

The following list should provide you with just about all the terms you'll need to enter the marketing game.

back order (to be on) *exp.* said of merchandise ordered by a customer yet is temporary unavailable • *The chair you requested is on back order;* The chair you requested will be sent to you as soon as it is available.

back-to-school sale *exp.* a popular sale occurring toward the end of summer when schools reopen. ◗ NOTE: This expression is commonly used on television and radio commercials and well as newspaper and magazine advertisements.

bangtail *n.* a coupon or order form attached to an envelope flap, usually separated by a perforation, which presents a new product the consumer can readily order • *When we send the customer the bill, let's include a remittance envelope with a bangtail announcing our new product;* When we send the

customer the bill, let's include a remittance envelope with an order form attached to the envelope flap announcing our new product.

barter (to) *v.* to trade advertising time or print space for merchandise rather than money • *The Burke Soap Company bartered with the television station to give them 10,000 bars of free soap in exchange for 30 seconds of free broadcasting time;* The Burke Soap Company negotiated with the television station to give them 10,000 bars of free soap in exchange for 30 seconds of free broadcasting time.

bell cow *n.* a sales item that sells well and makes a good profit • *Our new foot massager is a real bell cow!;* Our new foot massager sells extremely well and makes a good profit!

bingo card *n.* a postcard advertisement bound into a publication which the consumer may return to the manufacturer for additional information on a product • *Almost all of the bingo cards we put into the magazine have come back! I think this product is going to be popular!;* Almost all of the postcard advertisements we put into the magazine have come back! I think this product is going to be popular!

bribe *n.* a special deal offered to a customer as a way to entice him/her to make a purchase • *We need to come up with a good bribe so the customer becomes a member of our video club. How about, "Join now and receive ten free video rentals!;"* We need to come up with a special offer to entice the customer so he/she becomes a member of our video club. How about, "Join now and receive ten free video rentals!"
▶ SYNONYM: **up-front offer** *n.*

cannibalize (to) *v.* to create a "new and improved" version of one's own product under a different name.
▶ NOTE: It is hoped that this strategy causes sales to drop for the original product yet soar for the new one, making the company a substantial profit all around.

category business *n.* a company which makes different products in the same category such as a book publisher, a toy company, etc. • *A category business may make several different sales to the same customer, whereas an "item business" (such as a mattress manufacturer) usually sells only a single item to the customer;* A business which makes different products in the same category may make several different sales to the same customer, whereas an "item business" (such as a mattress manufacturer) usually sells only a single item to the customer.

clearance sale *n.* a sale to get rid of old merchandise • *Smith's Furniture is having a clearance sale tomorrow!;* Smith's Furniture is having a sale tomorrow to get rid of old merchandise!

container premium *n.* the packaging of a product which, when empty, is actually a gift of a reusable container.

continuity series *n.* a product which is made up of several parts (such as a series of books), each one sent to the consumer at specific intervals.

corporate license *n.* an entitlement given by a corporation to use its own product's image to help sell another company's merchandise (such as popular cartoon characters created by a television studio printed on shirts manufactured by another company) • *If you want to print the cartoon character's face on shirts, you'll have to get a corporate license from the manufacturer;* If you want to print the cartoon character's face on shirts, you'll have to get a written entitlement from the manufacturer.

designer *adj.* made by the best designers • *Have you tried on our new designer jeans?;* Have you tried on our new jeans made by some of the world's best designers?

direct premium *n.* a free gift offered to a consumer along with a purchase • *Let's offer a direct premium to the customer to entice them to buy our product;* Let's offer a free gift to the customer to entice them to buy our product.
♦ SYNONYM: **GWP** *n.* abbreviation for *"Gift With Purchase."*

direct response *n.* a way in which the advertiser gets an immediate response from the potential customer by approaching the customer directly, through phone sales, flyers, brochures, catalogues, etc. (as opposed to through a retail store) • *We've had more sales with direct response on this product than we have had through stores;* We've had more sales on this product by approaching the customers

directly than we have had through stores.

door *n.* branch of a chain of stores • *If we can get our product to every door in this chain store, profits should increase substantially;* If we can get our product to every branch of this chain store, profits should increase substantially.

drip method *exp.* a type of marketing approach where an interested, yet undecided, buyer is solicited at regular intervals by telephone until he/she has decided whether or not to make a purchase • *I think we're going to have to apply the drip method on this customer. He seems interested but just can't make up his mind right now;* I think we're going to have to make regular calls to this customer. He seems interested but just can't make up his mind right now.
♦ NOTE: This expression conjures up an image of telephone calls made to a potential consumer as regularly and steadily as a slow-dripping faucet.

drop (to) *v.* to mail out • *Our fall book catalogue drops in October;* Our fall book catalogue mails out in October.

drop back order *n.* an order made with a coupon from a previously purchased item • *We've received a large number of drop back orders from "Biz Talk -1" requesting copies of "Biz*

Talk -2; "We've received a large number of orders made with a coupon from *Biz Talk -1* requesting copies of *Biz Talk -2.*"

flagship *n.* the first in a group • *This store is the flagship in a chain of stores;* This store is the first in a chain of stores.

flanker *n.* new merchandise carrying the same name as another well-established and profitable product of the same company • *Since our product Dazzle Floor Cleaner is selling so well, maybe it's time to introduce some flankers such as "Dazzle Window Cleaner" or "Dazzle Wood Polish;"* Since our product "Dazzle Floor Cleaner" is selling so well, maybe it's time to introduce some new merchandise carrying the same name such as "Dazzle Window Cleaner" or "Dazzle Wood Polish."

gatekeeper *n.* one who decides what another person should or should not buy • *In our next series of toy commercials, we need to try to appeal to the parents. Since parents are the gatekeepers for their children, we need to stress safety as well as low cost;* In our next series of toy commercials, we need to try to appeal to the parents. Since parents are the ones who decided what their children should have, we need to stress safety as well

as low cost.
‣ SYNONYM: **decision-maker** *n.*

generation X *n.* consumers in their twenties • *Sexy clothing is usually aimed at generation X;* Sexy clothing is usually aimed at consumers in their twenties.
‣ ORIGIN: **The term** *"baby boomer"* was given to the many babies born after World War II between 1947 and 1961. This generation gained a great deal of media attention to the point where the next generation seemed secondary and remained nameless.

generic product *n.* (term also known by those outside marketing) merchandise which is marketed without a brand name and is consequently sold at a lower price • *Whenever I buy paper towels, I always buy generic ones since they're cheaper than the name brands;* Whenever I buy paper towels, I always buy ones without a brand name since they're cheaper than the well known ones.

gray market *n.* the senior citizen population (those people at or over the age of retirement) • *These magazines have a wide appeal to the gray market;* These magazines have a wide appeal to senior citizens.

image marketing *n.* a marketing strategy where a celebrity with a good public image endorses a product • *I think if we do some* *image marketing, we could really sell your product;* I think if we get a well-liked celebrity to endorse you, we could really sell your product.

keeper *n.* a gift (which accompanies a product) that the customer may keep whether or not he/she ends up buying the product • *For good public relations, let's offer a keeper with the product;* For good public relations, let's offer the customer a free gift whether or not he/she buys the product.

pitch *n.* a speech that a salesperson aims at a potential customer in the hope of selling a product • *She makes at least twenty sales a day! She must have a great sales pitch!;* She makes at least twenty sales a day! She must have a great sales speech!

preferred customer *n.* a consumer who gets special buying-privileges (such as special discounts, gifts, advance notice about sales, etc.) from a retailer as a way of enticing the consumer to make more purchases.

preemptive marketing *n.* a marketing strategy used by a company where products are announced before they are ready to be distributed — a way of keeping consumers from buying products made by other companies.

premium *n.* an extra cost incurred in order to make a special arrangement for advertising • *We paid a premium to be the first ad in the magazine;* We paid an additional fee to be the first ad in the magazine.

sale-a-bration *n.* a play-on-words using the word "sale" and "celebration," often seen in advertisements • *June Clothing Company is having a sale-a-bration!;* June Clothing Company is celebrating by having a sale!
♦ VARIATION: **sale-a-thon** *n.* a play-on-words using "sale" and "marathon."

scent strips *n.pl.* actual scented advertisements for perfumes and colognes which are inserted in magazines • *With scent strips, the potential customer can get a preview of what the particular perfume or cologne smells like before deciding whether or not to make a purchase.*

scratch and sniff *adj.* a popular marketing tool among manufacturers of colognes and perfumes where the consumer can sample a fragrance by scratching on a designated part of a magazine advertisement, releasing the scent of the product • *Scratch and sniff ads are a great way to sample colognes before making a purchase.*

skyrocket (to) *v.* said of sales which go up considerably and

quickly • *After we ran the series of commercials, sales skyrocketed!;* After we ran the series of commercials, sales went up considerably!
♦ SYNONYM: **to go through the roof** *exp.*

spiffs *n.pl.* enticements (considered bribes by some people) usually in the form of gifts or money offered to store managers who agree to give favorable treatment to a specific product • *If we offer the store manager some spiffs, I'm sure we can get her to display our product next to the cash register;* If we offer the store manager an enticement, I'm sure we can get her to display our product next to the cash register.

state-of-the-art *adj.* the most advanced current technology has to offer • *We sell hundreds of state-of-the-art speakers;* We sell hundreds of speakers which are the most advanced current technology has to offer.

telemarketing *n.* telephone solicitation to prospective customers • *Although telemarketing is considered to be intrusive by many people, it can be a very effective marketing strategy;* Although soliciting potential customers by telephone is considered to be intrusive by many people, it can be a very effective marketing strategy.

top-of-the-line *adj.* the best within a specific category • *This car is top-of-the-line;* This car is the best one in its category.

trademark *n.* a name, emblem, or logo associated with a product (whose use by another person or company is prohibited by law) • *The trademark used by Universal Publishing is a drawing of an opened book on the top of Mount Olympus;* The logo associated with Universal Publishing is a drawing of an opened book on the top of Mount Olympus.

white sale *exp.* a special discount on linens, towels, etc.
♦ NOTE: This expression originated when linens, towels, etc. were white. Although this is no longer the case, the expression is still used to refer to items of any color.

window *n.* the time between two events • *The window between a movie release and home video release is shrinking;* The time between a movie release and home video release is shrinking.

Practice Advanced Marketing Jargon

(Answers, p. 228)

A. Underline the word that best completes the phrase.

1. Today everyone is wearing (**designated, destined, designer**) jeans.

2. If we can get our product to every (**floor, door, gate**) in this chain store, profits should increase substantially.

3. Our fall book catalogue (**falls, rises, drops**) in October.

4. This store is the (**flagship, battleship, spaceship**) in a chain of stores.

5. Since our product, Dazzle Floor Cleaner, is selling so well, maybe it's time to introduce some (**banker, flanker, thanker**) such as Dazzle Window Cleaner or Dazzle Wood Polish.

6. Since parents are the (**gatekeepers, housekeepers, bookkeepers**) for their children, we need to stress safety as well as low cost.

7. Marketers call the senior citizen population the (**white, black, gray**) market.

8. She makes at least twenty new sales a day! She must have a great sales (**pitch, itch, stitch**)!

9. We sell hundreds of (**city, state, country**)-of-the-art television sets.

10. The (**door, chimney, window**) between a movie release and home video release is shrinking.

Advertising Jargon

– *"Plugging a Product"* –

**"Let's put some ideas on the ground
and see if any of them walk."**

Lesson Six - ADVERTISING JARGON

Dialogue In Slang

"Plugging a Product"

DIALOGUE

Karen Stevens, the **A.E.** of McMaine & Tote Advertising Agency, has called a meeting.

Karen: We need to come up with a **PR** strategy for the client's product. As they say on **Madison Avenue**, "Let's **put some ideas on the ground and see if any of them walk**."

Jim: What if we do a **30-second spot** during **prime time** with a catchy **jingle** and a **donut** where we can really **plug** the product? We could write up some **copy**, do a **storyboard**, and hire some **talent** within a few days!

Peggy: Why don't we **blow in an ad** in a magazine or maybe even **run a double-truck**?

Tom: Too expensive. Getting a free **blurb** in a national newspaper could really **pull**. A good **puff piece** could generate a lot of **word-of-mouth** advertising.

Karen: I've got it! I think we should run a **display ad** right away in some of the national magazines. I want to see a **dummy ad** by this afternoon and a **paste-up** with a **beauty shot** of the product first thing tomorrow.

Lesson Six - ADVERTISING JARGON

"Plugging a Product"

DIALOGUE

Karen Stevens, the **Account Executive** of McMaine & Tote Advertising Agency, has called a meeting.

Karen: We need to come up with a **public relations** strategy for the client's product. As they say in **the advertising business,** "Let's **discuss some ideas and see if any of them are acceptable.**"

Jim: What if we do a **30-second commercial** during **the period of 7:00 P.M. and 11:00 P.M.** with a catchy **little song** and an **opening** where we can really **promote** the product? We could write up some **spoken text,** do a **series of illustrations demonstrating the commercial idea,** and hire some **actors** within a few days!

Peggy: Why don't we **insert a small advertisement** in a magazine or maybe just go ahead and **insert an advertisement on two facing pages**?

Tom: Too expensive. Getting a free **article** in a national newspaper could really **attract customers.** A good **flattering article** could generate a lot of **advertising where one satisfied customer tells a friend, and so on.**

Karen: I've got it! I think we should insert an **advertisement with illustrations** right away in some of the national magazines. I want to see a **a preliminary version of the advertisement first to get an idea of how the final one could look** by this afternoon and a **final version** with an **enhanced photo** of the product first thing tomorrow.

Lesson Six - ADVERTISING JARGON

Dialogue in slang as it would be heard

"Plugging a Product"

DIALOGUE

Karen Stevens, the **A.E.** of McMaine 'n Tote Advertising Agency, has called a meeding.

Karen: We need ta come up with a **PR** stradegy fer the client's product. As they say on **Madis'n Avenue**, "Let's **put s'm ideas on the ground 'n see if any of 'em walk**."

Jim: Whad if we do a **30-secon' spot** during **prime time** with a catchy **jingle** 'n a **donut** where we c'n really **plug** the product? We could wride up s'm **copy**, do a **storyboard**, 'n hire s'm **talent** within a few days!

Peggy: Why don't we jus' **blow in 'n ad** 'n a magazine 'r maybe go ahead 'n **run a double-truck**?

Tom: Too expensive. Gedding a free **blurb** 'n a nashn'l newzpaper could really **pull**. A good **puff piece** could generade alodda **word-a-mouth** advertising.

Karen: I've god it! I think we should run a **display ad** ride away in some'a the nashn'l magazines. I wanna see a **dummy ad** by this afternoon an' a **paste-up** with a **beaudy shod** 'a the product firs' thing t'morrow.

Vocabulary

A.E. *n.* an abbreviation for *"Account Executive,"* the person who personally handles a client's account • *I just got assigned as AE for our biggest client!;* I just got assigned as Account Executive for our biggest client!

beauty shot *n.* a view of a product, taken for either a commercial or print ad, which has been greatly enhanced in order to make the product look enticing through lighting, coloring, or whatever it takes to attract consumers • *It took almost three hours to get a beauty shot of this product;* It took almost three hours to get the ideal photo of this product.

blow-in an ad (to) *v.* to insert an advertisement between two pages in a book or magazine (by stitching it in with the other pages) • *I just found the perfect magazine where we should advertise our product. If the magazine hasn't gone to press yet, let's see about blowing-in an ad!;* I just found the perfect magazine where we should advertise our product. If the magazine hasn't gone to press yet, let's see about inserting an ad!
  ♦ ALSO: **blow-in** *n.* an insert.
    ⇨ SYNONYM: **stitch-in** *n.*

blurb *n.* a short (free) article written about a product or event • *Did you see the blurb about our play in today's newspaper?;* Did you see the short article about our play in today's newspaper?
  ♦ SYNONYM: **mention** *n.* • *Our company just got a mention in a national magazine!;* Our company just got mentioned in a short article in a national magazine!
  ♦ ALSO: **write-up** *n.* a detailed article about a product or event • *After reading the write-up about the movie, I can't wait to see it!;* After reading the detailed article about the movie, I can't wait to see it!

copy *n.* the written text in a commercial • *Now that you've had a chance to look over the copy, are you ready for your audition?;* Now that you've had a chance to look over the written text for the commercial, are you ready for your audition?

display advertising *n.* the technique of using illustrations in an advertisement to attract the potential customer's attention.

donut *n.* the middle of a commercial where the advertiser may fill in with an appropriate narration for the product.
  ♦ NOTE: A typical donut begins with music and singing, then music only

while the advertiser may do a narration for the product followed by more music and singing.

double-truck *n.* a large advertisement which spreads across two facing pages • *A double-truck may cost a lot of money to run, but it should attract a lot of new customers;* An advertisement which spreads across two facing pages may cost a lot of money to run, but it should attract a lot of new customers.

‣ SYNONYM: **spread** *n.*

dummy ad *n.* a preliminary version of an advertisement used to get an idea of how the final advertisement could look • *I'm not sure I'm understanding your idea is for the ad. Why don't you create a dummy ad and let me see it?;* I'm not sure I'm understanding your idea is for the advertisement. Why don't you create a preliminary version of the ad and let me see it?

jingle *n.* a short, irresistible combination of melody and lyrics used during a commercial to make consumers remember a particular product • *I can't get that jingle out of my head! It sure does make me remember the product;* I can't get that commercial song out of my head! It sure does make me remember the product.

Madison Avenue *n.* a common nickname for the advertising business since this avenue is known as the center for advertising agencies in New York City.

paste-up *n.* the final composite of elements (photographs, illustrations, and text), pasted onto a stiff piece of cardboard, needed to create a final advertisement • *You can see exactly how the final ad will appear in the magazine by looking at the paste-up;* You can see exactly how the final advertisement will appear in the magazine by looking at the final pasted-up composite.

‣ SYNONYM (1): **boards** *n.pl.* • *The boards look great! Go ahead and photograph them for the ad;* The final pasted-up composites look great! Go ahead and photograph them for the ad.

‣ SYNONYM (2): **comps** *n.pl.* short for "composites" • *I can see by the comps that the ad is really going to attract potential customers;* I can see by the comps that the advertisement is really going to attract potential customers.

⇨ NOTE: The terms *"rough comp"* or *"roughs"* refer to a preliminary version of the final comps.

‣ ALSO: **slicks** *n.pl.* the final composite ready for reproduction (usually mounted on glossy paper).

plug a product (to) *v.* to promote a product • *Once we plug the product on national television, sales should go way up;* Once we promote the product on national television, sales should go way up.

P.R. *n.* • **1.** a common abbreviation for *"Public Relations"* meaning "the way the public views a company" • *Ever since our last product failed, the public has lost confidence in our company. We need to get out there and do some P.R. right away in order to save our reputation!* • **2.** refers to publicity which consists of free promotions of a product through reviews, interviews, and feature stories in both print and television • *Once we've exhausted all of our P.R. possibilities for our product, we'll begin running ads;* Once we've exhausted all the free publicity possible for our product, we'll begin running advertisements.

prime time *n.* the hours between 7:00 P.M. and 11:00 P.M. when the largest number of people are watching television • *If we run the commercial during prime time, sales will be sure to go up!;* If we run the commercial between 7:00 P.M. and 11:00 P.M. sales will be sure to go up!

puff piece *n.* a flattering article written about a product, service, or person • *The Times just released a nice puff piece about our product today!;* The Times just released a nice flattering article about our product today!

pull (to) *v.* • **1.** said of an advertisement which attracts customers • *Our ad really pulled;* Our advertisement really attracted a number of customers. • **2.** to withdraw (an advertisement for lack of effectiveness or lack of funds) • *Our ad doesn't seem to be working very well. I think we should just pull it;* Our advertisement doesn't seem to be working very well. I think we should just withdraw it.

put some ideas on the ground and see if any of them walk *exp.* (humorous) to discuss some ideas and if any of them have merit. ◗ NOTE: The advertising business has invented several clever and fun ways of saying, "Let's try it and see what kind of response we get from the public!" Here are just a few of these *"ad agencyisms:"*
• *"Let's run it up the flagpole and see if anyone salutes!;"*
• *"Let's toss it around and see if it makes salad!;"*
• *"Let's drop it down the well and see what kind of splash it makes!;"*
• *"Let's put it in the water and see if it floats!"* etc.

spot *n.* a commercial • *We need to familiarize the public with your product by running a few 30-second spots;* We need to familiarize the public with your product by running a few 30-second commercials.

⟩ ALSO (1): **a thirty** *n.* a 30-second commercial.

⟩ ALSO (2): **a sixty** *n.* a 60-second commercial.

storyboard *n.* a step-by-step series of illustrations (and sometimes text or *"copy"*) demonstrating a copywriter's idea for a particular television commercial • *I'm not quite sure what kind of commercial you want to write. Do you have a storyboard I can look at?;* I'm not quite sure what kind of commercial you want to write. Do you have a step-by-step series of illustrations demonstrating your ideas that I can look at?

talent *n.* performers in a commercial • *We need to hire some talent by tomorrow to get the commercial done by Friday;* We need to hire some actors by tomorrow to get the commercial done by Friday.

word-of-mouth advertising *n.* an extremely effective and important strategy in advertising where a satisfied customer tells friends about a particular product, and so on • *I heard about this product by word-of-mouth;* I heard about this product through friends.

⟩ SYNONYM: **endless chain** *n.*

PRACTICE THE VOCABULARY

[Answers to Lesson Six, p. 228]

A. Complete the sentences by choosing the appropriate word(s) from the list below.

blurb	copy	truck
jingle	paste	plug
puff	spot	storyboard
pull	dummy ad	prime time

1. _____ *n.* the hours between 7:00 P.M. and 11:00 P.M. when the largest number of people are watching television.

2. _____ *n.* a step-by-step series of illustrations (and sometimes text or "copy") demonstrating a copywriter's idea for a particular television commercial.

3. _____ *n.* a short, irresistible combination of melody and lyrics used during a commercial in order to make consumers remember a particular product.

4. _____ **- up** *n.* the final composite of elements (photographs, illustrations, and text), pasted onto a stiff piece of cardboard, needed to create a final advertisement.

5. _____ *n.* a short (free) article written about a product or event.

6. _____ *n.* a preliminary version of an advertisement used to get an idea of how the final advertisement could look.

7. **double-**_____ *n.* an advertisement written on two facing pages.

8. _____ **(to)** *v.* • **1.** said of an advertisement which attracts customers • **2.** to withdraw (an advertisement for lack of effectiveness or lack of funds).

9. _____ *n.* a commercial.

10. _____ **a product (to)** *v.* to promote a product.

11. _____ **piece** *n.* a flattering article written about a product, service, or person.

12. _____ *n.* the written text in a commercial.

B. Underline the word(s) in parentheses that best complete(s) the sentence.

1. That commercial has the greatest (**jingle, mingle, tingle**). I just can't get the melody out of my head!

2. Tell the photographer we need to get a beauty (**spot, slot, shot**).

3. Why don't we (**blow, breathe, wheeze**) an ad into the magazine?

4. Did you see the (**burp, blob, blurb**) about us in the newspaper today?

5. These actors are terrible! I think we'd better hire some new (**talent, spots, puff pieces**) right away.

6. Congratulations! I heard you've just been made (**A.E.I.O.U., B.O., A.E.**) for our biggest client!

7. We only have 30 minutes left before our paste-(**up, down, in**) is due for the advertisement!

8. What a great ad! I'm sure it'll (**push, tug, pull**) well.

9. I'm not quite sure I understand your idea for the commercial. Do you have a (**scoreboard, storyboard, skateboard**)?

10. Word-of-(**ear, elbow, mouth**) is a great vehicle for advertising.

C. Match the columns.

☐ 1. We need to find some actors for the commercial.

☐ 2. An advertisement spread across two facing pages may cost a lot of money, but it should attract a lot of new customers.

☐ 3. How are things in the world of advertising?

☐ 4. I love the short melody and lyrics in your commercial!

☐ 5. I'd like to see a preliminary version of your ad to get a good idea of what you're describing.

☐ 6. Let's see if it's effective.

A. **I'd like to see a dummy ad to get a good idea of what you're describing.**

B. **A double-truck may cost a lot of money, but it should attract a lot of new customers.**

C. **I love the jingle in your commercial!**

D. **How are things on Madison Avenue?**

E. **We need to find some talent for the commercial.**

☐ 7. This ad is really attracting a lot of new customers!

☐ 8. We need to do some public relations in order to get a good reputation with potential customers.

☐ 9. I saw your television spot last night.

☐ 10. If we run the commercial during prime time, we'll reach a larger number of consumers.

F. **If we run the spot during prime time, we'll reach a larger number of consumers.**

G. **I saw your TV commercial last night.**

H. **This ad is really pulling!**

I. **Let's put it on the ground and see if it walks.**

J. **We need to do some P.R. in order to get a good reputation with potential customers.**

A CLOSER LOOK:
Advertising Slang & Jargon

Since advertising is all about being creative, clever, and unique, it stands to reason that the jargon it has produced is just as imaginative. Below are some of the most common terms known to just about everyone on Madison Avenue.

account side *n.* the half of an advertising agency which actively recruits clients • *I could never work on the account side. I'm not a good enough salesperson;* I could never work in the half of the advertising agency which goes out and recruits clients. I'm not a good enough salesperson.
 ▶ ALSO: **creative side** *n.* the other half of an advertising agency which "creates" and produces the advertisements for the clients.

ad *n.* a popular abbreviation for "advertisement" (used by everyone, not just those in the advertising industry) • *The client said we have until tomorrow to come up with an ad he likes for the magazine or we'll lose the* *account!;* The client said we have until tomorrow to come up with an advertisement he likes for the magazine or we'll lose the account!

advertorial *n.* an advertisement made to look like a publications' editorial section • *Since so many people are tired of reading ads, let's make ours look more like an editorial. We'll create an advertorial which is very effective at attracting potential customers;* Since so many people are tired of reading ads, let's make our look more like an editorial. We'll create an advertisement made to look like an editorial which is very effective at attracting potential customers.
♦ ORIGIN: **advertisement + editorial** = *advertorial.*

advid *n.* a video used to advertise a product • *Let's produce an advid that we could send to potential customers;* Let's produce a video about our product that we could send to potential customers.
♦ ORIGIN: **advertisement + television video** = *advid.*

air (to) *v.* to broadcast (on the airwaves) • *Let's start airing the commercials tomorrow;* Let's start broadcasting the commercials tomorrow.

art *n.* anything visual used to enhance an advertisement such as illustrations, photographs, etc. • *We'll need the art by Monday in order to meet our deadline;* We'll need the visual elements for the advertisement by Monday in order to meet our deadline.

bait and switch *exp.* an unethical marketing practice where customers are lured into a store by an advertised special deal on a product (which may not exist) and pursuaded to buy a more expensive item.

bait and wait *exp.* a technique used in commercials where something extremely intriguing is mentioned (not always having to do with the product) at the beginning of the commercial to grab the potential customer's attention — the product name is then mentioned at the end, ensuring the customer doesn't change channels.
♦ SYNONYM: **borrowed interest spot** *exp.*

billings *n.pl.* the total amount of money made by an advertising agency in a given amount of time • *What were our billings for the month of August?;* How much money did we make in the month of August?

bleed *n.* a print advertisement whose image extends to the very edge of the page (as if the image were "bleeding" off the page) • *Make sure to tell the artist that we want the colors in the ad to bleed off the page;* Make sure to tell the artist that we want the colors in the advertisement to extend to the very edge of the page.

boutique *n.* a specialized advertising agency that creates the "look" for a particular advertisement or commercial • *Let's hire a boutique to create the commercial and then we'll broadcast it;* Let's hire a specialized agency to create the commercial and then we'll broadcast it.

circular *n.* a flyer or card advertising a product • *I'm so tired of receiving all these circulars in the mail every day!;* I'm so tired of receiving all these flyers in the mail every day!
◗ NOTE: The term *"circular"* refers to the flyer or card being "circulated" to a number of people at the same time; not the shape of the advertisement.
◗ SYNONYM: **junk mail** *exp.* (a term known by those in and out of the advertising industry).
⇨ NOTE: Since consumers are constantly barraged with circulars in the mail, these advertisements tend to lose their effectiveness and are considered to be nothing more than junk by many people.

clutter *n.* a series of television commercials • *At night, the clutter on television seems to get worse;* At night, the series of television commercials seems to get worse.
◗ SYNONYM: **pod** *n.*

co-op *n.* short for "cooperative" where the manufacturer of a product and the retailer cooperate together in sharing advertising costs • *Let's form a co-op for our product. That way, we can cut our advertising costs in half;* Let's form a cooperative plan for our product. That way, we can cut our advertising costs in half.

creative *n.* artwork representing how a particular advertisement or commercial will look • *His creative looks great!;* The artwork representing his idea for the commercial looks great!

direct mail *n.* a common and effective strategy where advertisements are mailed directly to consumers who have purchased similar items in the past • *Over 300,000 thousand people have ordered our product in the past. Now that we have a* *new product, it would be a good idea to do a direct mail campaign to our current customers;* Over 300,000 thousand people have ordered our product in the past. Now that we have a new product, it would be a good idea to send an advertisement directly to our current customers.

▶ SEE: **marriage mail** *n.*

drive time *n.* the ideal time (usually morning and late afternoon rush hours) to broadcast a radio commercial since many people are in their cars listening to the radio • *Drive time is the best time to broadcast a commercial;* The morning and late afternoon rush hours (when many people are in their cars listening to the radio) is the best time to broadcast a commercial.

exclusivity *n.* an arrangement made whereby a television network allows an advertiser to be the only agency to advertise a particular type of product during a broadcast, eliminating competing commercials • *During tomorrow's special broadcast, our product will have exclusivity;* During tomorrow's special broadcast, our product will be the only one of its category to be advertised.

face *n.* short for "typeface" which refers to the style of type for an advertisement • *Let's use a different face for this ad. The one we're using now looks too serious;* Let's use a different typeface for this advertisement. The one we're using now looks too serious.

▶ SYNONYM: **font** *n.*

flack/flak (to) *v.* to act as a public relations person • *I'm flacking for a brand new company;* I'm acting as public relations person for a brand new company.

greek text (to) *exp.* to use jumbled characters in place of text for position only (used in cases where the advertisement must be laid out but the text has not yet been written) • *Since we don't know what the ad is going to say yet, just greek the text;* Since we don't know what the advertisement is going to say yet, just use jumbled characters for position.

gutter *n.* the blank space between columns of text • *The columns of the ad look too close together. I think you need more gutter space;* The columns of the advertisement look too close together. I think you need more blank space between them.

horizontal publication *n.* a publication with a wide-spread circulation • *TV Guide, which is bought by millions of people, is a horizontal publication.*
◆ VARIATION: **vertical publication** *n.* a publication with a limited circulation • *Skydiving News, which is bought by a limited number of people, is a vertical publication.*

infomercial *n.* a paid advertisement, disguised to look like a news program, which gives detailed information to the potential consumer and usually lasts about 30 minutes (whereas most commercials last 30 seconds) • *Infomercials are an extremely effective way of selling a product since they look like news programs and lead the consumer to believe everything that is being said!*
◆ ORIGIN: **information + commercial** = *infomercial.*

insert *n.* an intriguing question or statement which is "inserted" before the commercial and answered only after the commercial to insure the audience will not change channels • *Let's put in an insert right here so that the audience stays with us;* Let's put in an intriguing question right here and answer it after the commercial so that the audience stays with us.

magalog *n.* a company's catalogue which carries advertisements for other company's products as well.
◆ ORIGIN: **magazine + catalogue** = *magalog.*

makegood *n.* a rerun of an advertisement due to an error in reproduction • *Did you see our ad in today's newspaper? It looked terrible! We need to run a makegood right away;* Did you see our advertisement in today's newspaper? It looked terrible! We need to run a better version of the advertisement right away.

marriage mail *n.* several advertisements (by different advertisers) which have been grouped together and sent directly to the consumer's house or office • *I receive packets of marriage mail almost every day!;* I receive packets of advertisements from different advertisers almost every day!

news release *n.* a one-page informational sheet which describes a product in news format so a piece may be readily pulled for a feature story • *Before we decide whether or not to do a story on your product, could you please send us a news release first?;* Before we decide whether

or not to do a story on your product, could you please send us an informational sheet first?
▶ VARIATION: **release** *n.*
▶ SYNONYM: **press release** *n.*

Nielsens *n.* short for *"A.C. Nielsen Company,"* an organization which determines the number of people watching a particular television broadcast at a particular time.
▶ NOTE: Advertisers want to invest their advertising dollars in the most popular television shows to reach the largest number of people possible. Since the *"Nielsens"* or *"Nielsen Ratings"* determine the popularity of a particular television broadcast, any broadcast which has a low Nielson Rating is subject to cancellation.
▶ SYNONYM: **ratings** *n.pl.* • *I wonder how the ratings were for the TV show last night?;* I wonder how many people were watching the TV show last night?

peg *n.* that which makes an advertisement intriguing such as *"This product saved my life!"* • *We need to find a good peg to put at the top of the ad;* We need to find an intriguing caption to put at the top of the ad.
▶ SYNONYM (1): **handle** *n.*
▶ SYNONYM (2): **hook** *n.*

▶ SYNONYM (3): **slant** *n.*
▶ SYNONYM (4): **spin** *n.*

perfect bound (to be) *v.* said of a book whose pages are bound together by glue (as opposed to a magazine whose pages are bound together with staples or *"saddle-stitched"*).

piggyback (to) *v.* to broadcast two separate 15-second commercials (advertising separate products) one after the other which have been produced by the same sponsor.
▶ SYNONYM: **to do a split-30** *exp.*

pony unit *n.* a smaller version of an advertisement • *Let's put a pony unit in their regional magazine;* Let's put a smaller version of the advertisement in their regional magazine.

PSA *n.* an abbreviation for *"Public Service Announcement"* which is a message (free of charge to the company generating the PSA) used to inform the public about a particular event or service • *Did you see the PSA on television yesterday about child abuse?;* Did you see the Public Service Announcement on television yesterday about child abuse?

puffery *n.* exaggerated claims made by a product • *Look at this ad: "Our soap is the absolute best,* *most incredible, best smelling, best-feeling soap ever to be introduced to the market!" Can you believe all this puffery?;* Look at this ad: "Our soap is the absolute best, most incredible, best smelling, best feeling soap ever to be introduced to the market!" Can you believe all these exaggerated claims?

put a product on the map (to) *v.* to make a product known to the public • *If all of the advertising efforts we have planned don't put this product on the map, nothing will!;* If all of the advertising efforts we have planned don't make this product well known, nothing will!

reach *n.* the percentage of people being exposed to an advertisement • *Our reach in the L.A. market is about 38%;* The percentage of people being exposed to our product in Los Angeles is about 38%.
♦ SYNONYM: **CUME** *n.* (pronounced *"kyoom"*) short for Cumulative Audience Ratings which report the approximate number of people being exposed to an advertisement or broadcast • *The CUME of our radio program is about 80,000 people;* The number of people being exposed to our radio program is about 80,000.

run an ad (to) *exp.* to place an advertisement in a publication • *It's very expensive to run ads in national publications;* It's very expensive to place advertisements in national publications.

saddle-stitched (to be) *v.* said of a publication, such as a magazine, whose pages are bound together by staples (as opposed to a book whose pages bound together with glue or *"perfect bound"*).

sandwich board *n.* two large posters that are worn by a person, one poster hanging in front and one in back (as a way to advertisement a product or event) ⊛ *Why don't we just put a sandwich board on him and let him walk the streets? Since it's a small town, everyone is bound to see him;* Why don't we just have him wear two large posters advertising the product and let him walk the streets? Since it's a small town, everyone is bound to see him.

shoot (to) *v.* to photograph • *Let's shoot the ad tomorrow morning;* Let's photograph the advertisement tomorrow morning.
♦ ALSO: **photo shoot** *n.* photography session where various elements for an

advertisement are photographed either in a studio or outdoors.

snipe *n.* something which has been printed separately (or *looks* like it's been printed separately) then attached on top of another printed page to draw attention (such as a sticker that says *"New!"* placed on the package of a product).
> ALSO: **burst** *n.* a snipe in the shape of a sun burst.

space *n.* short for *"advertising space"* bought and reserved in a newspaper or on television • *It's probably worthwhile it to buy some space on TV for the product;* It's probably worthwhile it to buy some advertising space on TV for the product.

spot TV / spot radio *n.* a commercial running regionally only (not nationally) • *Spot TV and spot radio is much less expensive than running a commercial nationally;* Regional commercials for TV and radio are much less expensive than running a commercial nationally.

spread *n.* an advertisement, article, photograph, etc. which starts on the left-hand page of a magazine and continues or *"spreads"* over onto the right-hand page; • *I saw the spread you ran in the*

magazine today!; I saw the two-page advertisement you placed in the magazine today.

suds *n.* beer clients • *Suds are great clients because they pull in a lot of money!;* Beer clients are great because they pull in a lot of money!
> NOTE: Due to the suds on top of a glass of beer, the term *"suds"* has become a popular slang term for beer in general.

sweeps *n.pl.* period when television ratings are recorded (ratings determine which television shows are the most popular) • *During sweeps week, television programs are the most enticing to attract a majority of the viewers;* During the week when television ratings are taken, television programs are the most enticing to attract a majority of the viewers.

tag line *n.* the last few words in a commercial • *… Now playing at a theater near you!*

throw-away *n.* a flyer which the advertiser hopes will be effective even though he/she knows it will be glanced at quickly by the potential customer and then "thrown-away" • *Let's print up some throw-always that we can distribute at the fair;* Let's print up some flyers that we can distribute at the fair.

trade dress *n.* a combination of colors designed to be associated with a product • *Yellow and orange would be an ideal trade dress for your product. When we're finished with our advertising campaign, anytime a consumer sees those two colors, they'll automatically think of your product;* Yellow and orange would be ideal colors to be associated with your product. When we're finished with our advertising campaign, anytime a consumer sees those two colors, they'll automatically think of your product!

"Truth in Advertising" *exp.* a law which enforces truth in advertising claims.

voice-over *n.* the narration over a television or radio commercial where the narrator is heard but not seen • *Let's have John do a voice-over while the actor demonstrates how to use the product;* Let's have John do some narration while the actor demonstrates how to use the product.

♦ VARIATION: **V.O.** *n.*

wearout *n.* exposure level at which a commercial, because of excess repetition, loses its ability to be effective • *The ad ran so many times that it reached its wearout level in a month!;* The ad ran so many times that it became ineffective in a month!

"White Coat Rule" *exp.* a restriction by the Federal Trade Commission prohibiting advertisers to use actors dressed as doctors (wearing white lab coats) when making claims about a product.

zap (to) *n.* to fast forward a videotape past the commercials • *Since more and more people videotape programs to view at night, advertisers are concerned about zapping;* Since more and more people videotape programs to view at night, advertisers are concerned about consumers fast forwarding past the commercials.

Practice Advertising Slang & Jargon

(Answers, p. 229)

A. Circle the letter which corresponds to the correct definition of the words in boldface.

1. **bleed**:
   a. a costly advertisement
   b. a print advertisement whose image extends to the very edge of the page

2. **circular**:
   a. a flyer or card advertising a product
   b. a short television commercial

3. **creative**:
   a. the narration used in a television commercial
   b. artwork representing how a particular advertisement or commercial will look

4. **to greek text**:
   a. to use jumbled characters in place of text for position only
   b. to translate text into another language

5. **gutter**:
   a. a flyer or card advertising a product
   b. the blank space between columns of text

6. **makegood**:
   a. a rerun of an advertisement
   b. a colorful advertisement

7. **puffery**:
   a. a series of commercials
   b. exaggerated claims made by a product

8. **reach**:
   a. the percentage of people being exposed to an advertisement
   b. a free commercial also known as a public service announcement

Finance
Slang & Jargon
– *"In the Black"* –

*"Since you're **flat broke**, let me **float you a loan**."*

Lesson Seven - FINANCE SLANG & JARGON

"In the Black"

DIALOGUE

Rick has good news for his partner, Dan.

Rick: I just looked at the **books** today and we're finally **in the black**! We should be making money **hand over fist** in no time. And you thought this company was going **to go belly up**!

Dan: Well, you have to admit we've been spending **big bucks** for the past eight months. Even our new computer system **cost an arm and a leg**. I don't mean to sound like a **penny pincher** but frankly, I still think we were **throwing money down a rat hole**. You can **bet your bottom dollar** that computer salesman is getting some **kickback** for that sale, too.

Rick: I don't know why you're always so worried we're going to **nickel-and-dime** ourselves out of business. Look, **the bottom line** is that the company's finally **turning a profit** even though it had a few **lean** years. I think we should go celebrate over lunch and since I know you're **short on** cash, I'll even **pick up the check**. Besides, you **floated me a loan** last week and now we can **call it even**.

Dan: Well, if you're going **to bankroll** the meal, I'm accepting! Besides, I'm **flat broke** today.

Lesson Seven - FINANCE SLANG & JARGON

Translation of dialogue in standard English

"In the Black"

DIALOGUE

Rick has good news for his partner, Dan.

Rick: I just looked at the **financial records** today and we're finally **making a profit**! We should be making money **continuously** in no time. And you thought this company was going **to fail**!

Dan: Well, you have to admit we've been spending **a lot of money** for the past eight months. Even our new computer system was **extremely expensive**. I don't mean to sound like a **miser** but frankly, I still think we were **wasting our money**. You can **bet all your money** that computer salesman is getting some **unethical payment** for that sale, too.

Rick: I don't know why you're always so worried we're going to **ruin our business financially**. Look, **the central issue** is that the company's finally **making a profit** even though it had a few **financially meager** years. I think we should go celebrate over lunch and since I know you're **lacking** cash, I'll even **pay for your meal**. Besides, you **loaned me money** last week and now we can **cancel the debt**.

Dan: Well, if you're going **to buy** the meal, I'm accepting! Besides, I'm **completely without money** today.

Lesson Seven - FINANCE SLANG & JARGON

Dialogue in slang as it would be heard

"In the Black"

DIALOGUE

Rick has good news for 'is partner, Dan.

Rick: I jus' lookt'it the **books** t'day 'n we're fin'lly **in the black**! We should be making money **hand over fist** 'n no time. And you thought this company was gonna **go belly up**!

Dan: Well, ya have to admit we've been spending **big bucks** fer the past eight months. Even our new compuder system **cost 'n arm 'n a leg**. I don't mean ta soun' like a **penny pincher** but frankly, I still think we were **throwing money down a rat hole**. You c'n **bet ch'r bodom dollar** that compuder salesm'n's gedding s'm **kickback** fer that sale, too.

Rick: I dunno why y'r always so worried we're gonna **nickel-'n-dime** ourselves oudda business. Look, **the bottom line** is that the company's fin'lly **turning a profit** even though it had a few **lean** years. I think we should go celebrate over lunch an' since I know y'r **shord on** cash, I'll even **pick up the check**. B'sides, you **floaded me a loan** last week an' now we c'n **call it even**.

Dan: Well, if y'r gonna **bankroll** the meal, I'm accepting! B'sides, I'm **flat broke** t'day.

Vocabulary

bankroll someone (to) *v.* to pay for someone • *This is the last time I'm bankrolling you. Next time you'd better remember to bring your wallet;* This is the last time I'm paying for you. Next time you'd better remember to bring your wallet.

‣ NOTE: A *"bankroll"* is literally a roll of paper money.

belly up (to go) *exp.* to go out of business (usually due to reasons beyond the control of the owner such as financial trouble) • *If our company isn't profitable within the next few months, we'll go belly up;* If our company isn't profitable within the next few months, we'll go out of business.

‣ ORIGIN: This expression was derived from the fact that when a fish dies, it floats belly up on the surface of the water.

‣ SYNONYM (1): **to close up shop** *exp.* to go out of business (voluntary or otherwise) • *My father decided to close up shop and retire;* My father decided to go out of business and retire. • *My father was forced to close up shop because he couldn't renew his lease;* My father was forced to go out of business because he couldn't renew his lease.

‣ SYNONYM (2): **pull the plug (to)** *exp.* • **1.** to go out of business • *Goober Printing couldn't make a profit so they had to pull the plug;* Goober Printing couldn't make a profit so they had to go out of business. • **2.** to discontinue a business project • *The editor just pulled the plug on publishing any more books on travel;* The editor just discontinued publishing any more books on travel.

‣ SYNONYM (3): **to shutter** *v.* to terminate or close up a business • *The largest car manufacturer in the city just decided to shutter its oldest plant;* The largest car manufacturer in the city just decided to close its oldest plant.

⇨ ORIGIN: A *"shutter"* is a hinged door, usually made of wood, used to protect windows and/or close up a home (in the event of a storm or a prolonged vacancy).

‣ SYNONYM (4): **to go toes** *exp.* to go out of business • *The business went toes in just six months;* The business went out of business in just six months.

⇨ ORIGIN: This is a shortened version of the expression *"to go toes up"* which refers to someone who has fallen dead on his/her back with the toes pointed straight up.

bet one's bottom dollar (to) *exp.* to be willing to gamble all one's money (down to the last dollar in the very bottom of one's pockets) because of having enormous faith in something • *You can bet your bottom dollar that if she says a product will sell well, it will!;* You can bet all of your money that if she says a product will sell well, it will!

big bucks (to spend) *exp.* to spend a lot of money • *I spent big bucks getting my car repaired;* I spent a lot of money getting my car repaired.
  ▶ SYNONYM: **to spend money like it's going out of style** *exp.* to spend a lot of money quickly.

books *n.pl.* the financial records of a company • *The books show we're losing money every month;* Our financial records show we're losing money every month.

bottom line (the) *exp.* the central issue of a discussion • *There are all sorts of reasons why I don't want to hire Tim, but the bottom line is that I just don't like him;* There are all sorts of reasons why I don't want to hire Tim, but the central issue is that I just don't like him.
  ▶ ORIGIN: A financial report lists a company's earnings and expenses followed by a calculation of the final profit shown on the *"bottom line"* of the report. The bottom line is considered the most important part of a financial report since it clearly indicates the worth of the company.

call it even (to) *exp.* to cancel another person's debt since he/she has returned something equal in value • *I know I paid for your lunch yesterday, but since you let me borrow your car today, let's just call it even;* I know I paid for your lunch yesterday, but since you let me borrow your car today, I'm canceling the debt.

cost an arm and a leg (to) *exp.* to cost a lot of money • *That new computer system must have cost an arm and a leg!;* That new computer system must have cost a lost of money!
  ▶ SYNONYM: **to cost a pretty penny** *exp.*

flat broke (to be) *exp.* to be completely without money • *He's been flat broke for several months because he can't find a job;* He's had no money at all for several months because he can't find a job.
  ▶ ANTONYM: **to be loaded** *exp.* • **1.** to be extremely rich • **2.** to be intoxicated.

float someone a loan (to) *exp.* to loan someone money • *Can you float me a loan until next Friday?;* Can you loan me some money until next Friday?

hand over fist (to make money) *exp.* to make a lot of money on a continuous basis • *Ever since we started selling our cologne worldwide,*

we've been making money hand over fist! Ever since we started selling our cologne worldwide, we've been making a lot of money continuously!
♦ NOTE: This expression conjures up an image of someone pulling in money, one hand over the other.

in the black (to be) *exp.* said of a company which is making a profit • *It took a long time, but we're finally in the black;* It took a long time, but we're finally making a profit.
♦ ANTONYM: **to be in the red** *exp.* to be making a loss.
♦ ORIGIN: Years ago, financial reports were traditionally filled in with two different colored inks; profits were listed in black and losses were listed in red. Although this method is no longer used, the expression still remains.

kickback *n.* an unethical payment made to someone • *Every time he hires a printer for the company's brochures, the printer pays him. He's been getting kickbacks like this for years!;* Every time he hires a printer for the company's brochures, the printer pays him. He's been getting unethical payments like this for years!
♦ NOTE: This is an unethical payment made to someone who hires a company which agrees to pay (or *"kickback"*) money to the hiring-individual.

lean *adj.* financially meager • *This has been a very lean year for our company;* This has been a very financially meager year for our company.

nickel-and-dime (to) • **1.** *v.* to ruin financially bit by bit • *If you don't stop nickeling-and-diming the company, we'll be out of business in no time!;* If you don't stop spending the company's money on everything, we'll be out of business in no time! • **2.** *v.* to collect little by little • *Over the years, we've been able to nickel-and-dime ourselves a good profit;* Over the years, we've been able to earn ourselves a good profit little by little. • **3.** *adj.* said of something that pays very little • *I can't believe you accepted a nickel-and-dime job like that!;* I can't believe you accepted a low-paying job like that! • **4.** *adj.* said of a business which makes little money • *It's hard to believe that we started as a nickel-and-dime operation and now we have offices overseas;* It's hard to believe that we started as a very small business and now we have offices overseas.

penny pincher (to be a) *n.* to be a miser • (lit); one who holds on very tightly to his/her money, even to coins with as little value as a single penny • *On my birthday, he didn't even give me a card because he didn't want to spend the money. What a penny pincher!;* On my birthday, he didn't even give me a card because he didn't want to spend the money. What a miser!
♦ SYNONYM (1): **to be a cheapskate** *adj.*

♦ SYNONYM (2): **to be a money grubber** *adj.*

♦ SYNONYM (3): **to be a skin flint** *adj.*

♦ SYNONYM (4): **to be a tightwad** *adj.*

pick up the check (to) *exp.* to pay for one or more people at a restaurant
• *Since today is your birthday, I'm picking up the check;* Since today is your birthday, I'm paying for your meal.

♦ SYNONYM (1): **to pick up the tab** *exp.*

♦ SYNONYM (2): **to foot the bill** *exp.*

short on something (to be) *exp.* to be lacking in something • *He's really short on looks;* He's not very handsome. • *She's short on patience;* She lacks patience.

throw money down a rat hole (to) *exp.* to waste one's money on worthless items • *Why do you keep getting your car repaired by the same mechanic if he isn't doing a good job? You're just throwing your money down a rat hole;* Why do you keep getting your car repaired by the same mechanic if he isn't doing a good job? You're just wasting your money.

♦ ORIGIN: Anything that falls into a rat hole is probably lost forever since it would most likely be chewed up or destroyed.

turn a profit (to) *exp.* to make a profit • *The company turned a profit its first month in business;* The company made a profit its first month in business.

PRACTICE THE VOCABULARY

[Answers to Lesson Seven, p. 229]

A. Fill in the blank with the letter that corresponds to the most appropriate answer.

1. You can bet your _____ dollar that if he tells you something, it's the truth.
   a. **top**   b. **bottom**   c. **side**

2. Your new car must have cost an arm and a _____ .
   a. **thigh**   b. **face**   c. **leg**

3. We started making money hand over _____ our second month in business.
   a. **head**   b. **stomach**   c. **fist**

4. We're finally in the _____ ! At this rate, we should be able to hire more employees soon.
   a. **black**   b. **red**   c. **green**

5. This has been a very _____ year for our company. Hopefully we'll make a lot more money next yext.
   a. **skinny**   b. **lean**   c. **fat**

6. Do you need me to _____ you a loan?
   a. **float**   b. **sink**   c. **fly**

7. I thought their company was in good financial shape. I can't believe they went _____ up!
   a. **bottom**   b. **belly**   c. **feet**

8. Could you loan me a few dollars? I'm _____ on cash today.
   a. **short**   b. **tall**   c. **huge**

9. Why do you keep lending him money when he never pays you back? You're just throwing money down a _____ hole.
   a. **elephant**   b. **rat**   c. **giraffe**

10. The company _____ a profit its first month in business.
    a. **turned**   b. **spun**   c. **twirled**

B. Fill in the crossword on the opposite page by using the words from the following list.

fist	**bankroll**	**short**
kickback	**books**	**bucks**
bottom	**rat**	**belly**
	broke	

ACROSS

3. _____ *n.* an unethical payment made to someone.

5. **throw money down a** _____ **hole (to)** *exp.* to waste one's money on worthless items.

6. _____ **line (the)** *exp.* the central issue of a discussion.

7. _____ **up (to go)** *exp.* said of a company which goes out of business usually due to financial trouble.

8. _____ **on something (to be)** *exp.* to be lacking in something.

DOWN

1. **hand over** _____ **(to make money)** *exp.* to make a lot of money on a continuous basis.

2. _____ **someone (to)** *v.* to pay for someone.

4. **flat** _____ **(to be)** *exp.* to be completely without money.

6. **big** _____ **(to spend)** *exp.* to spend a lot of money.

7. _____ *n.pl.* the financial records of a company.

CROSSWORD PUZZLE

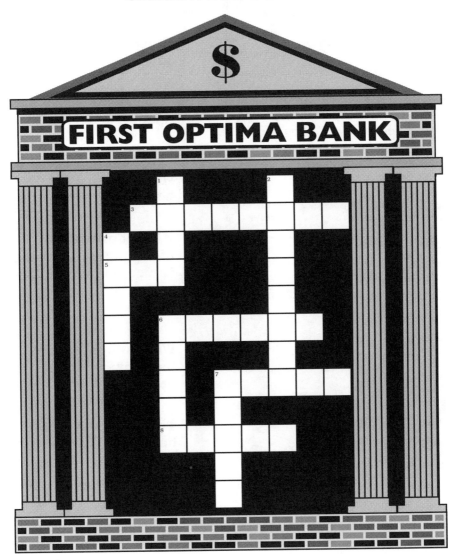

C. Match the columns.

☐ 1. She's such a miser.

☐ 2. If you don't stop spending the company's money on everything, we'll be out of business in no time.

☐ 3. It's my turn to pay for our meal.

☐ 4. She's been getting unethical payments from her clients for years.

☐ 5. She pays for all his expenses.

☐ 6. That was expensive.

☐ 7. Our new accountant wants to see our financial records.

☐ 8. We made a lot of money this year.

☐ 9. I don't have any money at all.

☐ 10. The company failed.

A. **She bankrolls all of his expenses.**

B. **That cost an arm and a leg.**

C. **Our new accountant wants to see our books.**

D. **If you don't stop nickeling-and-diming the company, we'll be out of business in no time.**

E. **We made money hand over fist this year.**

F. **The company went belly up.**

G. **I'm flat broke.**

H. **She's been getting kickbacks from her clients for years.**

I. **It's my turn to pick up the check.**

J. **She's such a penny-pincher.**

A Closer Look (1):
Slang & Jargon Relating to Finance

As seen in the opening dialogue, there are several terms and expressions having to do with money and finance that are commonly used by the general population. However, there is yet an additional lingo used primarily by those who are in the professions of finance, economics, banking, and accounting.

The following is a list of some of the more popular terms used by businesses and people dealing with everything from personal finances to corporate stocks.

advance *n.* an amount paid to someone on credit or before it is earned • *I know I'm starting work for you next week but I'll need an advance to purchase some important materials first;* I know I'm starting work for you next week but I'll need some money right now to purchase some important materials first.
▶ ALSO: **cash-advance** *n.* money which one may borrow against a credit card and may back with interest • *I'm going to get a cash-advance on my credit card;* I'm going to borrow money against my credit card.

annuity *n.* an investment which consistently pays the investor a fixed amount on a regular basis • *I'm never going to sell that property, it's my annuity;* I'm never going to sell that property, it's an investment from which I'll receive money regularly for the rest of my life.

arbs *n.pl.* abbreviation for "arbitrageurs," those who purchase stocks in one market in order to sell them quickly in another market where the price is higher • *The arbs are buying stock in McKay Enterprises on the New York market and selling them on the London market;* The arbitrageurs are buying stock in McKay Enterprises on the New York market and selling them on the London market.

asset *n.* any person or thing which is useful or valuable • *Susan has really turned out to be an asset to this company;* Susan has really turned out to be useful and valuable to this company. • *Our inventory is the only asset we have to secure a loan;* Our

inventory is the only thing of value we have to secure a loan.
⟩ ANTONYM: **liability** *n.*

at the market (to be) *exp.* the present stock market price at which the stock is being bought and sold • *Adams Trombone Company stock is a good value if bought at the market;* Adams Trombone Company stock is a good value if bought at the present stock market price.

Baby Bells *n.pl.*
⟩ NOTE: Ruled a monopoly, the federal government divided American Telephone and Telegraph (also called "AT&T" or "Ma Bell") into many small companies, called *"Baby Bells,"* which were allowed to serve specific communities or needs. • *Southwest Bell used to be part of Ma Bell, now it's just one of the Baby Bells;* Southwest Bell used to be part of American Telephone and Telegraph, now it's just a regional telephone company.
⟩ NOTE: Alexander Graham Bell was the inventor of the telephone.

balance sheet *n.* a list of what a company possesses and owes at a given time (the two lists must be equal, or *"balanced"*) • *Before you invest in Berkshire Cup & Saucer, you should check their most recent balance sheet;* Before you invest in Berkshire Cup & Saucer, you should check a list of what they have versus what they owe.

bear market *exp.* a market condition in which the majority of stock prices are falling (sometimes rapidly) • *Our current losses are the result of the recent bear market;* Our current losses are the result of the recent declining market.
⟩ ANTONYM: **bull market** *exp.* a market condition in which the majority of stock prices are rising (sometimes rapidly).

Big Blue *n.* slang for International Business Machines (also known as IBM) • *Big Blue cut its dividends for the first time this quarter;* International Business Machines cut its dividends for the first time this quarter.

Big Board (the) *n.* the New York Stock Exchange (also commonly known as the NYSE) • *Our company is finally on the Big Board!;* Our company is finally listed on the New York Stock Exchange!

black hole *n.* a company or project which, in order to maintain operation, pulls in unlimited amounts of money from its investors without the apparent possibility of yielding any profit

• (lit); an area in outer space with an extremely powerful gravitation field into which everything around it is pulled • *No matter how much money Bob's Flying Car Company raises from its investors, they'll never produce a working car. It's nothing but a black hole;* No matter how much money Bob's Flying Car Company raises from its investors, they'll never produce a working car. It's nothing but a business which takes investors' money with no apparent possibility of yielding a profit.

Black Monday *n.* Monday, October 19th, 1987 - the day the stock declined considerably causing many to lose large amounts of money • *This was our biggest loss since Black Monday;* This was our biggest loss since Monday, October 19th, 1987.

blue chip *n./adj.* a stock which sells at a high price due to the company's longstanding record of profit and growth • *My father always said you can't lose money investing in blue chips;* My father always said you can't lose money investing in stocks which sell at a high price owing to the company's longstanding record of profit and growth.

boiler room *n.* a company (often illegal) with little or no real assets, employing telephone salespeople who use high-pressure tactics to sell overpriced product • *You bought something from the Ace Furniture Company? It's just a boiler room;* You bought something from the Ace Furniture Company? It's not a real company, just a high-pressure phone-sales force.

bond *n.* a certificate sold at a discount which the issuing corporation or government promises to redeem for the full value (printed on the front of the certificate) at a later date.
  ▶ ALSO: **junk bond** *n.* a bond which sells at a much larger discount but also involves a much greater potential of never being redeemed.

boost • **1.** *n.* assistance • *An early rainy season was just the sales boost that Manhattan Umbrella Company needed;* An early rainy season was just the assistance Manhattan Umbrella Company needed for sales. • **2.** *v.* to raise, lift, or increase • *The Pinewood Pencil Company is hoping that their new color pencil line will boost profits this year;* The Pinewood Pencil Company is hoping that their new color pencil line will raise profits this year.

boutique *adj.* small and highly specialized • *If you only want to invest in drapery manufacturing stock, you should call Jones & Johansen Investments because they're a boutique firm;* If you only want to invest in drapery manufacturing stock, you should call Jones & Johansen Investments because they're a very small and highly specialized firm.

break even (to) *v.* to make back only what was put into something, showing no profit or loss • *I don't know why the editor decided to publish this type of book. He'll be lucky to break even!;* I don't know why the editor decided to publish this type of book. He'll be lucky to make back his investment!
♦ NOTE: Past tense: *"to have broken even"* • Past participle: *"broke even."*
♦ ALSO: **break-even point** *exp.* the point at which one's proceeds are exactly equal to one's expenses • *We're finally at the break-even point. From now on, anything we make will be profit;* We're finally at the point where our proceeds are exactly equal to our investment. From now on, anything we make will be profit.

bull market *n.* a stock market condition in which the majority of stock prices are rising (sometimes rapidly) or increasing in value • *Our current gains are the result of the recent bull market;* Our current gains are the result of the recent rising prices in the stock market.
♦ ANTONYM: **bear market** *n.*

call a loan (to) *v.* to demand for immediate and complete payment of a debt • *I missed two mortgage payments and the bank called my loan;* I missed two mortgage payments and the bank demanded my loan be paid immediately and in full.

capital *n.* money and other resources a company uses to conduct business • *We are considering manufacturing deck chairs instead of alarm clocks because it would require less capital;* We are considering manufacturing deck chairs instead of alarm clocks because it would require less money.

cash flow *n.* the amount of money a company has coming in compared to how much it has going out • *All of our bills are due in thirty days but we won't be getting paid by our customers for another sixty days! I wonder when we're going to stop having problems with cash flow;* All of our bills are due in thirty days but we won't be getting paid by our customers for another sixty days! I wonder when we're going to stop having problems with spending money faster than we make it!

cash-strapped (to be) *adj.* to have an insufficient amount of money • *Our company needs to get a loan soon because we're really cash-strapped;* Our company needs to get a loan soon because we're lacking money.

chapter 11 (to be in/to go) *n.* a situation where a company declares that it is insolvent but continues, with court protection, to reorganize and do business while it works with its debtors to pay its debts • *After Century Airlines had its third bad year, they had to declare Chapter 11 or go out of business;* After Century Airlines had its third bad year, they had to declare their company insolvent, but they will continue under court protection, to do business while they work with their debtors to find a way to pay their debts.
◗ ORIGIN: This comes from chapter 11 of the Bankruptcy Code.

corner the market (to) *v.* to own (or control) more of a specific commodity then anyone else,

usually in an attempt to control the price • *They tried to buy enough silver to corner the market;* They tried to buy enough silver to control the market so they could drive up the price.

credit risk *n.* a person (or company) who is unreliable at repaying a debt • *Since John has never had a consistent source of income, lenders consider him a credit risk;* Since John has never had a consistent source of income, lenders consider him unreliable at repaying his debts.

crown jewels *n.* those assets which are the most valuable part of a company's operation • *The new computers are the crown jewels of Wright Typesetting Service;* The new computers are the most valuable assets of Wright Typesetting Service.

disclosure *n.* a declaration, required by the government, made by a company to its investors (and potential investors) revealing everything good and bad about the company's condition • *Before I choose to invest in your company, I need to see a disclosure;* Before I choose to invest in your company, I need to see a declaration about your company's current condition.
◗ SYNONYM: **prospectus** *n.*

disposable income *n.* money that a person has available after paying taxes • *I have more disposable income this year than I had last year;* I'm left with more money after paying taxes this year than I had last year.

dividend *n.* the part of a company's profit which is distributed among its investors • *Investors are angry because Manitoba Window Company didn't make much profit this year, so their dividend will be small;* Investors are angry because Manitoba Window Company didn't make much profit this year, so the portion of the profit distributed to its investors will be small.

dividend reinvestment *n.* a program through which any portion of money owed to an investor is automatically used to buy more stock instead of being paid to the investor directly • *Instead of receiving money from my stock in The Tremblay Tractor Company, I am in a dividend reinvestment plan;* Instead of receiving money from my stock in The Tremblay Tractor Company, I am in a plan which automatically uses my money to buy more stock in the company.

downside *n.* • **1.** that which one is at risk of losing • *If I invest a million dollars in Torpedo Cruise Lines, the downside would be a half million dollars;* If I invest a million dollars in Torpedo Cruise Lines, I risk losing a half million dollars. • **2.** the negative aspect of a project • *The downside to working at Salt-Sea Fisheries is that your clothes smell like fish;* The negative aspect of working at Salt-Sea Fisheries is that your clothes smell like fish.

dump (to) *v.* to place large quantities of a product on the market to drive down prices, often done to force competitors out of business • *Venus Vertical Blinds has been accused of dumping;* Venus Vertical Blinds has been accused of putting huge quantities of its products on the market in order to drive down prices and force competitors out of business.

enterprise zone *n.* a selected area, often in a poor neighborhood, where the government gives rewards (such as low-cost loans, tax decreases, etc.) to help people start new businesses • *Graul Garments is considering opening their new store downtown in an enterprise zone;* Graul Garments is considering opening their new store downtown in an area where the government rewards people for starting new businesses.

equity financing *n.* a way for a company to raise money by dividing up and selling some or all of its ownership through issuing stock • *Our company was able to get enough money to expand through equity financing;* Our company was able to get enough money to expand by dividing up and selling ownership of the company.
‣ ANTONYM: **debt financing** *n.* a way for a company to raise money by borrowing from lenders with the promise of paying the loan back with interest • *Our company was able to get enough money to expand by debt financing;* Our company was able to get enough money to expand by borrowing money and promising to pay it back with interest.

escrow (to be in) *n.* said of something of value (money, ownership of property, etc.) which two sides agree to have held by a third party until the conditions of an agreement are met • *The deed to our new house has been in escrow for a week. Hopefully it will be ours by next Tuesday;* The deed to our new house has been held by an third party for a week. Hopefully, we'll meet the conditions of our agreement with the seller by next Tuesday.

exchange rate *n.* the worth of one currency in terms of a foreign currency • *I want to buy $100 worth of Japanese yen. What is the exchange rate today?;* I want to buy $100 worth of Japanese yen. What are yen worth in U.S. dollars today?

face value *n.* • **1.** The amount printed or written on the front (or *"face"*) of a document such as a bill or a bond • *In ten years, I can redeem my bonds for their face value;* In ten years, I can redeem my bonds for the amount printed on their face. • **2.** the apparent worth or literal meaning of something • *I didn't think she was joking, so I took her remark about my performance at face value;* I didn't think she was joking, so I took her remark about my performance literally.

fall (to) *v.* to decline • *Prices on Wall Street are expected to fall when the market opens again on Monday;*Prices on Wall Street are expected to decline when the market opens again on Monday.
‣ ANTONYM: **to climb** *v.*

Fannie Mae *n.* slang shorthand for the "Federal National Mortgage Association" • *My student loan was sold to Fannie Mae;* My student loan was sold to the Federal National Mortgage Association.

Fed (The) *n.* slang shorthand for "The Federal Reserve" • *The Fed is trying to control inflation;* The Federal Reserve is trying to control inflation.

fiduciary *n.* a person (or group) entrusted with the responsibility of investing someone else's money wisely and carefully • *Because she is too young to take care of her own money, Shelley has a fiduciary;* Because she is too young to take care of her own money, Shelley entrusts someone else with the responsibility of carefully investing her money for her.

financial statements *n.* a written account a company makes on its activities and financial condition for a specific period • *I think that the James Power Tool Company has done good business for the past three months, but I won't know for sure until I read their financial statement;* I think that the James Power Tool Company has done good business for the past three months, but I won't know for sure until I read the written account they'll make on their activities and financial condition for that period.

floor (the) *n.* that place in a stock exchange where trading actually takes place, known to be extremely chaotic • *I want to buy*

and sell stocks for a living, but I wouldn't want to be on the floor; I want to buy and sell stocks for a living, but I wouldn't want to be where trading actually takes place in the stock exchange.

front money *n.* money paid before the start of a project or before services have been rendered, often needed to begin that project • *If we can find an investor to pay us some front money, we can begin our Language School;* If we can find an investor to pay us some money now before we have started the business, we can begin our Language School.

fund *n.* a group of assets (usually a sum of money) set aside for a determined purpose • *We have decided to establish a fund to help art students go to college;* We have decided to establish a sum of money set aside specifically for the purpose of helping art students go to college.
　♦ SEE (1): **mutual fund** *n.*
　♦ SEE (2): **pension fund** *n.*

golden parachute *exp.* an agreement which promises an executive large amounts of money (or other valuables) in the event that his/her job is eliminated • *We lost everything when The Convex Tobacco Company went out of business, but the president wasn't affected* *because he had a golden parachute;* We lost everything when The Convex Tobacco Company went out of business, but the president wasn't affected because he had an agreement which promised him a large amount of money in the event his job was eliminated.

hand-hold (to) *v.* to reassure and coddle a nervous client, as one would hold the hand of a frightened child • *The clients got nervous about the project, so Tom had to meet with them for some hand-holding;* The clients got nervous about the project, so Tom had to meet with them to reassure and coddle them.

hard numbers *n.* specific financial figures (as opposed to an approximation) • *If you want to know if a company is healthy, you have to ignore all the projections and predictions and look at the hard numbers;* If you want to know if a company is healthy, you have to ignore all the projections and predictions and look at the specific financial figures.

hype *n.* overstatements and exaggerations usually used to pressure the sale of something • *Most of what the salesman told us was hype;* Most of what the salesman told us was

overstatement and exaggeration to pressure us to buy what he/she was selling.

index *n.* a way to gauge a current economic or financial condition by relating it statistically to the same condition at a previous time • *In order to find out if the Tippy-Top Timber Company is paying more for spruce wood then it did in 1956, you have to look at a price index for lumber costs;* In order to find out if the Tippy-Top Timber Company is paying more for spruce wood then it did in 1956, you have to look at a gauge of how the price of lumber this year compares statistically to the price of lumber in 1956.

inflation *n.* a situation where consumer prices rise and money buys less • *I'm planning on buying a house soon unless there is significant inflation over the next few years;* I'm planning on buying a house soon unless there is significant increase in consumer prices over the next few years.

insider • **1.** *n.* one who has special knowledge or access to information about a company because of an association with that company • *I found out that Davis Pencil Company is struggling by talking to an* *insider;* I found out that Davis Pencil Company is struggling by talking to someone who has special knowledge or access to information as a result of an association with that company. • **2.** *adj.* • *I was able to get insider information regarding our two competitors;* I was able to get information regarding our computer from someone with special access.

▶ ALSO: **insider trading** *n.* trading by insiders which is illegal due to their information and special access giving them an unfair advantage.

January effect (the) *n.* the phenomenon whereby the beginning of a new year seems to cause a rise in the stock market • *Andersen Company stock rose, but it's probably due to the January effect;* Andersen Company stock rose, but it's probably due to the phenomenon whereby the beginning of a new year seems to cause a rise in the stock market.

lackluster (to be) *adj.* to be unimpressive • *With such a rainy summer season, our sunscreen sales were lackluster;* With such a cool wet summer season, our sunscreen sales were unimpressive.

line of credit *n.* the maximum amount of money a bank (or other financial institution) will lend an individual or company • *Although we have had some unforeseen expenses, we should be able to pay them without exhausting our line of credit;* Although we have had some unforeseen expenses, we should be able to pay them without exhausting the maximum amount of money the bank will lend us.

liquid *adj.* said of something which can be converted into money quickly and easily • *You should sell some of your real estate and invest in some business ventures which are more liquid;* You should sell some of your real estate and invest in some business ventures which will bring you money quickly.

loan shark *n.* one who is in the business of loaning money at an excessively high interest rate to people or companies • *I know you're having trouble getting a loan from the bank, but keep trying. It's just not worth going to a loan shark;* I know you're having trouble getting a loan from the bank, but keep trying. It's just not worth going to someone in the business of providing loans at an excessively high interest rate.

lock, stock, and barrel *exp.* absolutely everything pertaining to a person or company • *Carlos bought the Greenway Greeting Card Company lock, stock, and barrel;* Carlos bought absolutely everything pertaining to the Greenway Greeting Card Company.

long on (to be) *exp.* to have a large amount of something • *I'm long on McKee Rubber;* I own a large amount of McKee Rubber.
‣ ANTONYM: **to be short on something** *exp.*
⇨ NOTE: This expression can also be used in other contexts, for example: *She's long on brains and short on looks;* She very smart but not very pretty.

maturity *n.* the date a loan (or other debt) is due and must be repaid • *When our loan reaches maturity next year, we are going to need a lot of cash;* When our loan reaches the date when it is due next year and must be repaid, we are going to need a lot of cash.

mentor *n.* a counselor or master, usually an executive with experience and seniority, who teaches inexperienced executives how to do a job • *When I first started at Thomas Sod & Seedlings, they made Mr. Jones my mentor;* When I first started at Thomas Sod & Seedlings, they

made Mr. Jones my counselor who taught me how to do my job.

mutual fund *n.* a fund (typically a sum of money set aside for a specific purpose) which is divided up into equal parts called "shares" and managed by an investment company.
‣ NOTE: The shares are sold, to the public, and the mutual fund invests the proceeds (usually in stocks, bonds or securities).The intent is that the majority of those investments will show profits and the shares will increase in value. • *Instead of buying stock in a particular company, I've decided to invest in a mutual fund;* Instead of buying stock in a particular company, I've decided to buy shares in a mutual fund which will then combine my money with that of other investors and buy a variety of stocks, a majority of which should show profit.

net 30 (to pay) *exp.* to pay an invoice in 30 calendar days (as opposed to 30 work days which are typically Monday through Friday in the U.S.) • *According to this invoice, we have to pay it net 30;* According to this invoice, we have to pay it in 30 calendar days.
‣ ALSO: **to pay 2/net 10** *exp.* to pay within ten days and receive a 2% discount.

no-load *adj.* sold (without a fee) directly to the investor • *I'm looking for a no-load mutual fund.;* I'm looking for a mutual fund which does not charge me a fee for investing.

north of (to be) *exp.* to be more than • *They would not say how much the company sold for but the price is rumored to be north of thirty million dollars;* They would not say how much the company sold for but the price is rumored to be more than thirty million dollars.
  ◗ ANTONYM: **to be south of** *exp.*

note *n.* a written document pledging to repay a debt (usually to a bank) • *Jim says the bank holds the note on his new sports car;* Jim says the bank holds a written document in which he pledges to repay the debt on his new sports car.
  ◗ SYNONYM: **paper** *n.*

off (to be) *adj.* said of a stock which has declined • *Pierre Dress Company stock closed off three points today;* Pierre Dress Company market declined three points today.

offshore *adj.* used to describe any enterprise originating or operating outside the United States • *Ken has offered me a chance to invest in an offshore corporation, but I found out it produces more pollution then products;* Ken has offered me a chance to invest in a corporation conducting business outside the United States, but I found out it produces more pollution then products.

out of the woods (to be) *exp.* to be out of danger or trouble • *Tom's Glue Company made a small profit last year, but it's not out of the woods yet;* Tom's Glue Company made a small profit last year, but it's still not out of trouble.

paper (on) *n.* in written form such as in a contract or a financial report • *The Adams Company looks like a good investment on paper, but soon it's going to be worthless;* The Adams Company looks like a good investment in financial reports, soon it's going to be worthless.

pay on time (to) *exp.* to pay a portion at a time determined by the terms of a particular loan (such as every 30 days, at the beginning of the month, etc.). • *Do we have to pay the entire amount now or may we pay on time?;* Do we have to pay the entire amount now or may we pay a portion at a time?.
  ◗ NOTE: The expression *"to pay on time"* literally means "to pay

by the due date." The difference between the two definitions depends on the context.

penny ante *adj.* a derogatory reference to a person or enterprise being small and insignificant • *Barney's Fishing Hats is a penny ante operation;* Barney's Fishing Hats is a small and insignificant operation.

pension fund *n.* a pool of money set aside by a company and invested in by the workers to be paid back on a regular basis when they retire • *As soon as I retire, I'll be able to get money on a regular basis from my pension fund;* As soon as I retire, I'll be able to get money on a regular basis from the pool of money set aside by my company.

plastic *n.* a credit card • *I didn't have enough cash, so I put it on plastic;* I didn't have enough cash, so I put it on a credit card.

player *n.* in the investment business, an active and powerful person who is taken seriously • *Homer is the only player at Beekman Investments, everyone else just follows him;* Homer is the only active and powerful person who is taken seriously at Beekman Investments, everyone else just follows him.

plunge (to take the/a) *exp.* to engage in a risky, sometimes reckless investment gamble • *I know I could lose everything, but I decided to take the plunge and invest in silver;* I know I could lose everything, but I decided to make a risky investment in silver.

portfolio *n.* a group of various investments held by an individual (or institution) • *Collin says I should have Spanish Seed Company stock in my portfolio;* Collin says I should have Spanish Seed Company stock in my collection of various investments.

pricey (to be) *adj.* to be expensive or high-priced • *Experts say the Anthony Shoe Company is not doing well because its products are too pricey for the average buyer;* Experts say the Anthony Shoe Company is not doing well because it's products are too expensive for the average buyer.

product *n.* that which a company or enterprise produces • *Longwood Gifts has a good sales force, but it has a mediocre product;* Longwood Gifts has a good sales force, but it makes mediocre products.
▶ NOTE: Although the term *"product"* is used in the singular form, its definition refers to several items.

profitability *n.* the likelihood that something will make more money then it costs to produce • *There is good profitability in manufacturing T-shirts;* There is a good likelihood that manufacturing T-shirts will make more money than they cost to produce.

pure profit (to be) *exp.* said of a venture which is completely profitable • *Now that all of our expenses have been covered, everything else we make is pure profit;* Now that all of our expenses have been covered, everything else we make is nothing but profit.

rally • *n.* **1.** an increase in activity, value, and price of a stock • *Drubind Chemical stock fell three points early in the day but was able to rally back by six at closing time;* Drubind Chemical stock fell three points early in the day but was able to increase in value by six at closing time. • **2.** to arouse a company or group and motivate them to act • *The accounting department was gloomy after the audit, but Janet was able to rally them to work even harder;* The accounting department was gloomy after the audit, but Janet was able to arouse and motivate them to work even harder.

realize a profit (to) *exp.* to make a profit • *We hope to realize a profit in just a few weeks;* We hope to make a profit in just a few weeks;
▶ VARIATION: **to show a profit** *exp.*

rebound (to) *v.* to stop getting worse and start getting better • *The Allstead Unicycle Company is hoping sales will rebound after next year;* The Allstead Unicycle Company is hoping sales will stop getting worse and start getting better after next year.
▶ VARIATION: **to bounce back** *exp.*

return *n.* profit • *I'm hoping to make a return on my investment within a year;* I'm hoping to make a profit on my investment within a year.

revolving credit (line) *n.* an amount of money available for an individual or business to borrow which can be repaid and then borrowed again immediately • *Since I have a good job, I have up to $4,000 in revolving credit at the bank;* Since I have a good job, I have up to $4,000 available for me to borrow, which I can repay and then borrow again immediately.

rig (to) *v.* to influence through dishonest means • *The manager* *rigged the stock price by lying about his inventory;* The manager influenced the stock price dishonestly by lying about his inventory.

rollover (to) *n.* to move one's money from one investment directly to another (instead of turning it back into cash) usually to avoid paying taxes • *Instead of getting money back from my investment and just spending it, I'm going to let it rollover into other investments;* Instead of getting money back from my investment and just spending it, I'm going to move it to other investments.

run *n.* a large number of depositors who, having lost confidence in a bank's financial condition, are demanding their money back all at once • *If it becomes public knowledge that the bank's loans are not being paid back, there will certainly be a run on the bank;* If it becomes public knowledge that the bank's loans are not being paid back, there will be a large number of depositors who, losing confidence in the bank, will demand all their money back at once.
 ♦ NOTE: Since banks keep only a small percentage of their cash available, a large *"run"* can cause a bank to fail.

scorched earth *exp.* used literally in the Vietnam war, when an area would be destroyed completely, so that nothing was left alive (used figuratively in business) • *With all the budget reductions, this company is going to be scorched earth;* With all the budget reductions, this company will have nothing and nobody of any value left.

shake-out *n.* the elimination of investors too weak to survive or too cautious to remain during a crisis in the market, such as a sharp decline • *He hasn't invested in stock since the last shake-out when the market dropped six percent in a day;* He hasn't invested in stock since the last time many strong investors were eliminated when the market was in crisis and dropped six percent in a day.

short run (in the) *exp.* within a short period of time • *In the short run, we stand to make a lot of money;* In a short period of time, we stand to make a lot of money.
 ♦ ANTONYM: **in the long run** *exp.* over an extended period of time • *If we spread our advertising dollars over a period of five years, we'll make more money in the long run;* If we spread our advertising dollars over a period of five years, we'll make more

money over an extended period of time.

spin-off *n.* a company which was once a part of another company but now operates on its own • Sigma Graphics is a spin-off of Elevated Printing Company; Sigma Graphics, once a part of Elevated Printing Company, now operates on its own.

stake in something (to have a) *exp.* to have part ownership of a company or enterprise • *Now that he has purchased part of Treeline Television, Barry has a stake in three different media companies;* Now that he has purchased part of Treeline Television, Barry has part ownership of three different media companies.

stock option plan *n.* a form of payment (usually for executives) which involves giving someone the right to purchase stock in the company at a price less than what the stock is currently worth. ◗ NOTE: Both the company and the employee benefit from such a plan: The company avoids spending money immediately to pay the employee and actually receives money from the sale of its stock to the employee. In addition, an employee who is "part owner" will work harder for "his/her" company. The employee makes more money by purchasing stock at a discount (through the option plan) than the company would have paid the employee in cash. Furthermore, the employee (now a *"stock holder"*) makes additional money if the value of the stock goes up.

subpar (to be) *adj.* to be substandard • *Our line of tennis socks didn't lose money last season, but profits were subpar;* Our line of tennis socks didn't lose money last season, but profits were less than standard.

T-bill *n.* short for "treasury bill" which is a written promise by the government to pay the purchaser a set amount of money after a future date • *Gary has given up trying to guess what the stock market will do next, so now he only buys T-bills;* Gary has given up trying to guess what the stock market will do next, so now he only buys treasury bills, which are written promises by the government to pay him a set amount of money at a future date. ◗ NOTE: *"Treasury bills"* are redeemable in five years or less whereas *"treasury bonds"* are redeemable <u>after</u> five years.

takeover *n.* the purchase of controlling interest in a company by another individual, group or company • *I heard a rumor that Holzhaus Shoes is planning a takeover of Rawhide Footwear;* I heard a rumor that Holzhaus Shoes is planning to purchase controlling interest in Rawhide Footwear.

♦ ALSO (1): **to take over** *v.*

♦ ALSO (2): **friendly takeover** *exp.* a takeover in which the target company is agreeable to the situation.

⇨ ANTONYM: **hostile takeover** *exp.* a takeover in which the target company is not agreeable to the situation.

turn a corner (to) *exp.* said of a situation whose outlook is changing for the better • *We've been losing money but with the start of the new season we've finally turned a corner;* We've been losing money but with the start of the new season, we've finally been able to make a profit.

undercapitalized (to be) *adj.* said of a (typically new) company having so little money available to operate that it is in danger of failing • *In its second year of operation, the Burke Chocolate Company is badly undercapitalized;* In its second year of operation, the Burke Chocolate Company has so little money available to operate that it is in danger of failing.

up-front money *exp.* money which must be paid before a project can begin • *We would love to start a company which would produce thousands of laptop computers, but it would require too much up-front money;* We would love to start a company which would produce thousands of laptop computers, but it would require too much money which must be paid before production can begin.

venture capitalist *n.* one who provides money and other resources for young companies offering higher then average risk of loss yet higher potential for profit • *Marcia wants to start a company to manufacture communication satellites, so she's looking for a venture capitalist;* Marcia wants to start a company to manufacture communication satellites, so she's looking for someone who provides money and other resources for young companies offering higher then average risk of loss yet higher potential for profit.

widget *n.* an unnamed gadget or device, often used as the product in hypothetical discussions about business • *The company that can make more widgets per dollar has the advantage;* The company that can make more products per dollar has the advantage.

Practice Advanced Finance Terms

(Answers, p. 230)

A. Fill in the blanks using the list below.

escrow	front	return
balance	bear	Board
capital	bull	dividend
asset	annuity	board

1. **across the** _____ *exp.* everything in a given group or category, usually without exception.

2. _____ *n.* an investment which consistently pays the investor a fix amount on a regular basis.

3. _____ *n.* any person or thing which is useful or valuable.

4. _____ **sheet** *n.* a list of what a company possesses and owes at a given time.

5. _____ **market** *exp.* a market condition in which the majority of stock prices are falling (sometimes rapidly).

6. **The Big** _____ *n.* the New York Stock Exchange.

7. _____ **market** *n.* a stock market condition in which the majority of stock prices are rising (sometimes rapidly).

8. _____ *n.* money and other resources a company uses to conduct business.

9. _____ *n.* the part of a company's profit which is distributed among its investors.

10. _____ **(to be in)** *n.* said of something of value (often money, ownership of property, etc.) which two sides agree to have held by a third party until the conditions of an agreement are met.

11. _____ **money** *n.* money paid before the start of a project or before services have been rendered.

12. _____ *n.* profit.

A Closer Look (2):
Common Initials Pertaining to Finance

The following is a brief list of some of the more popular initials and abbreviations known by just about everyone having to do anything with money and finance.

AMEX *n.* *"American Stock Exchange,"* alternative to the New York Stock Exchange catering to those buying and selling stock in smaller companies.
♦ NOTE: Pronounced *"Am-ex."*

A.P.R. *n.* *"annual percentage rate,"* the interest rate on a loan or debt represented as a percentage per year.

A.T.M. *n.* *"automated teller machine,"* a machine connected to a financial institution which allows members to perform such functions as deposit money into accounts, transfer money between accounts, withdraw cash from accounts, etc.

C.D. *n.* • **1.** (finance) *"certificate of deposit,"* a contract whereby a person agrees to let a bank hold a certain amount of money for a fixed amount of time, after which the bank returns that money with interest • **2.** (music) *"compact*

disc," a disc used to store music which is encoded and retrieved digitally using a laser.

C.F.O. *n.* *"Chief Financial Officer,"* the person in a company who has control of (and responsibility for) the company's money.

C.O.D. *n.* *"cash on delivery,"* a type of shipping method where the price for the shipment and the cost of delivery is paid by the recipient at the time the delivery is made.

COLA *n.* *"cost-of-living adjustment,"* a modification in one's salary (usually annually) to salaries to provide for increases in costs of living such as food, shelter, clothing, etc.
♦ NOTE: Pronounced *"kola."*

E.E.C. *n.* *"European Economic Community,"* a partnership between many of the European countries designed to encourage trade and mutual cooperation and to allow collective bargaining with much larger countries.

F.D.I.C. *n. "Federal Deposit Insurance Corporation,"* a federal agency whose main responsibility is to insure (up to $100,000) deposits in most American banks.

F.S.L.I.C. *n. "Federal Savings and Loan Insurance Corporation,"* a federal agency whose main responsibility is to insure deposits in most American saving and loan institutions.

I.R.A. *n. "individual retirement account,"* a special kind of savings account into which an individual may make tax-deductible deposits (up to a certain limit each year), but from which no money may be taken until age 65 (when his/her tax rate will be lower).
◗ NOTE: Pronounced as individual letters (I-R-A) or as a word *"eye-ra."*

L.B.O. *n. "leveraged buyout,"* the purchase of a company with borrowed money, usually with the promise that the loan will be repaid from the profits or assets of the newly-acquired company.

M.B.A. *n. "Master of Business Administration degree,"* a graduate degree which requires

that a student spend two to three years studying every aspect of general business including a specialty (such as management, economics, accounting, etc.)

N.A.S.D.A.Q. *n. "National Association of Securities Dealers Automated Quotations,"* an alternative source, similar to the New York Stock Exchange, for brokers to find out the price of stocks which are being publicly bought and sold.

S&L *n. "Savings and Loan Association,"* originally an institution much like a bank but offering savings accounts and making home loans exclusively — in 1981 the government authorized them to function more like banks by offering checking accounts and making other kinds of loans — S&L's gained notoriety in the 1980s for widespread fraud and abuse.

S.E.C. *n. "Securities and Exchange Commission,"* a federal agency in charge of regulating the buying and selling of securities (such as stock) to assure fairness.

S.S. *n. "Social Security,"* a government plan which provides money to people for reasons of retirement, disability, unemployment, etc.

Sports Terms
Used In Business
– *"Batting a Thousand"* –

*"Let's **touch base** again tomorrow!"*

Lesson Eight - Sports Terms Used in Business

Dialogue In Slang

"Batting a Thousand"

DIALOGUE

Jeff is waiting for Austin to come out of the boss's office.

Jeff: So, did you **strike out** with the boss?

Austin: I've been doing nothing but **scoring points** with him! He was so agreeable **right off the bat**. I didn't even think I'd **make it to first base** with him but he really **threw me a curve**. He offered me a raise and a promotion because he likes the fact that I'm a **team player**. He even **went to bat for me** with the other executives. I've actually been **in the running** for a long time.

Jeff: **He shoots, he scores**! You're really **batting a thousand** these days. I guess it pays **to play by the rules**.

Austin: The last guy they hired **dropped the ball** so many times he was asked to resign. I was sure ready **to play hard ball** with him. I was even ready **to throw in the towel** if he didn't give me what I wanted.

Jeff: Did he give you a **ballpark** figure of what your new salary will be?

Austin: Not yet. I have **to touch base with him** later today regarding money.

Jeff: I guess I was **way off base** about him. So, I suppose you'll be **calling the shots** around here soon, huh?

Austin: Guess so. I'll be **off and running** first thing next week. I'll keep you posted. In the meantime, **"it's back to the ol' ball game!"**

Lesson Eight - Sports Terms Used in Business

Translation of dialogue in standard English

"Batting a Thousand"

DIALOGUE

Jeff is waiting for Austin to come out of the boss's office.

Jeff: So, did you **fail** with the boss?

Austin: I've been doing nothing but **gaining favor** with him! He was so agreeable **right from the beginning**. I didn't even think I'd **get to the preliminary step** with him but he really **surprised me**. He offered me a raise and a promotion because he likes the fact that I **work well with others**. He even **spoke favorably about me** with the other executives. I've actually been **a candidate** for a long time.

Jeff: **You attempted something and succeeded**! You're really **successful at everything you do** these days. I guess it pays **to conduct yourself by the policy set forth by the company**.

Austin: The last guy they hired **shirked his responsibilities** so many times he was asked to resign. I was sure ready **to resort to aggressive methods** with him. I was even ready **to resign** if he didn't give me what I wanted.

Jeff: Did he give you an **approximate** figure of what your new salary will be?

Austin: Not yet. I have **to meet with him briefly** later today regarding money.

Jeff: I guess I was **very wrong** about him. So, I suppose you'll be **making the rules** around here soon, huh?

Austin: Guess so. I'll be **well into my job** first thing next week. I'll keep you posted. In the meantime, **"I'd better get back to work!"**

Lesson Eight - Sports Terms Used in Business

Dialogue in slang as it would be heard

"Batting a Thousand"

DIALOGUE

Jeff's waiding fer Austin ta come oudda the boss's office.

Jeff: So, did ja **strike out** with the boss?

Austin: I've been doin' nothing but **scoring points** with 'im! He was so agreeable **ride off the bat**. I didn' even think I'd **make it ta firs' base** with 'im bud 'e really **threw me a curve**. He offered me a raise 'n a promotion b'cuz 'e likes the fact thad I'm a **team player**. He even **went ta bat fer me** with thee other execudivs. I've aksh'ly been **'n the running** fer a long time.

Jeff: **He shoots, 'e scores**! Y'r really **badding a thousan'** these days. I guess it pays **ta play by the rules**.

Austin: The las' guy they hired **dropped the ball** so many times 'e was asked ta resign. I was sher ready **ta play hard ball** with 'im. I was even ready **da throw in the towel** if 'e didn' gimme whad I wan'ed.

Jeff: Did e' give you a **ballpark** figure of what ch'r new salary will be?

Austin: Not chet. I haf **ta touch base with 'im** lader t'day r'garding money.

Jeff: I guess I was **way off base** about 'im. So, I suppose you'll be **calling the shots** aroun' here soon, huh?

Austin: Guess so. I'll be **off 'n running** firs' thing next week. I'll keep ya posted. In the meantime, **"it's back ta thee ol' ball game!"**

Vocabulary

ballpark figure *exp.* estimate • *"How much money do you think the company made this year?" "I can only give you a ballpark figure;"* "How much money do you think the company made this year?" "I can only give you an estimate."
♦ ORIGIN: baseball.

bat a thousand (to) *exp.* • **1.** to be successful at everything one does • *Every potential client you've brought into the company has decided to hire our services. You're really batting a thousand!;* Every potential client you've brought into the company has decided to hire our services. You're really successful every time! • **2.** to be unsuccessful at everything one does (used facetiously) • *I know it was an accident, but you insulted the boss for the third time today! You're really batting a thousand!;* I know it was an accident, but you insulted the boss for the third time today! You're really not being at all successful with him!
♦ ORIGIN: Baseball batting averages are determined by dividing the number of successful hits (by a specific batter) by the number of times at bat. The resulting number is traditionally carried out to the third decimal point. For example: a batter who has been at bat ten times and has hit the ball successfully three times, would be said to have a batting average of .300 (3 successful hits divided by 10 times at bat). However, since it is common in baseball to read the average as a three-digit number, the player would be said to be *"batting 300."* Therefore, a player who could hit the ball successfully every time at bat, would be *"batting a thousand."*

call the shots (to) *exp.* to make the rules • *I know you want to be able to start work later, but you don't call the shots here;* I know you want to be able to start work later, but you don't make the rules here.
♦ ORIGIN: This expression comes from pool where each player announces the target-pocket for each shot. This is known as *"calling the shots."*

drop the ball (to) *exp.* to shirk one's responsibilities suddenly • *For our big conference in Atlanta, Joe said he'd take care of all the travel arrangements. He got our plane tickets but didn't make the hotel reservations. This isn't the first time he's dropped the ball;* For our big conference in Atlanta, Joe said he'd take care of all the travel arrangements. He got our plane tickets but didn't make the hotel reservations. This isn't the first time he's shirked his responsibilities suddenly.

♦ ORIGIN: This expression comes from baseball where one of the goals of the players is to catch the ball after being hit by the other team's batter. (This forces the batter to lose his turn and prevents him from scoring a point.) However, if the player should *"drop the ball,"* the other team will have the advantage and may be able to score points.

make it to first base (to) *exp.* to get to the preliminary step (in conducting a potential business transaction) • *I know we're trying to get him as a client but he talks so much that I could hardly speak with him. I can't believe I couldn't even make it to first base with him!;* I know we're trying to get him as a client but he talks so much that I could hardly speak with him. I can't believe I couldn't even get to the preliminary step with him!

♦ ORIGIN: In baseball, the first step in getting closer to the home plate (where a point is earned), is to reach first base.

go to bat for someone (to) *exp.* to try and convince someone to do a favor or service for someone else • *I don't know if the executives will be willing to give you the promotion but I promise I'll go to bat for you;* I don't know if the executives will be willing to give you the promotion but I promise I'll try and convince them.

♦ ORIGIN: baseball.

"He/she shoots, he/she scores!" *exp.* "He/she attempted something and succeeded! • *I heard you just signed three new clients today! He shoots, he scores!;* I heard you just signed three new clients today! You attempted something and succeeded!

♦ NOTE: This expression is commonly announced during basketball games when a player makes two points.

"It's back to the ol' ball game!" *exp.* • **1.** "I'd better get back to work!" **2.** "It's back to the original plan" • *We've tried every possible plan but none of them work as well as the first one. I guess it's back to the ol' ball game;* We've tried every possible plan but none of them work as well as the first one. I guess we'd better go back to the original plan.

♦ ORIGIN: This expression is said about a baseball player who returns to the game after a short break.

in the running (to be) *exp.* to be a candidate • *I just found out I'm in the running for the position of vice president of the company!;* I just found out I'm a candidate for the position of vice president of the company!

♦ ORIGIN: Said of a horse which is running evenly with the other horses

during a race.
♦ ANTONYM: **to be out of the running** *exp.* to be no longer a candidate.

off and running (to be) *exp.* to be making significant progress in a project
 • *Susan was just given an assignment from the boss and she's already off and running!;* Susan was just given an assignment from the boss and she's already making significant progress!
 ♦ ORIGIN: Said of horses who are running aggressively from the start of a race.

play by the rules (to) *exp.* to conduct oneself by the accepted policy •
I'm afraid we cannot tolerate your tardiness every day. You have to play by the rules of this company or resign; I'm afraid we cannot tolerate your tardiness every day. You have to conduct yourself by the rules of this company or resign.
 ♦ ORIGIN: Every sport has rules under which the team members must play or risk being disqualified.

play hardball (to) *exp.* to resort to aggressive methods in order to attain a goal (even if it is to the detriment of another person) • *I've been trying to get a promotion here for five years. Now I just found out Johanna is being considered for the same promotion and she's only been here a month! It's time to play hardball;* I've been trying to get a promotion here for five years. Now I just found out Johanna is being considered for the same promotion and she's only been here a month! It's time to do whatever it takes for me to get this!
 ♦ ORIGIN: In professional baseball, a small hard ball is used which makes the game somewhat more aggressive than that played by teams who use a larger, soft ball.

right off the bat *exp.* from the very beginning • *The boss said he liked me right off the bat;* The boss said he liked me immediately.
 ♦ ORIGIN: In baseball, *"right off the bat"* refers to a baseball that is hit with full force after the first pitch.

score points (to) *exp.* to gain someone's favor • *You'd better start coming to work on time. You're not scoring many points with the boss;* You'd better start coming to work on time. You're not gaining the boss's favor.
 ♦ VARIATION: **to make points** *exp.*

strike out (to) *exp.* to fail • *I'm afraid we just couldn't effectively sell his product. We really struck out;* I'm afraid we just couldn't effectively sell his product. We really failed.

▶ ORIGIN: This expression is said of a baseball player at bat who misses the ball three times *(three "strikes")* and loses his turn at bat.

team player (to be a) *exp.* said of one who works easily in a group toward a common goal • *She's not much of a team player. She's the only one who never offers to stay late when we have deadlines!;* She's not much for working easily in groups toward a common goal. She's the only one who never offers to stay late when we have deadlines!

▶ ORIGIN: A *"team player"* is one who works well with other teammates during a game and is primarily concerned with bringing the entire team glory as a whole.

throw someone a curve [ball] (to) *exp.* to surprise someone by doing something unexpectedly • *He really threw me a curve [ball] when he called me into his office to offer me a raise. I thought I was going to be laid off!;* He really surprised me when he called me into his office to offer me a raise. I thought I was going to be laid off!

▶ ORIGIN: In baseball, the pitcher may decide to throw a ball which curves unexpectedly as it approaches the batter.

throw in the towel (to) *exp.* to quit • *This job is too difficult. I'm throwing in the towel;* This job is too difficult. I quit.

▶ VARIATION: **to throw in the sponge** *exp.*

▶ ORIGIN: These expressions comes from boxing where the manager of a losing boxer would literally throw in the *"towel"* (used to wipe the sweat of the boxer) or a *"sponge"* (used to put cool water on the boxer) into the ring, signifying defeat.

touch base with someone (to) *exp.* to contact someone briefly in order to exchange information • *I need to touch base with the boss before I leave on my business trip;* I need to meet with the boss briefly before I leave on my business trip.

▶ ORIGIN: In baseball, once a batter has hit the ball, he/she must run around the baseball diamond and tag each base with his/her foot in order to advance to home plate and score a run.

[way] off base (to be) *exp.* to be very wrong • *I thought he'd be an ideal employee. I guess I was [way] off base;* I thought he'd be an ideal employee. I guess I was [very] wrong.

▶ ORIGIN: This expression is said of a baseball player who is not on a base and is therefore vulnerable to being tagged.

PRACTICE THE VOCABULARY

[Answers to Lesson 8, p. 230]

A. Match the italicized word(s) in the left column with their slang equivalent from the right column.

☐ 1. Give me an *approximation* of how much money you think the company made this year.

A. **in the running**

☐ 2. You promised you'd take care of our hotel accommodations but you forgot? I can't believe you'd *shirk your responsibilites* like this!

B. **ballpark figure**

C. **threw me a curve [ball]**

☐ 3. It's time to *resort to aggressive methods in order to attain my goal.*

D. **calls the shots**

☐ 4. You're not *gaining favor* by coming in late to work every day.

E. **play hardball**

☐ 5. He really *surprised me* when he called me into his office to congratulate me on doing a good job!

F. **scoring points**

☐ 6. She *makes the rules* around here, not you!

G. **struck out**

☐ 7. I just found out I'm *a candidate* for the position of vice president.

H. **touch base**

☐ 8. I didn't get the promotion. I really *failed.*

I. **drop the ball**

☐ 9. I was *very wrong* about him.

☐ 10. I need to *meet* with her briefly.

J. **[way] off base**

B. Fill in the blanks by choosing the appropriate word(s) from the list below.

bat	ball	shots
base	running	points
towel	curve	hardball
scores	thousand	rules

1. **drop the** _____ **(to)** *v.* to shirk one's responsibilities suddenly.

2. **bat a** _____ **(to)** *exp.* • **1.** to be successful at everything one does • **2.** to be unsuccessful at everything one does (used facetiously).

3. **go to** _____ **for someone (to)** *exp.* to try and convince someone to do a favor or service for someone else.

4. **off and** _____ **(to be)** *exp.* to be making significant progress in a project.

5. **play** _____ **(to)** *exp.* to resort to aggressive methods in order to attain a goal (even if it is to the detriment of another person).

6. **call the** _____ **(to)** *exp.* to make the rules.

7. **"He/she shoots, he/she** _____ **!"** *exp.* "He/she attempted something and succeeded!"

8. **play by the** _____ **(to)** *exp.* to conduct oneself by the accepted policy.

9. **make it to first** _____ **(to)** *exp.* to get to the preliminary step (in conducting a potential business transaction).

10. **throw in the** _____ **(to)** *exp.* to quit.

11. **score** _____ **(to)** *exp.* to gain someone's favor.

12. **throw someone a** _____ **(to)** *exp.* to do something very unexpectedly.

C. In the scoreboard below, find and circle the words used in exercise B.

B	A	T	G	A	A	M	I	G	R	I	E
H	A	R	D	B	A	L	L	I	U	T	P
E	P	S	C	O	R	E	S	V	N	O	O
T	H	O	U	S	A	N	D	L	N	W	I
P	M	Y	R	S	H	O	T	S	I	E	N
E	I	K	V	R	S	C	O	E	N	L	T
B	A	S	E	R	U	L	E	S	G	R	S

A CLOSER LOOK (1):
General Sports Slang Used in American Business

Sports has given birth to a great deal of slang and jargon used not only in the individual sport but in our daily conversations as well having nothing to do with athletics at all. Below are some of the most typical expressions, used universally in any sport, which have been adopted into our day-to-day speech.

blow the whistle on someone (to) *exp.* to inform on someone • *If Monica hadn't blown the whistle on him, he would have continued to steal money from the company;* If Monica hadn't reported him, he would have continued to steal money from the company.
▶ ORIGIN: In many sports, the referee blows a whistle indicating that an illegal play has just been made.

bounce something off someone (to) *exp.* to test someone's reaction to an idea • *I just got a great idea for a new movie that I want to bounce off you;* I just got a great idea for a new movie that I want to get your opinion on.
▶ ORIGIN: When a ball is tossed toward a wall, it bounces back to the thrower. In this expression, the speaker hopes to have his/her idea bounced back in the form of a positive.

get the ball rolling (to) *exp.* to begin • *When do you think you'll get the ball rolling on the new advertising campaign?;* When do you think you'll begin the new advertising campaign?

hard to call (to be) *exp.* to be hard to determine • *I don't know whether or not all of his absences are legitimate or not. It's very hard to call;* I don't know whether or not all of his absences are legitimate or not. It's very hard to determine.
▶ ORIGIN: Referees are known for having to make difficult judgments or *"calls"* regarding whether or not a particular play is legal under the rules of the game.

play fair (to) *exp.* to work ethically • *When I told Mark I was trying to bring Mr. Nash's account to our company, Bill went over and had Mr. Nash sign with him that afternoon! He doesn't play fair;* When I told Mark I was trying to bring Mr. Nash's account into our company, Bill went over and had Mr. Nash sign with him that afternoon! He doesn't work ethically.

♦ ORIGIN: In all sports, the team members must play fairly by adhering to the rules of the game or risk getting disqualified.

referee (to) *v.* to mediate between two or more people • *I'm tired of having to referee between you two! If you can't work together, I'll reassign you both;* I'm tired of having to mediate between you two! If you can't work together, I'll reassign you both.

score big (to) *exp.* to earn one's high esteem • *You sure scored big with the boss today!;* You sure earned the boss's esteem today!

sport (to be a) *n.* said of one who is very cooperative at doing unpleasant tasks • *Thank you for agreeing to help the new employee during his first week on the job. You're a sport!;* Thank you for cooperating to help the new employee during his first week on the job. You're very cooperative!

♦ VARIATION: **to be a good/bad sport** *exp.* to be a good/bad loser • *When John wasn't chosen to get the new job position, he was such a bad sport!;* When John wasn't chosen to get the new job position, he was such a bad loser (and started yelling at everyone)!

"That's the way the ball bounces!" *exp.* "That's life!" • *I know you got fired your second day, but sometimes that's the way the ball bounces!;* I know you got fired your second day, but sometimes that's just the way life is!

"Time out!" *interj.* "Stop everything and listen to me!" • *Time out! This meeting is starting to focus on the wrong issue;* Stop! This meeting is starting to focus on the wrong issue.

♦ VARIATION: **to take a time out** *exp.* to stop the proceedings momentarily (usually for a private meeting) • *I'd like to take a time out from the meeting in order to discuss some important issues with my colleagues;* I'd like to take a brief pause from the meeting in order to discuss some important issues with my colleagues.

⇨ NOTE: This expression is commonly used by parents when disciplining children: *You children are being too wild! I want you to take a time out;* You children are being too wild! I want you to stop everything for a while.

♦ NOTE: The interjection *"Time out!"* is used in various sports by referees to stop the game momentarily.

A CLOSER LOOK (2):
Slang from Specific Sports Used in American Business

If *"getting your feet wet"* in the previous section was *"smooth sailing,"* you'll be anxious *"to dive right in"* to the next list.

The following is a collection of expressions used in American business which has been taken from specific sports such as baseball, basketball, boxing, football, horse racing, sailing, swimming, tennis, and track & field.

Don't stop now… you're almost in the *"home stretch!"*

Baseball

come out of left field (to) *exp.* to be completely unexpected • *I was just laid off! That totally came out of left field!;* I was just laid off! That totally took me by surprise!

field a call (to) *exp.* to pick up a telephone call • *Want me to field that call for you?;* Do you want me to pick up that telephone call for you?
♦ NOTE: This is a play-on-words from the expression *"to field a ball"* meaning "to catch the ball."
♦ ALSO: **to field** *v.* to give an unrehearsed answer • *He fielded questions at his presentation with great confidence;* He answered questions at his presentation with great confidence.

hit a home run (to) *exp.* to reach a big goal (and get more than

expected) • *After I sold him his new car, the rest of his family came in the next day and bought five new cars! I guess I really hit a home run!;* After I sold him his new car, the rest of his family came in the next day and bought five new cars! I guess I really reached an unexpected goal!
♦ ORIGIN: A *"home run"* is the goal in baseball where the batter hits the ball so far that he is able to run to all the bases and score.

home free (to be) *exp.* to be assured of attaining one's goal • *Once I get done with this last assignment, I'm home free;* Once I get done with this last assignment, I'll definitely achieve my goal.
♦ ORIGIN: In baseball, a player who is sure to get to home base

and score a run, is considered to be *"home free."*

in the ballpark (to be) *exp.* to be within the general range • *You're probably in the ballpark when you say the company has made four million dollars this year;* You're probably very close when you say the company has made four million dollars this year.
‣ ORIGIN: This expression describes a baseball which has not been hit outside the confines of the ballpark.

in the same league as someone or something (to be) *exp.* to be at the same level as someone (in expertise, wealth, beauty, etc.) • *We can't compete against that company. For now, we're just not in the same league;* We can't compete against that company. For now, we're just not on the same (high) level.
‣ ALSO: **major league** *n.* a team of highly skilled professionals • (lit); a team of highly skilled baseball players • *You're in the major league now. If you don't feel very confident in your abilities, please don't accept employment with our company;* You're working with highly skilled professionals now. If you don't feel very confident in your abilities, please don't accept employment with our company.
⇨ SYNONYM: **big league** *n.*

keep one's eye on the ball (to) *exp.* to pay careful attention to what one is doing • *Rick has the potential of being a great employee if he'd just learn to keep his eye on the ball;* Rick has the potential of being a great employee if he'd just learn to pay careful attention to what he's doing.
‣ ORIGIN: In baseball, the best way for a batter to effectively hit the ball is to *"keep his eye on the ball"* from the moment it is thrown by the pitcher.

pinch hit (to) *exp.* to take someone's place • *Can you pinch hit at the meeting for me? I have to leave town suddenly;* Can you substitute for me at the meeting? I have to leave town suddenly.
‣ NOTE: **pinch hitter** *n.* one who takes over for another person • (lit); a baseball player who takes over for another player at bat usually because he is a superior batter and it is a crucial point in the game.

pitch one's ideas (to) *exp.* to present one's concepts about something (like a baseball pitcher who throws one ball after the other) • *Tomorrow I'm going to pitch my movie ideas to some big Hollywood producers!;* Tomorrow I'm going to present my concepts to some big Hollywood producers!

◗ VARIATION: **to make a pitch** *exp.*

rain check (to take a) *exp.* to postpone • *I think I'm just too sick to meet with you today. Can I take a rain check?;* I think I'm just too sick to meet with you today. Can I postpone it?
◗ ORIGIN: Baseball is commonly called off if rain occurs. Instead of giving the fans their money back, they are typically offered a *"rain check"* in the form of a ticket stub to see the game at a later date.

"Three strikes and you're out!" *exp.* "You've attempted that three times and now it's time to give up!"
◗ ORIGIN: In baseball, when a batter misses the ball three times *(three "strikes"),* he strikes out and ends his turn at bat.

two strikes against oneself (to have) *exp.* to have done two offensive deeds with only one remaining before severe consequences occur • *First you told the president of the company you didn't like his shirt, and then you suggested he should lose weight! That's two strikes against you!;* First you told the president of the company you didn't like his shirt, and then you suggested he should lose weight! If you make one more offensive comment, you're going to have to face the consequences!
◗ ORIGIN: In baseball, the batter is allowed two misses or *"strikes."* A third strike will get him disqualified.

Basketball

shoot (to) *v.* to begin • *"I have a great idea for a new advertising campaign." "Okay, shoot!;"* "I have a great idea for a new advertising campaign." "Okay, tell me!"

Boxing

go a few rounds with someone (to) *exp.* to fight with someone on several issues • *I just went a few rounds with the boss;* I just had a fight with the boss on several issues.

◗ ORIGIN: In boxing, the match is divided into rounds.

heavyweight (to be a) *exp.* to be an important and powerful person within the organizational structure of a company • *My* *mother is a heavyweight at Star Oil Company;* My mother is an important and powerful person at Star Oil Company.

♦ ANTONYM: **to be a lightweight** *exp.* • (lit); to be a boxer whose low weight puts him in the "lightweight" category • *Don't*

let him tell you what to do. He's just a lightweight around here; Don't let him tell you what to do. He has a low position around here.

♦ ORIGIN: Said of a boxer whose weight puts him in the "lightweight" category.

Football

game plan *n.* strategy • *If this company is to make more money this year, we're going to have to change our game plan and start working more efficiently;* If this company is to make more money this year, we're going to have to change our strategy and start working more efficiently.

♦ ORIGIN: In football, the coach devises a strategy or *"game plan"* before the start of each game determining which moves the players will make to beat the other team.

huddle (to) *v.* to have a private meeting • *We need to huddle in my office right away;* We need to meet in my office right away.

make a fumble (to) *exp.* to make a mistake • *I told everyone the meeting was for noon tomorrow and I just found out it's for today! I guess I really made a fumble;* I told everyone the meeting was for noon tomorrow and I just found out it's for

today! I guess I really made a mistake.

♦ ORIGIN: In football, when a player accidentally drops the ball during a play, this "mistake" is called a *"fumble."*

run interference for someone (to) *exp.* to block a potential problem from going to someone else • *I really appreciate that you took care of that angry client for me. Thank you for running interference for me;* I really appreciate that you took care of that angry client for me. Thank you for sparing me the aggravation.

run with it (to) *exp.* to implement something • *I like your idea for the client's advertising campaign. I want you to run with it;* I like your idea for the client's advertising campaign. I want you to implement it.

♦ VARIATION: **to take the ball and run with it** *exp.* to take charge and implement something.

♦ ORIGIN: In football, the player with the ball must do everything possible to *"run with it"* without stopping, in order to make the goal.

tackle a problem (to) *exp.* to attack a problem with full force (as a football player "tackles" another player) • *Many of our employees are leaving earlier than they should. We need to tackle this problem before it gets any worse;* Many of our employees are leaving earlier than they should. We need to attack this problem before it gets any worse.

Horse Racing

down to the wire (to be) *exp.* to be very close to the moment when something is due • *Your report is due in the president's office in ten minutes! You're really down to the wire!;* Your report is due in the president's office in ten minutes! You're really close to the time it's due!
♦ ORIGIN: In horse racing, the *"wire"* indicates the finishing line.

first out of the gate (to be) *exp.* to be the first person to begin a project • *Although we were just given assignments by the boss a few minutes ago, Allen has already started! He's always the first out of the gate;* Although we were just given assignments by the boss a few minutes ago, Allen has already started! He's always the first to begin a project.
♦ ORIGIN: Said of a horse which leaves the starting gate before the other horses during a race.

in the homestretch (to be) *exp.* to be close to completion • *We're finally in the homestretch with this project;* We're finally close to completing this project.
♦ ORIGIN: In horse racing, the final distance the horses have to travel (between the last turn and the finish line) is called the *"homestretch."*

jockey for position (to) *exp.* to maneuver for an advantage • *We'll have to jockey for position if we want to get a good contract;* We'll have to maneuver for an advantage if we want to get a good contract.

left at the gate (to be) *exp.* to be abandoned • *I left the office for a few minutes and when I got back, everyone had gone to lunch without me. That's the second time this week I got left at the gate;* I left the office for a few minutes and when I got back, everyone had gone to lunch

without me. That's the second time this week I got abandoned.
 ◗ ORIGIN: During a horse race, any horse not leaving the starting gate with the others is considered to be *"left at the gate."*

neck and neck (to be) *exp.* to be even in a contest • (lit); said of horses in a race who are even with one another • *The two candidates are neck and neck. This election is going to be close!;* The two candidates are running even. This election is going to be close!

right out of the chute (to be) *exp.* to be inexperienced • (lit); said of a horse who dashes out of the starting gate at a race • *Don't give him too many responsibilities right away. He's right out of the chute and may*

need to get some more experience first; Don't give him too many responsibilities right away. He's brand new and may need to get some more experience first.
 ◗ NOTE: This expression is also used in the rodeo where a steer, bull, or untrained horse crashes out of the gate of the holding pen.

win by a nose (to) *exp.* to win by a very small margin • *I can't believe she was voted the best employee of the year. At least she only won by a nose;* I can't believe she was voted the best employee of the year. At least she only won by a very small margin.
 ◗ ORIGIN: Said of a horse race where one horse wins over the other by the length of a nose.

Sailing

"Every man for himself!" *exp.* "Every person must take care of himself (since no one else will)" • *In business, it's "every man for himself;"* In business, it's "each person must take care of himself (since no one else will)."
 ◗ ORIGIN: During times of war, the maritime tradition has been that each man must take care of himself and do whatever he can in order to stay alive.

even keel (to be on an) *exp.* to be steady and well balanced • *We had a lot of problems with this project but it's finally on an even keel;* We had a lot of problems with this project but it's finally steady.
 ◗ ORIGIN: The bottommost part of a boat or ship which runs lengthwise from the front (*"the bow"*) of the vessel to the back (*"the stern"*). When a vessel is

tilting to either side, it is said to be on an *"uneven keel."*

go down with the ship (to) *exp.* to stay with a project right down to its collapse • *Our new product isn't generating sales yet, but I'm still going to promote it because I believe in it. I may go down with the ship in the process, but at least I didn't give up!;* Our new product isn't generating sales yet, but I'm still going to promote it because I believe in it. The whole project may collapse, but at least I didn't give up!
♦ ORIGIN: In Maritime tradition a captain never gave up his vessel even if it meant *"going down with the ship."*

like the cut of someone's jib (to) *exp.* to like someone • *He's the kind of person I want working with us. I really like the cut of his jib;* He's the kind of person I want working with us. I really like him.
♦ NOTE: A *"jib"* is an additional triangular sail used in larger sail boats.

rough seas ahead (to have) *exp.* to have many difficulties and challenges in the near future • *The project may seem easy at first look, but I can assure you we have rough seas ahead;* The project may seem easy at first look, but I can assure you we're going to have many difficulties

and challenges with it in the future.

shape up or ship out (to) *exp.* to conduct oneself in accordance with a company's policy or resign • *I'm tired of you coming in to work late every morning. I'm warning you, you'd better shape up or ship out!;* I'm tired of you coming in to work late every morning. I'm warning you, you'd better conduct yourself in accordance with this company's policy or resign!

smooth sailing (to be) *exp.* said of a project which is working out well with no obstacles • *Now that we've solved all the problems with this project, the rest should be smooth sailing;* Now that we've solved all the problems with this project, the rest should work out easily.

take the wind out of one's sails (to) *exp.* to lose one's enthusiasm due to discouragement • *I was so excited about my new job until I found out that I was only going to be paid half my normal salary. That took the wind out of my sails;* I was so excited about my new job until I found out that I was only going to be paid half my normal salary. That made me lose my enthusiasm because I got so discouraged.
♦ ORIGIN: This expression is used

to describe a sailboat that loses speed due to the lack of wind.

walk the plank (to make someone) *exp.* to kill someone (figuratively) • *The boss is gonna make you walk the plank when he hears how much of the company's money you spent!;* The boss is going to punish you severely when he hears how much of the company's money you spent!
‣ ORIGIN: In the days of pirates, enemies were killed by being forced to walk off the end of a wooden plank into the ocean. This was referred to as *"walking the plank."*

Swimming

dive [right] in (to) *exp.* to begin a task without hesitation • *I'm very excited about being part of your company. I can't wait to dive [right] in;* I'm very excited about being part of your company. I can't wait to begin working right away.
‣ ORIGIN: Many people who swim need to determine whether or not the water temperature before jumping in. Others are able to *"dive right in"* without having to adapt first.

drowning in something (to be) *exp.* to be submerged in something • *I'm drowning in work today;* I'm submerged in work today.
‣ ORIGIN: If a person goes in a large body of water without the proper swimming skills, he/she may *"drown"* (i.e. risk falling below the surface of the water, unable to breathe).

get one's feet wet (to) *exp.* to start a new project cautiously • *If you need some important decisions made about the project, you may want to ask Ms. Newman and not me. I just started working here last week and I'm still getting my feet wet;* If you need some important decisions made about the project, you may want to ask Ms. Newman and not me. I just started working here last week and am still very new to the project.
‣ ORIGIN: Instead of jumping right into a body of water, some people prefer to adjust to the water temperature by *"getting their feet wet"* then gradually move their entire bodies in the water.

go in headfirst (to) *exp.* to do something impulsively without researching the consequences • *He took a big risk by going in headfirst with an expensive*

advertising campaign.
Fortunately it brought sales way
up; He took a big risk by starting
an expensive advertising
campaign without regard for
the financial consequences.
Fortunately it brought sales
way up.
  ▶ ORIGIN: A swimmer who dives
into the water without checking
the water temperature is said to
"go in headfirst."

in deep water (to be) *exp.* to be in
  trouble • *If we don't sell at least*
  thirty thousand dollars worth of
  products within the next month,
  we're going to be in deep water;
  If we don't sell at least thirty
  thousand dollars worth of
  products within the next month,
  we're going to be in big trouble.
  ▶ ORIGIN: When a swimmer is in
  deep water for an extended
  period of time, he/she risks
  exhaustion and, consequently,
  drowning.

jump off the deep end (to) *exp.* to
  take immediate and drastic action
  • *Our competitor is about to*
  introduce a new product which
  will take sales away from us. I
  think it's time to jump off the
  deep end and begin whatever
  advertising campaign it takes to
  publicize our product; Our
  competitor is about to introduce a
  new product which will take
  sales away from us. I think it's
  time to take immediate and

drastic action and begin whatever
advertising campaign it takes to
publicize our product.
  ▶ ORIGIN: When a swimmer
jumps off the deep end of the
pool, there is no immediate
bottom in sight. In business, this
expression refers to the
open-ended limit in spending.

sink or swim (to) *exp.* to be time to
  exert a big effort in order to get
  something done or face the
  consequences of failure • *This*
  business is so competitive that
  it's sink or swim; This business is
  so competitive that you have to
  either exert a lot of effort in what
  you do or fail.
  ▶ ORIGIN: In business, this
  expression refers to a worker
  who has the choice of either
  working hard (*"swimming"*) or
  being terminated due to loafing
  (*"sinking"*).

test the water (to) *exp.* to verify
  whether or not one's plan will
  work before proceeding • *Before*
  we proceed with our advertising
  campaign for this product, let's
  test the water and get people's
  reaction; Before we proceed
  with our advertising campaign
  for this product, let's verify
  whether or not it will be effective
  by getting people's reaction.
  ▶ ORIGIN: Before swimming,
  people often *"test the water"*
  temperature to make sure it's not
  too cold before jumping in.

Tennis

"The ball's in your court" *exp.*
"It's up to you to make the next move" • *This is the best salary I can offer you to take this job. The ball's in your court;* This is the best salary I can offer you to take this job. It's up to you to make the next move.
♦ ORIGIN: This expression is said to a tennis player who has received the ball on his/her side of the court and must therefore make the next move.

Track & Field

a close second (to come in) *exp.* to come close to being chosen as first choice for something • *We could only hire one person and decided to choose someone else. You came in a close second;* We could only hire one person and decided to choose someone else. You did come very close to being chosen.
♦ ORIGIN: Said of a track and field runner who misses getting first place by an extremely short distance.

clear a hurdle (to) *exp.* to overcome an obstacle • *There are only a few more hurdles we have to clear before the company starts making a profit;* There are only a few more obstacles we have to overcome before the company starts making a profit.
♦ ORIGIN: In track and field, hurdles are set up on the track as obstacles which the runners must jump over without falling or breaking their stride.

inside track (to have the) *exp.* to have the advantage • *There are a lot of good candidates for the promotion but Pete has the inside track because the boss and he went to the same school;* There are a lot of good candidates for the promotion but Pete has the advantage because the boss and he went to the same school.
♦ ORIGIN: In track and field, the runner who runs on the inside track has an advantage over the others since he/she has the shortest distance to run.

jump the gun (to) *exp.* to start something before the time is right, to act prematurely • *The contractor jumped the gun and started the next phase of construction before the client approved it;* The contractor acted prematurely and started the next phase of construction before the client approved it.
♦ ORIGIN: In track and field, a gun is sounded which indicates the

beginning of the race. Sometimes in anticipation of the gun's explosion, a runner may inadvertently start forward or *"jump the gun."*

keep pace with someone or something (to) *exp.* to stay current • *As a clothing manufacturer, we need to keep pace with today's fashion;* As a clothing manufacturer, we need to keep current with today's fashion.
▶ ORIGIN: In track and field, it is important that the runners do not run faster than the first runner or they risk exhaustion later in the race. They must, therefore, *"keep pace with"* the front runner and conserve their energy.

marathon *n.* said of work which takes many long hours to complete • *It looks like I'm going to be home late. I'm doing a marathon at work;* It looks like I'm going to be home late. I have to work for several more hours at work.
▶ ORIGIN: A very long track and field race.

pace oneself (to) *exp.* to adjust one's speed in order not to reach exhaustion after beginning a job

• *Now that Nancy left on vacation, I'm doing her job as well as mine. If I don't pace myself, I'm going to be exhausted in just a few days;* Now that Nancy left on vacation, I'm doing her job as well as mine. If I don't adjust my speed, I'm going to be exhausted in just a few days.
▶ ORIGIN: In track and field, it is important that the runners adjust their speed or *"pace themselves"* in order not to expend all of their energy at once, leading to exhaustion before the end of the race.

set the pace (to) *exp.* to establish the speed at which everyone else will work • *Our supervisor is extremely relaxed and she's the one who sets the pace for the rest of the department;* Our supervisor is extremely relaxed and she's the one who establishes the speed at which the rest of the department works.
▶ ORIGIN: In track and field, the front runner establishes the speed or *"sets the pace"* at which the other runners will run toward the beginning of the race. This is a way for the other runners to conserve their energy until later in the race.

Practice Sports Terms in Business

(Answers, p. 231)

A. Circle the letter which corresponds to the correct definition of the words in boldface.

1. **to get the ball rolling**:
   a. to quit
   b. to begin

2. **to bounce something off someone**:
   a. to have a fight with someone
   b. to test someone's reaction to an idea

3. **to be in the ballpark**:
   a. to be within the general range
   b. to be tired

4. **to keep one's eye on the ball**:
   a. to pay careful attention to what one is doing
   b. to be careless

5. **to take a rain check**:
   a. to have a good time
   b. to postpone

6. **to go a few rounds with someone**:
   a. to eat with someone
   b. to fight with someone on several issues

7. **to run with it**:
   a. to implement something
   b. to steal something

8. **to be down to the wire**:
   a. to be depressed
   b. to be very close to the moment when something is due

9. **to be in the home stretch**:
   a. to be far from completion of a project
   b. to be close to completion of a project

10. **to be neck and neck:**
    a. to be even in a contest
    b. to strangle someone

11. **to be on an even keel:**
    a. to be confused and disorderly
    b. to be steady and well balanced

12. **to take the wind out of one's sails:**
    a. to lose one's enthusiasm due to discouragement
    b. to begin a project

ANSWERS TO LESSONS 1-8

LESSON ONE - General Office Slang
"The Big Wigs"

Practice the Vocabulary

A.
1. wigs
2. rug
3. down
4. head
5. down
6. jump
7. in
8. pounding
9. driver
10. buns

B.
1. J
2. D
3. A
4. E
5. I
6. G
7. C
8. H
9. B
10. F

C. WORD SEARCH

1. cover
2. contacts
3. kiss
4. carpet
5. can
6. scuttlebutt
7. kowtow
8. buckle
9. wig
10. pusher

N	A	R	K	O	W	T	O	W	S	A	N	A	A
B	B	G	B	U	B	B	L	T	B	T	U	B	K
C	U	C	O	R	C	H	C	A	R	P	E	T	I
I	C	O	D	X	D	A	D	W	C	D	B	D	S
S	K	I	E	W	T	E	B	I	E	A	E	E	S
W	L	O	O	N	Y	F	L	G	B	F	N	F	F
H	E	G	O	G	G	L	F	G	C	G	K	U	P
E	L	C	O	V	E	R	H	B	H	K	E	E	L
F	P	I	S	C	U	T	T	L	E	B	U	T	T
E	R	P	J	P	U	S	H	E	R	J	L	P	J

Practice Using Universal Business Slang, Idioms, & Jargon

A. 1. back
    2. blew
    3. blue
    4. breadwinner
    5. speed
    6. cush

    7. cut
    8. draw
    9. through
    10. clock
    11. cut
    12. red

Practice Using Office Party Jargon

B. 1. small talk
    2. mingle
    3. to be fashionably late
    4. bash

    5. make an entrance
    6. shmooze
    7. to put in an appearance

Practice Using Common Slang Synonyms for Business-Related Terms

C. 1. a, b, d, e
    2. a, c, d, e, f
    3. b, c, d, e
    4. c, d, e, f

LESSON TWO - Computer Slang
"The New PC Clone"

Practice the Vocabulary

A. 1. b   7. b
    2. a   8. a
    3. b   9. b
    4. b   10. a
    5. a   11. b
    6. b   12. a

B. 1. crashed   5. friendly   9. joystick
    2. boot   6. glitch   10. WYSIWYG
    3. BBS   7. down   11. backup
    4. PC   8. modem   12. clone

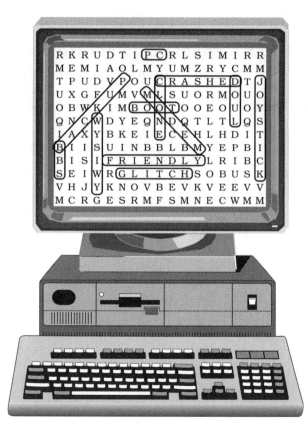

C. 1. J   6. D
    2. F   7. C
    3. G   8. E
    4. A   9. I
    5. H   10. B

Practice Using Advanced Computer Slang & Jargon

A. 1. abort   6. default
    2. bug   7. drive
    3. cache   8. end
    4. click   9. mainframe
    5. crunching   10. write

LESSON THREE - Meeting/Negotiation Jargon
"A Brainstorming Session!"

Practice the Vocabulary

A. 1. aye   6. move
    2. order   7. person
    3. brainstorm   8. table
    4. floor   9. minutes
    5. quorum   10. order

B. 1. brainstorm   6. floor
    2. recognizes   7. minutes
    3. adjourned   8. hold
    4. quorum   9. carries
    5. aye

C. 1. L   7. E
    2. H   8. K
    3. J   9. C
    4. D   10. I
    5. G   11. F
    6. B   12. A

Practice Jargon Used in Meetings & Negotiations

A. 1. stonewall   7. cut
    2. proxy   8. give and take
    3. standstill   9. rock-bottom
    4. back down   10. win-win
    5. barter
    6. come down

LESSON FOUR - Business Travel Jargon
"The Red-Eye"

Practice the Vocabulary

A. 1. c   6. c
    2. a   7. a
    3. c   8. c
    4. a   9. a
    5. b   10. a

B. 1. b   6. c
    2. c   7. a
    3. a   8. a
    4. c   9. c
    5. a   10. b

C. 1. to be in a ship, aircraft, car, etc.

T	O		B	E		O	N
B	**O**	**A**	**R**	**D**			

2. to commute with very little luggage.

T	O		T	R	A	V	E	L
L	**I**	**G**	**H**	**T**				

3. to reserve something (such as a hotel, flight, room, etc.)

T	O		**B**	**O**	**O**	**K**
S	O	M	E	T	H	I	N	G

4. said of an area which is so thick with fog as to impede all traffic.

T	O		B	E		**F**	**O**	**G**	**G**	**E**	**D**
I	N										

5. to upgrade someone's accommodations.

T	O		**B**	**U**	**M**	**P**
S	O	M	E	O	N	E		U	P

6. the front of the plane where the pilot controls the airplane.

C	O	C	K	P	I	T

7. winds which blow toward the aircraft.

| H | E | A | D | | W | I | N | D | S | | |

8. the class between first class and coast, also called "Executive Class."

| B | U | S | I | N | E | S | S | |
| C | L | A | S | S | | | | |

9. said of a flight which makes a stop before continuing to its final destination.

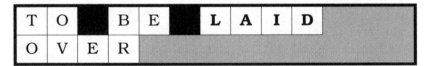

| T | O | | B | E | | L | A | I | D | |
| O | V | E | R | | | | | | | |

10. an economical class of accommodations in an airplane or train.

| C | O | A | C | H | | |

11. said of one who has traveled to a location in a different time zone and whose body has not yet adapted to the time change.

| T | O | | H | A | V | E | | J | E | T | |
| L | A | G | | | | | | | | | |

12. to register oneself into a hotel.

| T | O | | C | H | E | C | K | | I | N | T | O |
| A | | H | O | T | E | L | | | | | | |

Practice Using Business Travel Slang & Jargon

LESSON FIVE - **Marketing Jargon**
"A Cash Cow"

A. 1. b

2. a

3. c

4. a

5. b

6. a

7. b

8. b

B. 1. blitz

2. cutting

3. rebate

4. hook

5. tie

6. list

7. cold

8. Yuppies

9. target

10. launch

11. focus

12. line

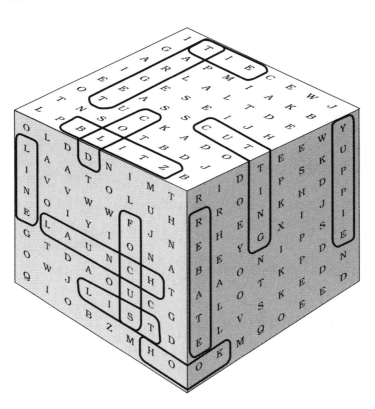

C. 1. E   5. F
    2. A   6. B
    3. H   7. C
    4. G   8. D

Practice Advanced Marketing Jargon

A. 1. designer   6. gatekeepers
    2. door   7. gray
    3. drops   8. pitch
    4. flagship   9. state
    5. flanker   10. window

LESSON SIX - **Advertising Jargon**
"Plugging a Product"

Practice the Vocabulary

A. 1. prime time   7. truck
    2. storyboard   8. pull
    3. jingle   9. spot
    4. paste   10. plug
    5. blurb   11. puff
    6. dummy ad   12. copy

B. 1. jingle   6. A.E.
    2. shot   7. up
    3. blow   8. pull
    4. blurb   9. storyboard
    5. talent   10. mouth

C. 1. E   6. I
    2. B   7. H
    3. D   8. J
    4. C   9. G
    5. A   10. F

Practice Advertising Slang & Jargon

A. 1. b   5. b
   2. a   6. a
   3. b   7. b
   4. a   8. a

LESSON SEVEN - Finance Slang & Jargon
"In the Black"

Practice the Vocabulary

A. 1. b   6. a
   2. c   7. b
   3. c   8. a
   4. a   9. b
   5. b   10. a

B.   **CROSSWORD PUZZLE**

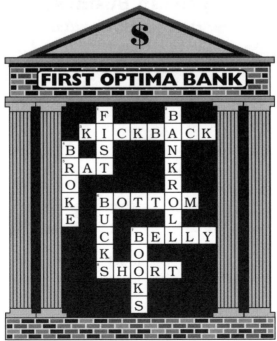

C. 1. J   6. B
    2. D   7. C
    3. I   8. E
    4. H   9. G
    5. A   10. F

Practice Advanced Finance Terms

A. 1. board   7. bull
    2. annuity   8. capital
    3. asset   9. dividend
    4. balance   10. escrow
    5. bear   11. front
    6. Board   12. return

LESSON EIGHT - Sports Terms Used In Business
"Batting a Thousand"

Practice the Vocabulary

A. 1. B   6. D
    2. I   7. A
    3. E   8. G
    4. F   9. J
    5. C   10. H

B. 1. ball   7. scores
    2. thousand   8. rules
    3. bat   9. base
    4. running   10. towel
    5. hardball   11. points
    6. shots   12. curve

C.

Practice Sports Terms in Business

A. 1. b
2. b
3. a
4. a
5. b

6. b
7. a
8. b
9. b

Glossary

-A-

A.E. *n.* an abbreviation for *"Account Executive,"* the person who personally handles a client's account • *I just got assigned as AE for our biggest client!;* I just got assigned as Account Executive for our biggest client!

antidote *n.* a program used to "cure" a computer of a "virus" • *I think the computer has a virus which is why it's having trouble saving each document. Hopefully, this new program is the antidote;* I think the computer has a virus which is why it's having trouble saving each document. Hopefully, this new program is the cure.
▶ SEE: **virus** *n.*

aye *n.* used to indicate a positive vote or "I am in favor" • *How many people are in favor of opening a new office downtown? Signify by saying "aye." The "ayes" have it;* How many people are in favor of opening a new office downtown? Signify by saying "yes." The "yes" votes prevail.
▶ SYNONYM: **yea / yah** *n.*
▶ ANTONYM: **nay** *n.* used to indicate a negative vote or "I am not in favor" • *The nays have it;* The majority of the members in this meeting are not in favor.

-B-

B&B *n.* This is a common abbreviation for a *"Bed and Breakfast"* which is an inn that offers sleeping accommodations as well as breakfast • *While we were on vacation, we found a great inexpensive B&B;* While we were on vacation, we found a great inexpensive inn which serves breakfast.

backup *n.* a copy of one's computer work on diskette or tape • *Be sure to make a backup of your work before leaving today;* Be sure to make a diskette (or tape) copy of your work before leaving today.
▶ VARIATION: **to backup** *v.* • *Don't forget to backup your work every day;* Don't forget to make a copy of your work on diskette (or tape) every day.

ballpark figure *exp.* estimate • *"How much money do you think the company made this year?" "I can only give you a ballpark figure;"* "How much money do you think the company made this year?" "I can only give you an estimate."
▶ ORIGIN: baseball.

bankroll someone (to) *v.* to pay for someone • *This is the last time I'm bankrolling you. Next time you'd better remember to bring your wallet;*

This is the last time I'm paying for you. Next time you'd better remember to bring your wallet.

♦ NOTE: A *"bankroll"* is literally a roll of paper money.

bat a thousand (to) *exp.* • **1.** to be successful at everything one does • *Every potential client you've brought into the company has decided to hire our services. You're really batting a thousand!;* Every potential client you've brought into the company has decided to hire our services. You're really successful every time! • **2.** to be unsuccessful at everything one does (used facetiously) • *I know it was an accident, but you insulted the boss for the third time today! You're really batting a thousand!;* I know it was an accident, but you insulted the boss for the third time today! You're really not being at all successful with him!

♦ ORIGIN: Baseball batting averages are determined by dividing the number of successful hits (by a specific batter) by the number of times at bat. The resulting number is traditionally carried out to the third decimal point. For example: a batter who has been at bat ten times and has hit the ball successfully three times, would be said to have a batting average of .300 (3 successful hits divided by 10 times at bat). However, since it is common in baseball to read the average as a three-digit number, the player would be said to be *"batting 300."* Therefore, a player who could hit the ball successfully every time at bat, would be *"batting a thousand."*

BBS *n.* an acronym for "Bulletin Board System" which is an electronic bulletin board system accessed through a modem-equipped computer where users may leave messages for each other or converse using the keyboard • *I wanted to find out where to buy a good printer so I left a message with one of the BBSs. Someone left me a reply that day;* I wanted to find out where to buy a good printer so I left a message with one of the electronic bulletin board systems. Someone left me a reply that day.

♦ SEE: **modem (to)** *v.*

beauty shot *n.* a view of a product, taken for either a commercial or print ad, which has been greatly enhanced in order to make the product look enticing through lighting, coloring, or whatever it takes to attract consumers • *It took almost three hours to get a beauty shot of this product;* It took almost three hours to get the ideal photo of this product.

bells and whistles *exp.* unnecessary yet enticing features • *This computer is so expensive because it comes with a special tape backup system, scanner, and modem. I just don't want to pay for all those bells and whistles!;* This computer is so expensive because it comes with a special tape backup system, scanner, and modem. I just don't want to pay for extra features I don't need!

belly up (to go) *exp.* to go out of business (usually due to reasons beyond the control of the owner such as financial trouble) • *If our company isn't profitable within the next few months, we'll go belly up;* If our company isn't profitable within the next few months, we'll go out of business.

♦ ORIGIN: This expression was derived from the fact that when a fish dies, it floats belly up on the surface of the water.

♦ SYNONYM (1): **to close up shop** *exp.* to go out of business (voluntary or otherwise) • *My father decided to close up shop and retire;* My father decided to go out of business and retire. • *My father was forced to close up shop because he couldn't renew his lease;* My father was forced to go out of business because he couldn't renew his lease.

♦ SYNONYM (2): **pull the plug (to)** *exp.* • **1.** to go out of business • *Goober Printing couldn't make a profit so they had to pull the plug;* Goober Printing couldn't make a profit so they had to go out of business. • **2.** to discontinue a business project • *The editor just pulled the plug on publishing any more books on travel;* The editor just discontinued publishing any more books on travel.

♦ SYNONYM (3): **to shutter** *v.* to terminate or close up a business • *The largest car manufacturer in the city just decided to shutter its oldest plant;* The largest car manufacturer in the city just decided to close its oldest plant.

⇨ ORIGIN: A *"shutter"* is a hinged door, usually made of wood, used to protect windows and/or close up a home (in the event of a storm or a prolonged vacancy).

♦ SYNONYM (4): **to go toes** *exp.* to go out of business • *The business went toes in just six months;* The business went out of business in just six months.

⇨ ORIGIN: This is a shortened version of the expression *"to go toes up"* which refers to someone who has fallen dead on his/her back with the toes pointed straight up.

bet one's bottom dollar (to) *exp.* to be willing to gamble all one's money (down to the last dollar in the very bottom of one's pockets) because of having enormous faith in something • *You can bet your bottom dollar that if she says a product will sell well, it will!;* You can bet all of your money that if she says a product will sell well, it will!

between jobs (to be) *exp.* an optimistic description of someone who is unemployed • *I'm between jobs at the moment;* I'm unemployed at the moment.

♦ SYNONYM: **to be in transition** *exp.*

big bucks (to spend) *exp.* to spend a lot of money • *I spent big bucks getting my car repaired;* I spent a lot of money getting my car repaired.

♦ SYNONYM: **to spend money like it's going out of style** *exp.* to spend a lot of money quickly.

big-wig *exp.* executive • *Someday, I'm going to be a big-wig in a large company;* Someday, I'm going to be an executive in a large company.

♦ NOTE: This expression comes from the old court system in England where the attorneys, jurors, and judge all wore similar white wigs.

blow-in an ad (to) *v.* to insert an advertisement between two pages in a book or magazine (by stitching it in with the other pages) • *I just found the perfect magazine where we should advertise our product. If the magazine hasn't gone to press yet, let's see about blowing-in an ad!;* I just found the perfect magazine where we should advertise our product. If the magazine hasn't gone to press yet, let's see about inserting an ad!

♦ ALSO: **blow-in** *n.* an insert.

⇨ SYNONYM: **stitch-in** *n.*

blurb *n.* a short (free) article written about a product or event • *Did you see the blurb about our play in today's newspaper?;* Did you see the short article about our play in today's newspaper?

♦ SYNONYM: **mention** *n.* • *Our company just got a mention in a national magazine!;* Our company just got mentioned in a short article in a national magazine!

♦ ALSO: **write-up** *n.* a detailed article about a product or event • *After reading the write-up about the movie, I can't wait to see it!;* After reading the detailed article about the movie, I can't wait to see it!

book a hotel, flight, room, etc. (to) *exp.* to reserve a hotel, flight, room, etc. in advance • *I had a lot of trouble booking my flight to Paris because all the planes were full! Luckily, there was a cancelation at the last minute;* I had a lot of trouble arranging my flight to Paris because all the planes were full! Luckily, there was a cancelation at the last minute.

books *n.pl.* the financial records of a company • *The books show we're losing money every month;* Our financial records show we're losing money every month.

boot (to) *v.* to start • *For some reason, the computer is having problems booting;* For some reason, the computer is having problems starting.

♦ SYNONYM: **to boot up** *v.* • *Your computer seems to take a long time booting up!;* Your computer seems to take a long time starting!

bottom line (the) *exp.* the central issue of a discussion • *There are all sorts of reasons why I don't want to*

hire Tim, but the bottom line is that I just don't like him; There are all sorts of reasons why I don't want to hire Tim, but the central issue is that I just don't like him.

♦ ORIGIN: A financial report lists a company's earnings and expenses followed by a calculation of the final profit shown on the *"bottom line"* of the report. The bottom line is considered the most important part of a financial report since it clearly indicates the worth of the company.

brainstorm (to) *v.* to gather in a group and spontaneously contribute ideas for solving problems • *We need to find a solution to this problem right away. I think we should have a meeting tomorrow with all the executives and brainstorm for a while;* We need to find a solution to this problem right away. I think we should have a meeting tomorrow with all the executives and study this for a while.

♦ ALSO (1): **brainstorming session** *exp.* a meeting where people gather and collectively arrive at decisions or solutions to a problem • *We're having a brainstorming session tomorrow to see how we can go about finding new clients;* We're having a decision-making meeting tomorrow to see how we can go about finding new clients.

♦ ALSO (2): **to have a brainstorm** *n.* to have a sudden clever idea • *I just had a brainstorm!;* I just had a great idea!

♦ SYNONYM (1): **to have a meeting of the minds** *exp.* • *We need to have a meeting of the minds in order to find a proper solution;* We need to have a meeting where we all try and arrive at a solution together.

♦ SYNONYM (2): **to put heads together** *exp.* • *I'm sure that if we put our heads together, we'll be able to come up with a great new product!;* I'm sure that if we think about this together, we'll be able to come up with a great new product!

buckle down (to) *exp.* to make an extra effort to get work done • *I just found out that the project is due in a week! That means for the next few days, we're really going to have to buckle down;* I just found out that the project is due in a week! That means for the few days, we're really going to have to make an extra effort to get work done.

bump someone up (to) *exp.* to upgrade someone's accommodations • (lit); to force someone to move by pushing him/her with a sudden jolt • *When the hotel manager found out my mother was a big executive, she was bumped up to the luxury suite!;* When the hotel manager found out my mother was a big executive, she was upgraded to the luxury suite!
♦ ALSO: **to bump someone** *exp.* to replace someone in a particular situation (such as a flight, a project, etc.) • *I got bumped from the flight for being a minute late!;* I got replaced on the flight for being a minute late!

business class *exp.* the class between first class and coach • *I couldn't afford to travel first class so I settled for business class;* I couldn't afford to travel first class so I settled for the class between first class and coach.
♦ NOTE: *"Business Class"* is also commonly referred to as *"Executive Class."*

bust one's buns (to) *exp.* to work excessively hard • (lit); to break one's buttocks • *I'm tired of busting my buns for such a low salary!;* I'm tired of working excessively hard for such a low salary!
♦ NOTE: In this expression, any synonym for "buttocks" may be used in place of *"buns."*

-C-

call in sick (to) *exp.* to call one's place of work and inform the proper authorities of one's absence due to illness • *She called in sick eight times this month!;* She called work eight times this month and told them she would be absent due to illness!

call it even (to) *exp.* to cancel another person's debt since he/she has returned something equal in value • *I know I paid for your lunch yesterday, but since you let me borrow your car today, let's just call it even;* I know I paid for your lunch yesterday, but since you let me borrow your car today, I'm canceling the debt.

call the shots (to) *exp.* to make the rules • *I know you want to be able to start work later, but you don't call the shots here;* I know you want to be able to start work later, but you don't make the rules here.
♦ ORIGIN: This expression comes from pool where each player announces the target-pocket for each shot. This is known as *"calling the shots."*

call to order (to) *exp.* to start a meeting • *The meeting was called to order at nine o'clock in the morning;* The meeting was started at nine o'clock in the morning.
♦ VARIATION: **to come to order** *exp.*
• *This meeting will now come to order.*

call up a document (to) *exp.* to retrieve a computer document on the screen • *Would you please call up the document we worked on yesterday? We need to make some changes;* Would you please retrieve the document we worked on yesterday? We need to make some changes.

called on the carpet (to be) *exp.* to be reprimanded by one's boss • *Tom got called on the carpet for being late to work again;* Tom got reprimanded by the boss for being late to work again.
♦ VARIATION: **to be called on the mat** *exp.*

can someone (to) *v.* • to fire someone • *She canned her secretary for working too slowly;* She fired her secretary for working too slowly.
♦ ALSO: **to get canned** *adj.* to get fired • *I got canned for no reason!;* I got fired for no reason!

cash cow *n.* a product which makes money simply by being on the market without expensive advertising • *This new food processor is a real cash cow! We haven't done any advertising at all and it just keeps selling!;* This new food processor attracts customers just by being on the market! We haven't done any advertising at all and it just keeps selling!

chairperson *n.* moderator • *She's going to be the chairperson for the conference;* She's going to be the moderator for the conference.
♦ NOTE: The term *"chairperson"* is a transformation of the noun "chairman." Since a chairman can be either a man or a woman, the term was deemed sexist by feminist groups and was transformed into a nongender-specific noun.

check into a hotel (to) *exp.* to register oneself into a hotel • *I believe Mr. Hammond just checked in;* I believe Mr. Hammond just registered himself (into the hotel).
♦ ANTONYM: **to check out of a hotel** *exp.*

check one's luggage (to) *exp.* to relinquish one's luggage to a special airline agent in exchange for a claim ticket • *We'd better arrive at the airport a little early so you can check your luggage;* We'd better arrive at the airport a little early so you can relinquish your luggage to the airline agent in exchange for a claim ticket.
♦ NOTE: A passenger usually checks his/her luggage at the *"Baggage Check-In"* desk. Although the term "luggage" is a common synonym for "baggage," it would be very rare to see a sign for "Luggage" Check-In.

clone *n.* a personal computer that has similar functions to a name brand such as the IBM Personal Computer • *I never thought I could afford a personal computer, so I bought a clone;* I never thought I could afford a personal computer, so I bought a reproduction which is really the same thing only cheaper.

coach *n.* an economical class of accommodations in an airplane or train • *I always travel coach so I can spend my money on the good restaurants!;* I always travel economically so I can spend my money on the good restaurants!

cockpit *n.* the front of the plane where the pilot controls the airplane • *My father is a pilot and always lets me sit with him in the cockpit;* My father is a pilot and always lets me sit with him in the front of the airplane.

cold call *n.* a marketing strategy where an unsolicited telephone call (or personal visit) is made to a potential customers in the hope of making a sale • *I hate making cold calls because many of the people who answer the phone resent that I'm bothering them at home;* I hate making unsolicited telephone calls to potential customers because many of the people who answer the phone resent that I'm bothering them at home.

copy *n.* the written text in a commercial • *Now that you've had a chance to look over the copy, are you ready for your audition?;* Now that you've had a chance to look over the written text for the commercial, are you ready for your audition?

corporate image *n.* the general impression the public has about a company's "personality" (i.e. friendly, helpful, service-oriented, etc.) • *We need to change your corporate image in order to attract more customers. Right now when people think of your company, they think of a company that is indifferent to their needs;* We need to change the general impression the public has about your corporation in order to attract more customers. Right now when people think of your company, they think of a company that is indifferent to their needs.

cost an arm and a leg (to) *exp.* to cost a lot of money • *That new computer system must have cost an arm and a leg!;* That new computer system must have cost a lost of money!
♦ SYNONYM: **to cost a pretty penny** *exp.*

countermarketing *n.* the act of a company convincing people *not* to buy the product of another company • *Did you hear about the countermarketing our competitor is doing? I just heard a radio commercial that said "Our new laundry soap is much more effective than SPIFF Soap which doesn't rinse out all the way!";* Did you hear how our competitor is trying to convince people not to buy our product? I just heard a radio commercial that said "Our new laundry soap is much more effective than SPIFF Soap which doesn't rinse out all the way!"

cover for someone (to) *exp.* • **1.** to do someone else's job during his/her absence • *Would you mind covering for me while I'm on vacation?;* Would you mind doing my job for me while I'm on vacation? • **2.** to lie in order to protect someone from getting into a predicament • *You've got to stop taking two-hour lunches! The boss is asking too many questions and I'm tired of covering for you!;* You've got to stop taking two-hour lunches! The boss is asking too many questions and I'm tired of lying to protect you from getting into a predicament!

crash (to) *v.* • **1.** said of a computer which stops working unexpectedly due to a slight malfunction • *I was in the middle of working on my document and suddenly my computer crashed!;* I was in the middle of working on my document and suddenly my computer stopped functioning! • **2.** said of a computer which stops working unexpectedly due to a serious malfunction causing lose of valuable data • *All the operators were working on their terminals when suddenly the entire mainframe crashed! Everyone's* *files were instantly destroyed!;* All the operators were working on their terminals when suddenly the entire mainframe lost data! Everyone's files were instantly destroyed!

▸ SEE: **mainframe** *n.* (p. 66).

▸ ALSO: **system crash** *n.* a serious computer failure (resulting in loss of data) • *At two o'clock in the afternoon, we had a system crash which destroyed all the files we had been working on for the past three weeks!;* At two o'clock in the afternoon, we had a serious computer failure which destroyed all the files we had been working on for the past three weeks!

cutting edge (to be on the) *exp.* to be the leader in setting trends, to be in the forefront • *Paris is on the cutting edge of fashion;* Paris is the leader in setting trends in fashion. • *MBI is on the cutting edge of computer technology;* MBI is the leader in computer technology.

-D-

demographics *n.* a popular marketing term which refers to the characteristics of the population by specific groups such as age, race, religion, sex, income, etc. • *The demographics of Los Angeles shows a growing number of women. Therefore, our marketing efforts for women's perfume should be concentrated in that city;* An increasing group in Los Angeles is made up of women. Therefore, our marketing efforts for women's perfume should be concentrated in that city.

desktop publishing *n.* (also called "DTP") a name given to the growing field of computer users who typeset in-house publications on a small scale using a personal computer • *We've just begun to do desktop publishing for all our newsletters;* We've just begun to do in-house typesetting for all our newsletters.

▸ ALSO: **to desktop publish** *v.* • *Did you desktop publish this brochure?;* Did you typeset this brochure in-house?

display advertising *n.* the technique of using illustrations in an advertisement to attract the potential customer's attention.

donut *n.* the middle of a commercial where the advertiser may fill in with an appropriate narration for the product.

▸ NOTE: A typical donut begins with music and singing, then music only while the advertiser may do a narration for the product followed by more music and singing.

double-truck *n.* a large advertisement which spreads across two facing pages • *A double-truck may cost a lot of money to run, but it should attract a lot of new customers;* An advertisement which spreads across two facing pages may cost a lot of money to run, but it should attract a lot of new customers.

▸ SYNONYM: **spread** *n.*

down (to be) *adj.* said of a computer which is inoperative • *This computer is down right now. Why don't you try the one in my office?;* This computer is not working right now. Why don't you try the one in my office?

▸ ANTONYM: **to be up** *adj.* to be functioning • *The computer will be down for a while. We hope to have it up around noon;* The computer will be down for a while. We hope to have it functioning around noon.

download (to) *v.* to receive a file from another computer via a modem • *Before I download your file, how large is it? I want to be sure I have enough room on my hard disk;* Before I receive your file, how large is it? I want to be sure I have enough room on my hard disk.
 ▶ SEE: "A CLOSER LOOK" section: **hard disk** *n.* (p. 65).
 ▶ ANTONYM: **upload (to)** *v.* to transfer a file from one computer to another via a modem • *I'm going to upload the file to you. As soon as you get it, print it out and give it to the president of our company;* I'm going to transfer the file to you. As soon as you get it, print it out and give it to the president of our company.

drop the ball (to) *exp.* to shirk one's responsibilities suddenly • *For our big conference in Atlanta, Joe said he'd take care of all the travel arrangements. He got our plane tickets but didn't make the hotel reservations. This isn't the first time he's dropped the ball;* For our big conference in Atlanta, Joe said he'd take care of all the travel arrangements. He got our plane tickets but didn't make the hotel reservations. This isn't the first time he's shirked his responsibilities suddenly.
 ▶ ORIGIN: This expression comes from baseball where one of the goals of the players is to catch the ball after being hit by the other team's batter. (This forces the batter to lose his turn and prevents him from scoring a point.) However, if the player should *"drop the ball,"* the other team will have the advantage and may be able to score points.

dummy ad *n.* a preliminary version of an advertisement used to get an idea of how the final advertisement could look

• *I'm not sure I'm understanding your idea is for the ad. Why don't you create a dummy ad and let me see it?;* I'm not sure I'm understanding your idea is for the advertisement. Why don't you create a preliminary version of the ad and let me see it?

-E-

exec *n.* • a popular abbreviation of "executive" • *So, how does it feel to be a big exec now?;* So, how does it feel to be a big executive now?

-F-

facility *n.* the location where a meeting will be held • *We're going to hold the meeting at a new facility in Chicago;* We're going to hold the meeting at a new location in Chicago.
 ▶ SYNONYM: **site** *n.*

file *n.* a computer-generated document • *Don't forget the name of the file you created or you'll have trouble retrieving it!;* Don't forget the name of the document you created on the computer or you'll have trouble retrieving it!

flat broke (to be) *exp.* to be completely without money • *He's been flat broke for several months because he can't find a job;* He's had no money at all for several months because he can't find a job.
 ▶ ANTONYM: **to be loaded** *exp.* • **1.** to be extremely rich • **2.** to be intoxicated.

float someone a loan (to) *exp.* to loan someone money • *Can you float me a loan until next Friday?;* Can you loan me some money until next Friday?

floppy *n.* a shortened version of *"floppy disk"* which is a removable disk (typically measuring either 3 1/2" or 5 1/4" in diameter) where data is stored • *Make sure not to expose your floppy disk to extreme heat or it could destroy the data;* Make sure not to expose your removable disk to extreme heat or it could destroy the data.
⧫ NOTE: The flexible or *"floppy"* disks are housed in a square plastic envelope.
⧫ SYNONYM: **diskette** *n.*

focus group *n.* a carefully selected cross section of consumers hired by a manufacturer to give their reaction to a particular product • *Let's bring in a focus group to test our new soft drinks. The drink that gets the best overall reaction is the one we'll release to the market;* Let's bring in a cross section of consumers to test our new soft drinks. The drink that gets the best overall reaction is the one we'll release to the market.

fogged in (to be) *exp.* said of an area which is so thick with fog as to impede all traffic • *The flight is delayed because the airport is fogged in;* The flight is delayed because the airport is thick with fog.
⧫ SYNONYM: **to be socked in** *exp.*

-G-

gender-biased (to be) *adj.* to be aimed more to one sex over the other • *It would be easier to market those tennis shoes if they weren't gender-biased. They need to look less masculine and more neutral;* It would be easier to market those tennis shows if they weren't aimed toward one sex over the other. They need to look less masculine and more neutral.

get away (to) *exp.* to leave one's problems by taking a vacation • (lit); to extricate oneself from a situation • *After working on this project for sixty hours a week, it'll be nice to get away tomorrow!;* After working on this project for sixty hours a week, it'll be nice to take a vacation away from work!
⧫ ALSO: **getaway** *n.* said of a vacation place far away from everyday pressures • *Our new cabin is the perfect mountain getaway;* Our new cabin is the perfect place in the mountains to escape from everyday pressures.

get in (to) *exp.* to arrive • *Can you believe this new employee? She got in at noon today! When the boss finds out, she could lose her job;* Can you believe this new employee? She arrived at noon today! When the boss finds out, she could lose her job.

glitch *n.* a minor computer malfunction • *This computer doesn't seem to be working very well. It must have a glitch;* This computer doesn't seem to be working very well. It must have a malfunction.

go to bat for someone (to) *exp.* to try and convince someone to do a favor or service for someone else • *I don't know if the executives will be willing to give you the promotion but I promise I'll go to bat for you;* I don't know if the executives will be willing to give you the promotion but I promise I'll try and convince them.
⧫ ORIGIN: baseball.

good contacts (to have) *exp.* to know many influential people • *She shouldn't have any trouble finding a new job. She has a lot of good contacts in her field;* She shouldn't have any trouble finding a new job. She knows a lot of influential people in her field.

-H-

hand over fist (to make money)

exp. to make a lot of money on a continuous basis • *Ever since we started selling our cologne worldwide, we've been making money hand over fist!* Ever since we started selling our cologne worldwide, we've been making a lot of money continuously!
‣ NOTE: This expression conjures up an image of someone pulling in money, one hand over the other.

hang it up (to) *exp.* to quit a task; to give up • *You're never going to get the boss to give you a raise. Just hang it up!;* You're never going to get the boss to give you a raise. Just forget it!
‣ SYNONYM (1): **to drop it** *exp.*
‣ SYNONYM (2): **to give it up** *exp.*
‣ ORIGIN: This expression conjures up an image of someone giving up a specific task and *"hanging it up"* where it will lay dormant.

have the floor (to) *exp.* to have permission to speak • *It's not your turn to speak. Mr. Smith has the floor;* It's not your turn to speak. Mr. Smith has permission to speak.
‣ VARIATION (1): **to obtain the floor** *exp.* to get permission to speak.
‣ VARIATION (2): **to yield the floor** *exp.* to relinquish one's right to speak in order that another topic be discussed.

"He/she shoots, he/she scores!" *exp.* "He/she attempted something and succeeded! • *I heard you just signed three new clients today! He shoots, he scores!;* I heard

you just signed three new clients today! You attempted something and succeeded!
‣ NOTE: This expression is commonly announced during basketball games when a player makes two points.

head hunter *exp.* (very popular) employment agent, usually from an elite agency, hired by an employer to find qualified candidates; executive recruiter • (lit); a warrior who kills his victims and collects the heads as trophies • *A head hunter called me today to see if I was interested in a job supervising an entire department in a major company!;* An elite employment agent called me today to see if I was interested in a job supervising an entire department in a major company!

head winds *exp.* winds which blow toward the aircraft, slowing it down • *We're going to be about ten minutes late arriving in Los Angeles due to head winds;* We're going to be about ten minutes late arriving in Los Angeles due to winds blowing toward the aircraft.
‣ ANTONYM: **tail winds** *exp.* winds which blow in the same direction as the aircraft helping to increase its speed.

hold a meeting (to) *exp.* to conduct a meeting • *The meeting will be held tomorrow at noon;* The meeting will be conducted tomorrow at noon.

hold down a job (to) *exp.* to have a job • *It's difficult to hold down a job and raise two children at the same time;* It's difficult to have a job and raise two children at the same time.
‣ VARIATION: **to hold down a 9-to-5** *exp.* to have a job which begins at 9:00 A.M. and ends at 5:00 P.M.

hook *n.* **1.** a marketing idea that attracts or *"hooks"* the customer or media • *The toy company recently came up with a good hook for their slogan: "Our toys are safe. If you care about your child's safety, you'll look at ours first."* The toy company recently came up with a good marketing slogan: "Our toys are safe. If you care about your child's safety, you'll look at ours first;" • **2. the part of a commercial which the customer remembers** • *The part of the commercial where the children sing the product name in harmony is a great hook;* The part of the commercial where the children sing the product name in harmony is extremely memorable.
♦ ALSO: **to hook a client** *exp.* • *Our new slogan should really hook clients;* Our new slogan should really attract clients.

-I-

in the black (to be) *exp.* said of a company which is making a profit • *It took a long time, but we're finally in the black;* It took a long time, but we're finally making a profit.
♦ ANTONYM: **to be in the red** *exp.* to be making a loss.
♦ ORIGIN: Years ago, financial reports were traditionally filled in with two different colored inks; profits were listed in black and losses were listed in red. Although this method is no longer used, the expression still remains.

in the running (to be) *exp.* to be a candidate • *I just found out I'm in the running for the position of vice president of the company!;* I just found out I'm a candidate for the position of vice president of the company!

♦ ORIGIN: Said of a horse which is running evenly with the other horses during a race.
♦ ANTONYM: **to be out of the running** *exp.* to be no longer a candidate.

"It's back to the ol' ball game!" *exp.* • **1.** "I'd better get back to work!" **2.** "It's back to the original plan" • *We've tried every possible plan but none of them work as well as the first one. I guess it's back to the ol' ball game;* We've tried every possible plan but none of them work as well as the first one. I guess we'd better go back to the original plan.
♦ ORIGIN: This expression is said about a baseball player who returns to the game after a short break.

-J-

jet lag (to have) *exp.* said of one who has traveled to a location in a different time zone and whose body has not yet adapted to the time change • *I know it's midnight but I'm wide awake. It must be jet lag from my trip;* I know it's midnight but I'm wide awake. It must be that my body hasn't adapted to the time change yet.

jingle *n.* a short, irresistible combination of melody and lyrics used during a commercial to make consumers remember a particular product • *I can't get that jingle out of my head! It sure does make me remember the product;* I can't get that commercial song out of my head! It sure does make me remember the product.

joystick *exp.* a cursor devise resembling the control stick of an aircraft used for positioning the cursor on the computer

screen • *Now that I have a joystick, I can play all sorts of computer games;* Now that I have a stick control, I can play all sorts of computer games.
▶ SEE: **mouse** *n.* (p. 66).

jump through hoops (to) *exp.* to go through a long and burdensome process in order to achieve something • *The owner of the company made me jump through a lot of hoops to get my new position;* The owner of the company made me go through a long and burdensome process to get my new position.
▶ ORIGIN: This expression comes from animal trainers who teach animals various tricks such as jumping through hoops. It is applied to people who are forced to take a great deal of seemingly unnecessary and possibly humiliating steps in order to attain a goal.

-K-

kickback *n.* an unethical payment made to someone • *Every time he hires a printer for the company's brochures, the printer pays him. He's been getting kickbacks like this for years!;* Every time he hires a printer for the company's brochures, the printer pays him. He's been getting unethical payments like this for years!
▶ NOTE: This is an unethical payment made to someone who hires a company which agrees to pay (or *"kickback"*) money to the hiring-individual.

kiss-up to someone (to) *exp.* to flatter someone in the hopes of being given preferential treatment • *Did you see that? The new guy just went and bought the boss lunch. I can't believe the way this guy is trying to kiss up to the boss!;* Did you see that? The new

guy just went and bought the boss lunch. I can't believe the way this guy is trying to get preferential treatment from the boss!

know-how (to have) *exp.* to have expertise; to "know how" to do something • *Let him handle the account. He has a lot of know-how in this area;* Let him handle the account. He has a lot of expertise in this area.

kowtow (to) *v.* to bow and cater to someone's every desire • *If you want to advance in this company, you'll learn that you have to kowtow to the executives;* If you want to advance in this company, you'll learn that you have to cater to every desire of the executives.
▶ ORIGIN: This verb comes from Chinese literally meaning "to knock the head."

-L-

laid over (to be) *exp.* said of a flight which makes a stop (of undetermined length) before continuing to its final destination • *It looks like we're going to be laid over here for a few hours due to fog;* It looks like we're going to be stopped here for a few hours due to fog.
▶ ALSO: **lay-over** *n.* a stop made by an aircraft before continuing to its final destination • *We're going to have an hour lay-over in San Francisco;* We're going to have an hour stop in San Francisco.

laptop *n.* a small portable computer which fits on the operator's lap • *Whenever I go on business trips, I bring my laptop with me;* Whenever I go on business trips, I bring my small portable computer with me.

launch a product (to) *exp.* to introduce a product to the public with an aggressive advertising campaign • *In just two weeks, we're going to launch our new shampoo product;* In just two weeks, we're going to introduce our new shampoo product to the public.

lay something on the table (to) *exp.* to present a matter for discussion • *I think we need to lay this matter on the table before we proceed;* I think we need to discuss this matter before we proceed.

lean *adj.* financially meager • *This has been a very lean year for our company;* This has been a very financially meager year for our company.

line *n.* (term also known by those outside marketing) a group of products carrying the same name within a specific category such as health products, bathroom products, etc. • *Let me show you our new line of evening wear;* Let me show you our new collection of evening wear.

list broker *n.* one who supplies (and sells) lists of potential clients to companies about to embark on a direct mail campaign • *Let's find a list broker who can give us the names and addresses of people who have a degree in linguistics;* Let's find a specialist who can give us the names and addresses of people who have degrees in linguistics.

-M-

Madison Avenue *n.* a common nickname for the advertising business since this avenue is known as the center for advertising agencies in New York City.

make a buck (to) *exp.* to make money • (lit); to make a dollar bill • *It's hard making a buck these days;* It's hard making money these days.
‣ VARIATION: **to make an honest buck** *exp.* to make money doing a reputable job • *No one wants to hire me! I just want to make an honest buck somewhere!;* No one wants to hire me! I just want to make money doing a reputable job somewhere!
‣ ORIGIN: The term *"buck,"* slang for "dollar," is a shortened version of "buckskin" which was used by American Indians for trade.

make it in (to) *exp.* to arrive at work • *I'm so exhausted after the party last night, I'm surprised I was able to make it in today;* I'm so exhausted after the party last night, I'm surprised I was able to arrive to work today.

make it to first base (to) *exp.* to get to the preliminary step (in conducting a potential business transaction) • *I know we're trying to get him as a client but he talks so much that I could hardly speak with him. I can't believe I couldn't even make it to first base with him!;* I know we're trying to get him as a client but he talks so much that I could hardly speak with him. I can't believe I couldn't even get to the preliminary step with him!
‣ ORIGIN: In baseball, the first step in getting closer to the home plate (where a point is earned), is to reach first base.

market • 1. *v.* to promote, distribute, and sell a product • *This new laundry soap will be easy to market. It's the only one like it!;* This new laundry soap will be easy to promote, distribute, and sell.

It's the only one like it! • **2.** *n.* a specific section of the general public made up of consumers • *There is a large market for skin care products;* There is a large section of the general public who will buy skin care products.

marketing blitz *n.* an extremely aggressive marketing campaign • *If this marketing blitz doesn't sell this product, nothing will!;* If this aggressive marketing campaign doesn't sell this product, nothing will!

minutes *n.pl.* a record of events of a previous meeting by times • *Please read the minutes from yesterday's meeting;* Please read the record of events from yesterday's meeting.

modem (to) *v.* to transmit a document electronically from one computer to another by way of a modem (a "computer-to-telephone" interface enabling one computer to communicate with another through the telephone lines) • *I'll modem the document to you tonight;* I'll transmit the document to you through the modem tonight. ♦ NOTE: The term *"modem"* is short for "**mo**dulator/**dem**odulator."

monitor *n.* a computer screen resembling a television screen • *I just bought a monochrome monitor because the color ones are just too expensive;* I just bought a computer screen which displays in a single color because the color ones are just too expensive.

move (to) *v.* to propose • *I move that we adjourn the meeting;* I propose that we adjourn the meeting.

move a product (to) *exp.* to sell a product • *Your product is certainly in demand. I don't think we'll have any*

problem moving it; Your product is certainly in demand. I don't think we'll have any problem selling it.

-N-

nickel-and-dime (to) • **1.** *v.* to ruin financially bit by bit • *If you don't stop nickeling-and-diming the company, we'll be out of business in no time!;* If you don't stop spending the company's money on everything, we'll be out of business in no time! • **2.** *v.* to collect little by little • *Over the years, we've been able to nickel-and-dime ourselves a good profit;* Over the years, we've been able to earn ourselves a good profit little by little. • **3.** *adj.* said of something that pays very little • *I can't believe you accepted a nickel-and-dime job like that!;* I can't believe you accepted a low-paying job like that! • **4.** *adj.* said of a business which makes little money • *It's hard to believe that we started as a nickel-and-dime operation and now we have offices overseas;* It's hard to believe that we started as a very small business and now we have offices overseas.

-O-

off and running (to be) *exp.* to be making significant progress in a project • *Susan was just given an assignment from the boss and she's already off and running!;* Susan was just given an assignment from the boss and she's already making significant progress! ♦ ORIGIN: Said of horses who are running aggressively from the start of a race.

officer *n.* an executive who holds a position of authority or trust in an organization • *Ms. Rich has just been appointed as one of the new officers in our corporation;* Ms. Rich has just been appointed as one of the new executives in our corporation.

on board (to be) *exp.* to be in a ship, aircraft, car, etc. • *We can't leave until the vice president is on board!* We can't leave until the vice president is in the aircraft!

▸ ORIGIN: The expression *"to be on board"* originally applied to being on a ship since the old vessels were all made of wood. The expression is still used today but refers to any means of transportation.

on the market (to be) *exp.* said of a product which is available in stores • *This is the best soap I've ever used. It's new on the market;* This is the best soap I've ever used. It's new in the stores.

out of order (to be) *exp.* said of one who is not adhering to the rules of a meeting such as speaking out of turn, yelling, etc. • *Mr. Chancer, you're out of order! I'll have to ask you to either take your seat or be excused from this meeting;* Mr. Chancer, you're not adhering to the rules of this meeting! I'll have to ask you to either take your seat or be excused from this meeting.

-P-

P.R. *n.* • **1.** a common abbreviation for *"Public Relations"* meaning "the way the public views a company" • *Ever since our last product failed, the public has lost confidence in our company. We need to get out there and do some P.R. right away in order to save our reputation!* • **2.** refers to publicity which consists of free promotions of a product through reviews, interviews, and feature stories in both print and television • *Once we've exhausted all of our P.R. possibilities for our product, we'll begin running ads;* Once we've exhausted all the free publicity possible for our product, we'll begin running advertisements.

paper-pusher *exp.* secretary; one who deals with a great deal of paper work • *I'm tired of being a paper-pusher in this company. I'm ready to do something more creative;* I'm tired of dealing with all this paper work. I'm ready to do something more creative.

▸ SYNONYM (1): **pencil-pusher** *exp.*
▸ SYNONYM (2): **pen-pusher** *exp.*

paste-up *n.* the final composite of elements (photographs, illustrations, and text), pasted onto a stiff piece of cardboard, needed to create a final advertisement • *You can see exactly how the final ad will appear in the magazine by looking at the paste-up;* You can see exactly how the final advertisement will appear in the magazine by looking at the final pasted-up composite.

▸ SYNONYM (1): **boards** *n.pl.* • *The boards look great! Go ahead and photograph them for the ad;* The final pasted-up composites look great! Go ahead and photograph them for the ad.

▸ SYNONYM (2): **comps** *n.pl.* short for "composites" • *I can see by the comps that the ad is really going to attract potential customers;* I can see by the comps that the advertisement is really going to attract potential customers.

⇨ NOTE: The terms *"rough comp"* or *"roughs"* refer to a preliminary

version of the final comps.
‣ ALSO: **slicks** *n.pl.* the final
composite ready for reproduction
(usually mounted on glossy paper).

PC *n.* an abbreviation for the IBM
"Personal Computer" but is commonly
used to describe any desktop computer
• *I finally threw away my old
typewriter and bought a PC;* I finally
threw away my old typewriter and
bought a personal computer.
‣ NOTE: In computer advertisements,
"PC" is rarely seen with periods: *P.C.*

penny pincher (to be a) *n.* to be a
miser • (lit); one who holds on very
tightly to his/her money, even to coins
with as little value as a single penny •
*On my birthday, he didn't even give
me a card because he didn't want to
spend the money. What a penny
pincher!;* On my birthday, he didn't
even give me a card because he didn't
want to spend the money. What a miser!
‣ SYNONYM (1): **to be a cheapskate**
adj.
‣ SYNONYM (2): **to be a money
grubber** *adj.*
‣ SYNONYM (3): **to be a skin flint**
adj.
‣ SYNONYM (4): **to be a tightwad**
adj.

phones (to be on) *exp.* to be assigned
to answer the telephones • *I hate being
on phones!;* I hate being assigned to
answer the telephones!

pick up the check (to) *exp.* to pay
for one or more people at a restaurant •
*Since today is your birthday, I'm
picking up the check;* Since today is
your birthday, I'm paying for your meal.
‣ SYNONYM (1): **to pick up the tab**
exp.
‣ SYNONYM (2): **to foot the bill** *exp.*

"plastic food" *exp.* humorous name
given to the institutional food served in
economy class on typical airlines
(which often comes wrapped in plastic).

play by the rules (to) *exp.* to
conduct oneself by the accepted policy •
*I'm afraid we cannot tolerate your
tardiness every day. You have to play
by the rules of this company or
resign;* I'm afraid we cannot tolerate
your tardiness every day. You have to
conduct yourself by the rules of this
company or resign.
‣ ORIGIN: Every sport has rules under
which the team members must play or
risk being disqualified.

play hardball (to) *exp.* to resort to
aggressive methods in order to attain a
goal (even if it is to the detriment of
another person) • *I've been trying to
get a promotion here for five years.
Now I just found out Johanna is being
considered for the same promotion
and she's only been here a month! It's
time to play hardball;* I've been trying
to get a promotion here for five years.
Now I just found out Johanna is being
considered for the same promotion and
she's only been here a month! It's time
to do whatever it takes for me to get this!
‣ ORIGIN: In professional baseball, a
small hard ball is used which makes the
game somewhat more aggressive than
that played by teams who use a larger,
soft ball.

plug a product (to) *v.* to promote a
product • *Once we plug the product
on national television, sales should go
way up;* Once we promote the product
on national television, sales should go
way up.

position a product (to) *exp.* to
generate product sales among a certain

group of the population by means of a well-conceived strategy • *The best way to position this book in a busy city like Los Angeles is to call it "The Ultimate Survival Guide for Every Driver;"* The best way to generate sales of this book in a busy city like Los Angeles is to call it "The Ultimate Survival Guide for Every Driver."

pound the pavement (to) *exp.* to look for employment • (lit); to walk from business to business seeking employment • *I've been pounding the pavement for three weeks and still can't find anything;* I've been looking for employment for three weeks and still can't find anything.

♦ SYNONYM: **to job search** *exp.*

pow-wow (to have a) *exp.* to hold a meeting • *We need to have a pow-wow in my office right away;* We need to have a meeting in my office right away.

♦ ORIGIN: This expression comes from American Indians who would regularly hold pow-wows (or meetings) with all the men in the tribe.

prime time *n.* the hours between 7:00 P.M. and 11:00 P.M. when the largest number of people are watching television • *If we run the commercial during prime time, sales will be sure to go up!;* If we run the commercial between 7:00 P.M. and 11:00 P.M. sales will be sure to go up!

puff piece *n.* a flattering article written about a product, service, or person • *The Times just released a nice puff piece about our product today!;* The Times just released a nice flattering article about our product today!

pull (to) *v.* • **1.** said of an advertisement which attracts customers • *Our ad*

really pulled; Our advertisement really attracted a number of customers. • **2.** to withdraw (an advertisement for lack of effectiveness or lack of funds) • *Our ad doesn't seem to be working very well. I think we should just pull it;* Our advertisement doesn't seem to be working very well. I think we should just withdraw it.

put some ideas on the ground and see if any of them walk *exp.* (humorous) to discuss some ideas and if any of them have merit.

♦ NOTE: The advertising business has invented several clever and fun ways of saying, "Let's try it and see what kind of response we get from the public!" Here are just a few of these *"ad agencyisms:"*

• *"Let's run it up the flagpole and see if anyone salutes!;"*

• *"Let's toss it around and see if it makes salad!;"*

• *"Let's drop it down the well and see what kind of splash it makes!;"*

• *"Let's put it in the water and see if it floats!"* etc.

-Q-

quorum *n.* (Latin) minimum number of persons present at the meeting of a committee or organization, usually a majority, needed to transact business • *The vote couldn't be taken because we didn't have a quorum;* The vote couldn't be taken because we didn't have the minimum number of persons needed to transact business present.

-R-

rebate *n.* a partial refund offered a consumer as an enticement to buy a product • *The dealer is offering a $150 rebate with the purchase of their computer;* The dealer is offering a partial refund of $150 with the purchase of their computer.

red-eye *n.* an airplane flight which travels during the night (causing the passenger to loose a night's sleep and arrive at the destination with *"red eyes"*) • *I'm catching a red-eye to New York tonight;* I'm catching a night-plane to New York tonight.

right off the bat *exp.* from the very beginning • *The boss said he liked me right off the bat;* The boss said he liked me immediately.
   ♦ ORIGIN: In baseball, *"right off the bat"* refers to a baseball that is hit with full force after the first pitch.

rollout *n.* the national distribution of a product • *When do you think the best time would be to do a rollout;* When do you think the best time would be to begin national distribution of the product?

-S-

score points (to) *exp.* to gain someone's favor • *You'd better start coming to work on time. You're not scoring many points with the boss;* You'd better start coming to work on time. You're not gaining the boss's favor.
   ♦ VARIATION: **to make points** *exp.*

scuttlebutt *n.* the current scandalous rumor, gossip • *So, what's the scuttle-butt in the office?;* So, what's happening in the office?
   ♦ ORIGIN: It is said that most office rumors are started around the drinking fountain or water cooler since this is a convenient place for employees to gather. Unbeknownst to many native-born Americans, a *"scuttlebutt"* is a nautical term for a drinking fountain on a ship. The term worked its way on land and is used today to mean "gossip in general."

second a motion (to) *exp.* to agree with a proposal • *"I second the motion." "The motion has been seconded;"* "I agree with the proposal." "The motion has been agreed upon by one of our members."
   ♦ NOTE: After a motion is made, it requires that one of the members in the meeting agree with its terms by saying *"I second the motion."* At that time, a general vote may be taken.
   ♦ ALSO: **to make a motion** *exp.* to make a proposal • *I make a motion to give all the employees a raise;* I make a proposal to give all the employees a raise.

short on something (to be) *exp.* to be lacking in something • *He's really short on looks;* He's not very handsome. • *She's short on patience;* She lacks patience.

skycap *n.* employee of an airline in charge of assisting passengers with checking in their luggage • *I think we'd better ask a skycap to assist us with our luggage.*

slave driver *n.* a supervisor who works his/her employees relentlessly as if they were slaves • *The boss insists we work the entire weekend! What a slave driver!*

smooth sailing (to be) *exp.* said of a situation or journey which is calm and steady • *Once we finish with the difficult drawings on this portion of the building, the rest will be smooth* *sailing;* Once we finish with the difficult drawings on this portion of the building, the rest will be calm and steady (like a sailboat traveling on a tranquil sea).

software *n.* refers to computer programs in general • *What kind of software are you using in your computer?;* What kind of computer programs are you using in your computer?

spot *n.* a commercial • *We need to familiarize the public with your product by running a few 30-second spots;* We need to familiarize the public with your product by running a few 30-second commercials.
♦ ALSO (1): **a thirty** *n.* a 30-second commercial.
♦ ALSO (2): **a sixty** *n.* a 60-second commercial.

stand adjourned (to) *v.* to be dismissed (said of a meeting) • *This meeting stands adjourned;* This meeting is dismissed.

stand-by (to be on) *exp.* said of a person who does not have a reserved seat on an airplane and must therefore wait at the airport for a cancelation • *I've been on stand-by for three hours!;* I've been waiting for a cancelation for three hours!

storyboard *n.* a step-by-step series of illustrations (and sometimes text or *"copy"*) demonstrating a copywriter's idea for a particular television commercial • *I'm not quite sure what kind of commercial you want to write. Do you have a storyboard I can look at?;* I'm not quite sure what kind of commercial you want to write. Do you have a step-by-step series of illustrations demonstrating your ideas that I can look at?

strike out (to) *exp.* to fail • *I'm afraid we just couldn't effectively sell his product. We really struck out;* I'm afraid we just couldn't effectively sell his product. We really failed.
♦ ORIGIN: This expression is said of a baseball player at bat who misses the ball three times *(three "strikes")* and loses his turn at bat.

system *n.* short for "computer system" • *Our expensive system isn't working correctly;* Our expensive computer system isn't working correctly.

-T-

table a discussion (to) *exp.* to postpone a discussion for a later time • *Let's table the discussion for now because we have something more important to address;* Let's postpone the discussion for now because we have something more important to address.

talent *n.* performers in a commercial • *We need to hire some talent by tomorrow to get the commercial done by Friday;* We need to hire some actors by tomorrow to get the commercial done by Friday.

target (to) *v.* to focus on a particular group of consumers • *We need to target our expensive perfumes toward the wealthy group of consumers and our swim wear toward students;* We need to focus our expensive perfumes toward the wealthy group of consumers and our swim wear toward students.

team player (to be a) *exp.* said of one who works easily in a group toward a common goal • *She's not much of a team player. She's the only one who never offers to stay late when we have deadlines!;* She's not much for working easily in groups toward a common goal. She's the only one who never offers to stay late when we have deadlines!

◆ ORIGIN: A *"team player"* is one who works well with other teammates during a game and is primarily concerned with bringing the entire team glory as a whole.

test-market a product (to) *v.* to test the effectiveness of a particular product before it is widely distributed by getting comments from people who have been chosen to use the product for a specified amount of time • *It's a good thing we test-marketed our new soft drink. We would have never known that only a few people like the taste!;* It's a good thing we tested the effectiveness on our new soft drink. We would have never known that only a few people like the taste!

"The chair recognizes [name]" *exp.* "As the chairperson, I give permission for [name] to speak."

◆ NOTE: This is a common expression used by the leader of a meeting who permits others to speak one at a time. In this expression, the *"chair"* refers to the "chairperson."

"The motion carries" *exp.* "The proposal will be acted upon."

◆ NOTE: This is a common expression used by the leader of a meeting to indicate that a vote for a particular proposal has been accepted.

throw in the towel (to) *exp.* to quit
• *This job is too difficult. I'm throwing in the towel;* This job is too difficult. I quit.

◆ VARIATION: **to throw in the sponge** *exp.*

◆ ORIGIN: These expressions comes from boxing where the manager of a

losing boxer would literally throw in the *"towel"* (used to wipe the sweat of the boxer) or a *"sponge"* (used to put cool water on the boxer) into the ring, signifying defeat.

throw money down a rat hole (to) *exp.* to waste one's money on worthless items • *Why do you keep getting your car repaired by the same mechanic if he isn't doing a good job? You're just throwing your money down a rat hole;* Why do you keep getting your car repaired by the same mechanic if he isn't doing a good job? You're just wasting your money.

◆ ORIGIN: Anything that falls into a rat hole is probably lost forever since it would most likely be chewed up or destroyed.

throw someone a curve [ball] (to) *exp.* to surprise someone by doing something unexpectedly • *He really threw me a curve [ball] when he called me into his office to offer me a raise. I thought I was going to be laid off!;* He really surprised me when he called me into his office to offer me a raise. I thought I was going to be laid off!

◆ ORIGIN: In baseball, the pitcher may decide to throw a ball which curves unexpectedly as it approaches the batter.

tie-in *n.* a campaign where two companies share advertising costs by combining or *"tying in"* each other's products • *World Amusement Park is interested in doing a tie-in with us where the consumer will receive a discount to the park for buying our product;* World Amusement Park is interested in combining advertising costs with us where the consumer will receive a discount to the park for buying our product.

touch base with someone (to)
exp. to contact someone briefly in order to exchange information • *I need to touch base with the boss before I leave on my business trip;* I need to meet with the boss briefly before I leave on my business trip.
♦ ORIGIN: In baseball, once a batter has hit the ball, he/she must run around the baseball diamond and tag each base with his/her foot in order to advance to home plate and score a run.

travel light (to) *exp.* to commute with very little luggage • *Whenever I go out of town on business, I try to travel light;* Whenever I go out of town on business, I try to take very little luggage with me.

turn a profit (to) *exp.* to make a profit • *The company turned a profit its first month in business;* The company made a profit its first month in business.

-U-

user-friendly (to be) *adj.* easy to use • *This typesetting program is very user-friendly. It tells you what to do every step of the way;* This typesetting program is very easy to use. It tells you what to do every step of the way.

-V-

virus *n.* a hidden instruction in a computer program intended to cause the computer to malfunction (causing possible loss of data) • *It's a good idea to backup the computer data every day in case it turns out to have a virus;* It's a good idea to backup the computer data every day in case it turns out to have a hidden instruction somewhere which may destroy the data.

[way] off base (to be) *exp.* to be very wrong • *I thought he'd be an ideal employee. I guess I was [way] off base;* I thought he'd be an ideal employee. I guess I was [very] wrong.
♦ ORIGIN: This expression is said of a baseball player who is not on a base and is therefore vulnerable to being tagged.

-W-

word-of-mouth advertising *n.* an extremely effective and important strategy in advertising where a satisfied customer tells friends about a particular product, and so on • *I heard about this product by word-of-mouth;* I heard about this product through friends.
♦ SYNONYM: **endless chain** *n.*

WYSIWYG *n.* (pronounced "wisee-wig" or "wizee-wig") an acronym for *"What you see is what you get"* meaning "What you see on the computer screen is exactly what you'll see when the page is printed" • *The display you see on the screen is WYSIWYG. So if it doesn't look right on the screen, it won't look any better when it's printed!;* The display you see on the screen matches what the printed page will look like. So if it doesn't look right on the screen, it won't look any better when it's printed!

-Y-

yuppie *n.* an abbreviation for *"young urban professional,"* a young, well-paid, pretentious, executive who tends to buy products of a trendy nature • *We need to target our new fashionable shoes to the yuppie;* We need to target our new fashionable shoes to the young, well-paid executive

who would be attracted to anything
fashionable.

♦ NOTE: In the gay world, the term has
been modified to *"guppi"* meaning
"gay urban professional."

♦ ALSO: **to be yuppified** *exp.* to
acquire the traits of a yuppie • *He
became so yuppified ever since he got
his new job;* He acquired all the traits
of a yuppie ever since he got his new
job.

-Z-

zap (to) *v.* to erase • *I don't need that
computer file anymore. Go ahead and
zap it;* I don't need that computer file
anymore. Go ahead and erase it.

9-to-5 *n.* a regular job (which begins at
9:00 A.M. and ends at 5:00 P.M.) • *I'm
so tired of working a 9-to-5. Maybe I
should become an artist;* I'm so tired
of working an ordinary job. Maybe I
should become an artist.

♦ ALSO: **9-to-5er** *n.* one who works a
9-to-5 • *Look at him carrying that big
gray lunch box. He's your typical
9-to-5er;* Look at him carrying that big
gray lunch box. He's your typical
person with an ordinary job.

ORDER FORM ON BACK

Prices subject to change

AMERICAN	BOOK	CASSETTE
STREET TALK -1 . . . . *How to Speak and Understand American Slang*	$16.95	$12.50
STREET TALK -2 . . . . *Slang Used in Popular American Television Shows*	$16.95	$12.50
STREET TALK -3 . . . . *The Best of American Idioms*	$18.95	$12.50
STREET TALK DICTIONARY . . . . *The Best of American Slang, Idioms, & Obscenities (available March '97)*	$18.95	
BIZ TALK -1 . . . . *American Business Slang & Jargon* 　(general office • finance • meetings & negotiations • 　business travel • "computerese" • marketing & advertising)	$16.95	$12.50
BIZ TALK -2 . . . . *More American Business Slang & Jargon (available December 1, 1996)* 　(more general office • international trade • commonly used initials 　in international trade • more "computerese" & on-line slang • 　management • "bureaucratese" • political slang & jargon)	$16.95	$12.50
BIZ TALK -3 . . . . *Even More American Business Slang & Jargon (available January '97)* 　(even more general office • more international trade • essential terms 　for political correctness • even more "computerese" & on-line slang • 　more management • tourism • political correctness in bureaucracy)	$18.95	$12.50
BIZ TALK DICTIONARY . . . . *The Best of American Business Slang & Jargon*	$18.95	
BLEEP! . . . . *A Guide to Popular American Obscenities*	$14.95	$12.50
FRENCH		
STREET FRENCH -1 . . . . *The Best of French Slang*	$15.95	$12.50
STREET FRENCH -2 . . . . *The Best of French Idioms*	$15.95	$12.50
STREET FRENCH -3 . . . . *The Best of Naughty French (available May '97)*	$15.95	$12.50
SPANISH		
STREET SPANISH . . . . *How to Speak and Understand Spanish Slang*	$15.95	$12.50
GERMAN		
STREET GERMAN -1 . . . . *The Best of German Idioms*	$16.95	$12.50

—— OPTIMA BOOKS Order Form ——

2820 Eighth Street · Berkeley, CA 94710

For U.S. and Canada, use our TOLL FREE FAX line: 1-800-515-8737
International orders FAX line: 510-848-8737 · Publisher direct: 510-848-8708

Name _____

(School/Company) _____

Street Address _____

City _____ State/Province _____ Postal Code _____

Country _____ Phone _____

Quantity	Title	Book or Cassette?	Price Each	Total Price

Total for Merchandise
Sales Tax (California Residents Only)
Shipping (See Below)
ORDER TOTAL

METHOD OF PAYMENT (check one)

☐ Check or Money Order ☐ VISA ☐ Master Card ☐ American Express ☐ Discover
(Money orders and personal checks must be in US funds and drawn on a US bank.)

Credit Card Number: **Card Expires:**

☐☐☐☐ ☐☐☐☐ ☐☐☐☐ ☐☐☐☐   ☐☐ ☐☐

Signature (important!):

SHIPPING

Domestic Orders: SURFACE MAIL (delivery time 5-7 days).
Add $5 shipping/handling for the first item · $1 for each additional item.
RUSH SERVICE available at extra charge.

International Orders: OVERSEAS SURFACE (delivery time 6-8 weeks).
Add $6 shipping/handling for the first item · $2 for each additional item.
OVERSEAS AIRMAIL available at extra charge.

BT1